# Dynamics Modeling and Maneuvering of Autonomous Underwater Vehicles

Xianbo Xiang · Faheem Ahmed · Gong Xiang

# Dynamics Modeling and Maneuvering of Autonomous Underwater Vehicles

## Theory and Practice

Springer

Xianbo Xiang
School of Naval Architecture and Ocean Engineering
Huazhong University of Science and Technology
Wuhan, Hubei, China

Faheem Ahmed
School of Naval Architecture and Ocean Engineering
Huazhong University of Science and Technology
Wuhan, Hubei, China

Gong Xiang
School of Naval Architecture and Ocean Engineering
Huazhong University of Science and Technology
Wuhan, Hubei, China

ISBN 978-981-95-1520-2 ISBN 978-981-95-1521-9 (eBook)
https://doi.org/10.1007/978-981-95-1521-9

This work was supported by National Natural Science Foundation of China (52071153).



This Springer imprint is published by the registered company Springer Nature Singapore Pte Ltd.
The registered company address is: 152 Beach Road, #21-01/04 Gateway East, Singapore 189721, Singapore

*To the scientific community working together to improve underwater vehicle technology.*

# Preface I

The field of autonomous underwater vehicles has witnessed significant advancements over the past few decades, driven by the growing need for robust, reliable, and intelligent systems capable of performing complex tasks in challenging underwater environments. As exploration and operations beneath the surface become increasingly vital for scientific, industrial, and defense applications, there is a critical demand for accurate modeling and maneuvering strategies that ensure performance, efficiency, and safety.

This book titled *Dynamics Modeling and Maneuvering of Autonomous Underwater Vehicles: Theory and Practice*, presents a comprehensive treatment of the fundamental and applied aspects of AUV dynamics. It bridges theoretical foundations with practical methodologies, offering insights into nonlinear dynamics modeling, hydrodynamic parameters estimation, and maneuvering strategies. The integration of experimental validations and computational techniques makes this work especially valuable for researchers, practitioners, and graduate students engaged in underwater robotics and marine engineering.

What distinguishes this volume is its focus on both classical and emerging approaches to dynamic modeling and hydrodynamic coefficients estimations, along with an emphasis on maneuvering analysis that supports mission-critical decision-making in real-world applications. By combining rigorous analysis with practical considerations, the authors have created a resource that contributes meaningfully to the continued development of autonomous marine systems.

This work reflects the collaborative effort and technical depth of its contributors and stands as an achievement to the progress and promise of autonomous underwater technology.

Wuhan, China
June 2025

Prof. Dr. Xianbo Xiang

# Preface II

AUV technology has experienced remarkable advances in recent years, driven by the demand for sophisticated platforms capable of exploring and operating in harsh underwater environments. AUVs play a critical role in applications ranging from offshore energy and environmental monitoring to deep-sea surveying and infrastructure inspection, where interactions with complex flow fields and dynamic forces significantly affect performance. Achieving high-precision operation and hydrodynamically efficient designs requires accurate modeling of vehicle–fluid interactions and an efficient estimation of hydrodynamic parameters under constrained computational and experimental resources.

Chapter 1 provides an introduction to AUV classifications, key applications, and the motivating challenges in modeling underwater vehicles, setting the stage for the in-depth treatments that follow.

Chapter 2 covers the fundamentals of AUV dynamics, including coordinate systems, reference frames, degrees of freedom, and basic motion principles. Building on this, Chap. 3 presents a rigorous derivation of the six-degree-of-freedom equations of motion, with detailed kinematic and kinetic formulations incorporating added mass, damping, hydrostatic forces, and control inputs.

Chapter 4 investigates analytical and semi-empirical methods for estimating hydrodynamic coefficients, leveraging strip theory, potential flow, slender-body theory, and related approaches.

Chapter 5 follows with high-fidelity computational fluid dynamics studies, addressing mesh generation, boundary conditions, and quantitative comparisons with analytical results.

Chapter 6 presents experimental and data-driven approaches for hydrodynamic coefficient estimation, combining ITTC-guided trials with system identification techniques to balance experimental fidelity and computational efficiency.

Chapter 7 analyzes maneuvering performance and experimental validations with practical examples of REMUS 100 AUV and a novel flight-style AUV to demonstrate how hydrodynamic coefficients affect real-world behavior and inform design optimization and control strategies.

In this book, researchers and engineers in marine engineering, naval architecture, and ocean engineering will find practical methodologies, detailed derivations, and case evaluations to support AUV design, testing, and operation. Advanced students and academic researchers will also benefit from the book's blend of analytical rigor and experimental validation, making it a valuable reference in both academic and industrial research environments.

Wuhan, China

Prof. Dr. Xianbo Xiang
Dr. Faheem Ahmed
Assoc. Prof. Dr. Gong Xiang

**Acknowledgements** We would like to express our sincere gratitude to the research community whose foundational work and continued innovation have made this book possible. The development of the book titled *Dynamics Modeling and Maneuvering of Autonomous Underwater Vehicles: Theory and Practice* has been shaped by years of collective progress in marine robotics, hydrodynamics, and control systems.

We are thankful to our respective institutions and research teams for their continuous support and for providing an environment that fosters collaboration, inquiry, and scientific growth. Special appreciation goes to the colleagues, peers, and reviewers who offered valuable feedback during the preparation of this manuscript.

This work also benefited from the availability of open-source tools, published experimental datasets, and scholarly resources that enabled us to validate and refine the technical content presented throughout the book.

Finally, we extend our thanks to the publishing team for their guidance and professionalism throughout the process. The completion of this book reflects not only our shared effort but also the broader spirit of collaboration that drives advancements in autonomous underwater vehicle research.

**Competing Interests** The authors have no competing interests to declare that are relevant to the content of this book.

This work is funded by National Natural Science Foundation of China [Grant No. 52131101, 52071153], National Key R&D Program of China-Intergovernmental International Scientific and Technological Innovation and Cooperation Program [Grant No. 2023YFE0115400], International Science and Technology Collaboration Project of Hubei Province [Grant No. 2024EHA030], and International Science and Technology Cooperation Project of Hubei Province [Grant No. 2023EHA024].

**Ethics Approval** This study did not involve human or animal subjects, and thus, no ethical approval was required. The study protocol adhered to the guidelines established by the publisher.

# Contents

# About the Authors

**Prof. Dr. Xianbo Xiang** is a Full Professor at the School of Naval Architecture and Ocean Engineering at Huazhong University of Science and Technology (HUST) in Wuhan, China. He is also the Director of the Laboratory of Advanced Robotic Marine Systems (ARMs). Professor Xianbo Xiang holds a Ph.D. in System Automation and Microelectronics from the University of Montpellier II, France, and has a solid academic background with earlier degrees from HUST. His research expertise spans autonomous marine robotics, intelligent control systems, and underwater vehicle technology. He has received several prestigious awards, including the Gold Medal with Congratulations of the Jury at the 48th International Exhibition of Inventions of Geneva, and has been recognized as one of the most cited Chinese researchers in Naval Architecture and Ocean Engineering since 2020. Professor Xianbo Xiang has been actively involved in various international research projects and collaborations, contributing to the advancement of autonomous marine technology. He has held prominent roles in several international conferences, including serving as the General Chair for IFAC CAMS 2025, IEEE USYS 2018, IMET 2023, IMET 2022 and serving on the editorial board for journals: IJME-Transactions of The Royal Institution of Naval Architects, Applied Ocean Research, China Ocean Engineering, etc. Professor Xianbo Xiang's research contributions have been supported by various national and international grants, including major projects on underwater vehicle control, subsea inspection and collaborative marine robotic systems. Professor Xianbo Xiang has authored more than 200 scholarly articles and publications in well-reputed international journals and conferences, showcasing his extensive contributions to the fields of autonomous underwater vehicles (AUVs), marine robotics, and intelligent control systems. His research focuses on advancing technologies for underwater vehicle control, fleet coordination, and sustainable marine systems, intelligent inspection and the integration of autonomous systems in challenging marine environments. These publications reflect his deep expertise and influence in the scientific community, with a commitment to addressing the complex challenges in underwater robotics and marine engineering.

**Dr. Faheem Ahmed** earned his Ph.D. degree in Marine Engineering from the School of Naval Architecture and Ocean Engineering at Huazhong University of Science and Technology (HUST) in Wuhan, China. With more than 15 years of experience in Naval Architecture and Ocean Engineering, he has specialized in Unmanned Underwater Technologies. His research interests include, but are not limited to: Underwater Vehicular Technologies, Underwater Vehicle Dynamics Modeling and Control, Hydrodynamic Modeling, Analytical and Semiempirical Methods, Computational Fluid Dynamics, Marine Robotics, Intelligent Systems, and Machine Learning. Currently, his research focuses on nonlinear dynamics and hydrodynamic modeling of Flight Style Autonomous Underwater Vehicles, with particular emphasis on maneuvering characteristics and experimental validation. Dr. Ahmed has an outstanding academic background. He received his Master's degree in Fluid Dynamics with distinction from Northwestern Polytechnical University (NPU) in Xi'an, China in 2013, and earned his Bachelor's degree in Mechanical Engineering in 2004, graduating in first position from Mehran University of Engineering and Technology in Pakistan. He has made substantial contributions to the field of Naval Architecture and Ocean Engineering, having published over 15 journal and conference papers as first author or co-author in high-impact international journals such as Ocean Engineering, Applied Ocean Research, as well as at prestigious IEEE conferences. His work has been presented at numerous esteemed international forums.

**Dr. Gong Xiang** is an Associate Professor at the School of Naval Architecture and Ocean Engineering, Huazhong University of Science and Technology (HUST) in Wuhan, China. He holds a Ph.D. in Naval Architecture and Marine Engineering from the University of New Orleans (UNO), a Master of Science in Ocean Engineering from Stevens Institute of Technology (SIT), and a Bachelor of Science in Naval Architecture and Ocean Engineering from HUST. His professional career is marked by extensive research experience, having servedas a Postdoctoral Researcher at the University of Lisbon in Portugal and a Research Engineer in Houston, Texas, USA. Dr. Gong Xiang's research interests encompass hydrodynamics and dynamics, computational fluid dynamics (CFD), marine robotics, intelligent ship systems. He has authored or co-authored over 60 scholarly articles and publications in well-reputed international journals and conferences. These publications span various topics such as hydrodynamic coefficient estimation, dynamic response analysis of marine structures, CFD studies for underwater applications, and optimization techniques for complex hydrodynamic problems. Dr. Gong Xiang's academic excellence has been recognized with numerous awards, including the "Young Elite Scientist" award from the China Association for Science and Technology and the "Best Paper Award" from the International Association of Ocean Engineers (IAOE). His role in advancing the field is further demonstrated by his active participation in organizing conferences, where he has served as Vice Chair, Program Chair, Session Chair, and Technical Committee Member for multiple high-profile events. Beyond his academic and research endeavors, Dr. Gong Xiang contributes to the scientific community as an Editorial Board Member for several international journals, where he lends his expertise in naval architecture, subsea engineering, and marine robotics. His dedication to research and innovation has made significant impacts, especially in areas that merge theoretical modeling with practical engineering solutions, advancing the development of next-generation marine technologies.

# Acronyms

| | |
|---|---|
| AMVs | Autonomous Marine Vehicles |
| AOA | Angle Of Attack |
| ARMs | Advanced Robotic Marine Systems |
| ASE | Analytical and Semi-empirical |
| AUV | Autonomous Underwater Vehicle |
| CB | Center of Buoyancy |
| CFD | Computational Fluid Dynamics |
| CG | Center of Gravity |
| CMT | Captive Model Testing |
| DARPA | Defense Advanced Research Projects Agency |
| DNS | Direct Numerical Simulation |
| DOF | Degrees Of Freedom |
| DTMB | David Taylor Model Basin |
| DTRC | David Taylor Research Center |
| DVL | Doppler Velocity Log |
| EMS | Electromagnetic Searcher |
| EXP | Experiment |
| FSAUV | Flight-Style AUV |
| FSI | Fluid–Structure Interaction |
| GPS | Global Positioning System |
| HCs | Hydrodynamic Coefficients |
| HEKF | Hybrid Extended Kalman Filter |
| IMD | Integrated Modular Design |
| IMU | Inertial Measurement Unit |
| INS | Inertial Navigation System |
| ITTC | International Towing Tank Conference |
| LBL | Long Base-Line |
| LES | Large Eddy Simulation |
| LSS | Laser Scanning System |
| ML | Machine Learning |
| NGC | Northrop Grumman Corporation |

| | |
|---|---|
| NWPU | Northwestern Polytechnical University |
| OUKF | Optimized Unscented Kalman Filter |
| PID | Proportional–Integral–Derivative |
| PMM | Planar Motion Mechanism |
| REMUS | Remote Environmental Monitoring UnitS |
| RANS | Reynolds-Averaged Navier–Stokes |
| RANSE | Reynolds-Averaged Navier–Stokes Equations |
| ROV | Remotely Operated Vehicle |
| SAROV | Semi-autonomous Remotely Operated Vehicle |
| SIM | Simulation |
| SI | System Identification |
| SNAOE | School of Naval Architecture and Ocean Engineering |
| SNDM | Symmetric Nonlinear Dynamics Model |
| SST | Shear Stress Transport |
| SVR | Support Vector Regression |
| SVM | Support Vector Machine |
| UKF | Unscented Kalman Filter |
| URANSE | Unsteady Reynolds-Averaged Navier–Stokes Equations |
| USBL | Ultra-Short Base-Line |
| USV | Unmanned Surface Vehicle |
| UUV | Unmanned Underwater Vehicle |
| UVMS | Underwater Vehicle Manipulator System |
| VIC | Video Imaging Complex |
| WBI | Wing-Body Lift Interference |
| WHOI | Woods Hole Oceanographic Institution |

# Symbols

| | |
|---|---|
| $A_{f_1}$ | Reference area of vertical control surfaces (e.g., rudders) |
| $A_{f_2}$ | Reference area of aft control surfaces |
| $A_{f_3}$ | Reference area of forward control surfaces |
| $A_{f_x}$ | Projected surface area along the longitudinal ($x$) axis |
| $A_{f_y}$ | Projected surface area along the lateral ($y$) axis |
| $A_{f_z}$ | Projected surface area along the vertical ($z$) axis |
| $A_{wf_1}$ | Combined surface area of vertical fins and wings |
| $A_{wf_2}$ | Combined surface area of stern-mounted fins and wings |
| $A_{wf_3}$ | Combined surface area of bow-mounted fins and wings |
| $A_p$ | Projected area of the vehicle hull |
| $B$ | Net buoyant force acting on the vehicle |
| $C$ | Composite matrix of Coriolis and centripetal terms |
| $C_A$ | Coriolis-centripetal matrix attributed to added mass |
| $C_{RB}$ | Coriolis-centripetal matrix of the rigid body |
| $CB$ | Geometric center of buoyancy |
| $CG$ | Geometric center of gravity |
| $D$ | Hydrodynamic damping matrix |
| $I_x$ | Roll moment of inertia |
| $I_y$ | Pitch moment of inertia |
| $I_z$ | Yaw moment of inertia |
| $J_\Theta$ | Kinematic transformation matrix relating linear and angular velocities |
| $K$ | Moment generated about the $x$-axis (roll) |
| $K_{\dot{p}}$ | Added inertia in roll due to angular acceleration |
| $K_{p\|p\|}$ | Nonlinear damping term in roll |
| $K_{prop}$ | Torque induced by propeller rotation |
| $l$ | Overall length of the AUV |
| $l_f$ | Forward section length excluding the tail |
| $l_m$ | Midsection length of a flight-style AUV |
| $l_n$ | Length of the nose section |
| $l_t$ | Tail section length of the AUV |
| $m$ | Mass of the vehicle |

| | |
|---|---|
| $m_f$ | Equivalent mass of displaced fluid |
| $M$ | Moment acting about the $y$-axis (pitch) |
| $M_A$ | Added mass matrix |
| $M_{\dot{q}}$ | Pitch-direction added mass due to angular acceleration |
| $M_{q\|q\|}$ | Pitch-direction damping coefficient |
| $M_{RB}$ | Rigid-body inertia matrix |
| $M_{uw}$, $M_{uq}$ | Lift-induced pitching moment coefficients |
| $n_o$ | Offset from center to nose section |
| $N$ | Yaw moment around the $z$-axis |
| $N_{\dot{r}}$ | Yaw-direction added mass due to angular acceleration |
| $N_{r\|r\|}$ | Nonlinear damping coefficient for yaw |
| $N_{ur}$, $N_{uv}$ | Lift-induced yaw moment coefficients |
| $N_{v\|v\|}$ | Yaw damping term due to sway motion |
| $p$ | Angular velocity about the $x$-axis (roll) |
| $q$ | Angular velocity about the $y$-axis (pitch) |
| $r$ | Angular velocity about the $z$-axis (yaw) |
| $R_b^n$ | Rotation matrix from body-fixed to inertial frame |
| $r_G$ | Location vector of the center of gravity |
| $r_B$ | Location vector of the center of buoyancy |
| $S_a$ | Surface area of the GPS antenna |
| $T_\theta$ | Transformation matrix between body and inertial frames |
| $t_o$ | Offset from center to tail section |
| $\theta_t$ | Deflection angle of tail surfaces |
| $u$ | Linear velocity in the surge direction ($x$-axis) |
| $v$ | Linear velocity in the sway direction ($y$-axis) |
| $w$ | Linear velocity in the heave direction ($z$-axis) |
| $W$ | Weight of the AUV |
| $x$ | Position along the $x$-axis in inertial frame |
| $x_{f_1}$ $x_{f_2}$ $x_{f_3}$ | Longitudinal centroid positions of vertical, stern, and bow fins relative to *CB* |
| $x_a$ | Longitudinal centroid of the antenna relative to *CB* |
| $X$ | Net surge force acting on the vehicle |
| $x_{\dot{u}}$ | Added mass in surge due to linear acceleration |
| $X_{u\|u\|}$ | Nonlinear damping in surge |
| $X_{prop}$ | Propeller thrust force in surge direction |
| $y_a$ | Lateral position of the antenna |
| $y_f$ | Lateral centroid of the vertical fin |
| $Y$ | Sway force acting on the AUV |
| $Y_{\dot{r}}$ | Added mass in sway due to yaw acceleration |
| $Y_{r\|r\|}$ | Sway damping due to yaw motion |
| $Y_{ur}$, $Y_{uv}$ | Lift-induced sway force coefficients |
| $Y_{v\|v\|}$ | Sway damping due to lateral motion |
| $z$ | Position along the $z$-axis in inertial frame |
| $Z$ | Net heave force acting on the vehicle |
| $Z_{\dot{q}}$, $Z_{\dot{w}}$ | Added mass in heave due to pitch or vertical acceleration |

| | |
|---|---|
| $Z_{q\|q\|}$ | Heave damping due to pitching motion |
| $Z_{uq}$, $Z_{uw}$ | Lift-induced vertical force coefficients |
| $Z_{w\|w\|}$ | Heave damping due to vertical motion |
| $\delta_b$ | Deflection angle of bow fins |
| $\delta_r$ | Deflection angle of vertical fin or rudder |
| $\delta_s$ | Deflection angle of stern fins |
| $\eta$ | Pose vector including position and orientation |
| $\nu$ | Body-fixed velocity vector |
| $\phi$ | Roll angle (rotation about $\nu$-axis) |
| $\psi$ | Yaw angle (rotation about $z$-axis) |
| $\rho$ | Fluid density (typically seawater) |
| $\theta$ | Pitch angle (rotation about $y$-axis) |

# Chapter 1
# Autonomous Underwater Vehicles

## 1.1 Introduction

Oceanography emerged as a formal scientific discipline in the late 19th century, marked notably by the HMS *Challenger* expedition conducted during the 1870s. This landmark voyage was instrumental in shaping the foundation of modern marine science, focusing on deep-ocean exploration, temperature profiling, chemical composition analysis, biological surveys, and seafloor characterization. As a multidisciplinary field, oceanography investigates the physical, chemical, and biological dynamics of the world's oceans, which encompass nearly 70% of Earth's surface. To conduct such investigations, researchers utilize a wide range of sophisticated marine technologies, including both autonomous surface platforms and underwater vehicles.

By the late 1950s, underwater vehicles developed for scientific and industrial applications in the deep sea. These platforms have since played a crucial role in advancing ocean-based research activities such as ecological monitoring, underwater construction, and subsea infrastructure assessment. Over the decades, the expanding demand for oceanic exploration and resource utilization has driven the advancement of intelligent, high-performance underwater systems capable of executing complex missions. This progression has been strongly supported by concurrent developments in computing, sensor technology, and robotics.

Unmanned Underwater Vehicles (UUVs) are robotic systems designed to operate below the ocean surface without direct human presence. They are generally classified into two main categories: Remotely Operated Vehicles (ROVs) and Autonomous Underwater Vehicles (AUVs). The distinction lies in their mode of control and operational behavior. ROVs are tethered platforms guided by operators through an umbilical cable, which provides power and facilitates real-time control and data transfer. These systems are well-suited for tasks demanding precise navigation and manipulation, such as subsea construction, repair operations, and intricate inspections.

In contrast, AUVs function without a tether, navigating based on pre-programmed instructions and on-board decision-making algorithms. Their autonomy allows for

 
X. Xiang et al., *Dynamics Modeling and Maneuvering of Autonomous Underwater Vehicles*, https://doi.org/10.1007/978-981-95-1521-9_1

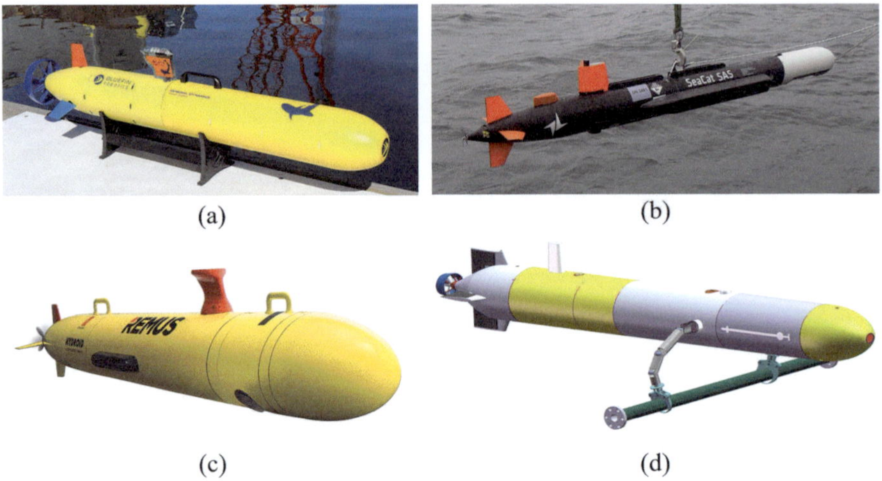


**Fig. 1.1** Torpedo-Shaped AUVs **a** Bluefin SandShark micro-AUV—Bluefin robotics products, General dynamics mission systems [19] **b** SeaCat AUV for mine countermeasures by ATLAS Elektronik GmbH [20] **c** REMUS AUV by oceanographic systems lab of woods hole oceanographic institution (WHOI) [15] **d** UVMS [5]

long-duration missions across vast oceanic areas, making them ideal for environmental assessment, oceanographic surveys, and the inspection of underwater pipelines and communication cables. Recent technological advancements–particularly in artificial intelligence, energy storage, and sensor integration–have significantly enhanced the operational efficiency and decision-making capabilities of AUVs. These innovations have enabled autonomous platforms to function reliably in dynamic and hostile marine environments, performing extended missions with minimal or no human intervention.

The AUVs can be broadly classified as: streamlined classical myring (torpedo-shaped), complex-shaped and open-frame (non-torpedo-shaped), and bio-inspired or biomimetic AUVs [1]. Torpedo-shaped AUVs, characterized by their streamlined hydrodynamic design, are ideal for long-distance missions and high-speed operations due to their efficient movement through water. Complex-shaped AUVs are designed with specialized features tailored to meet specific operational requirements, such as those involving intricate maneuvering or enhanced payload capacities. Open-frame AUVs, on the other hand, offer considerable flexibility, making them well-suited for research applications and the integration of various equipment. Bio-inspired AUVs, which draw design inspiration from aquatic organisms, provide superior maneuverability and improved energy efficiency, making them advantageous for navigating complex and dynamic underwater environments.

Additionally, the underwater vehicle manipulator system (UVMS) has emerged as an innovative marine robotic solution. By combining AUVs with integrated robotic arms or manipulators, the hybrid system is capable of autonomously performing complex underwater tasks, including object handling, sample collection, and equipment maintenance. UVMS designs can be based on either torpedo-shaped or complex-shaped AUV configurations [2–4]. For instance, Fig. 1.1d illustrates a UVMS equipped with a torpedo-shaped AUV integrated with robotic arms, demonstrating the capability to perform dynamic underwater tasks such as pipe grasping and installation operations, which also require precision [5].

## 1.2 From Classic-Myring AUVs to Latest Bio-Inspired AUVs

### *1.2.1 Classic-Myring (Torpedo-Shaped) AUVs*

#### Evolution and Development of Torpedo-Shaped AUVs

As described in [6], the conceptual origin of autonomous underwater vehicles (AUVs) can be traced back to the invention of the first self-propelled torpedo in 1866 by Robert Whitehead. This innovation, named after the torpedo fish–a ray capable of delivering electric shocks–was powered by compressed air, capable of reaching speeds of approximately 3.0 m/s, and had an effective range of 700 meters. Modern AUV development began in the late 1950s with the creation of the Self-Propelled Underwater Research Vehicle (SPURV), pioneered by Stan Murphy, Bob Francois, and Terry Ewart at the University of Washington's Applied Physics Laboratory. Designed for scientific rather than military applications, SPURV had a streamlined, torpedo-like shape [7], a cruising speed between 2 and 2.5 m/s, and an operational depth of up to 3650 meters [8, 9]. Its main objective was to collect oceanographic data while maintaining accurate underwater trajectories.

The development continued with SPURV-II in 1973, with over 400 documented deployments of SPURV until the late 1970s [6]. Its final known mission involved submarine wake experiments in 1979, though some sources suggest continued operation into the 1980s [7, 10]. During the same era, the University of Washington also introduced the Unmanned Arctic Research Submersible (UARS) for Arctic missions. Parallel initiatives included the Experimental Autonomous Vehicle (EAVE) developed at the University of New Hampshire in collaboration with the U.S. Navy, and the Russian Academy of Sciences' Institute of Marine Technology Problems, which focused on designing the earliest deep-diving AUVs. These foundational efforts catalyzed the global expansion of AUV technology, with recent developments strongly influenced by artificial intelligence to enhance autonomy in ocean operations.

Torpedo-shaped AUVs are characterized by their elongated, hydrodynamically efficient hulls that minimize drag and support high-speed propulsion through thrusters or propellers. These vehicles are equipped with control surfaces such as fins for maneuvering in both horizontal and vertical planes. To ensure precise motion control and orientation, they employ gyroscopes, inertial measurement units (IMUs), and accelerometers, along with advanced navigation aids such as GPS (for surface positioning) and underwater acoustic positioning systems.

This streamlined design not only reduces hydrodynamic resistance but also enhances endurance and range, making these AUVs particularly suitable for time-sensitive missions like rapid seabed mapping or underwater search and rescue. Their pressure-resistant, hermetically sealed hulls house mission-critical components such as power systems, sensors, and onboard control units, enabling operations at extreme depths–up to 6000 meters in the case of vehicles like the Autosub6000 [11, 12]. Recent advances have incorporated swarm coordination technologies, enabling multiple compact AUVs to operate collaboratively in mission-driven formations [13, 14]. These swarm-enabled systems support real-time task allocation, adaptive decision-making, and distributed sensing across large underwater areas.

Despite their advantages, torpedo-shaped AUVs are often limited by their compact size, which restricts payload capacity and onboard sensor variety. Additionally, many of these vehicles are underactuated–equipped with limited control actuators–posing challenges for precision control, especially in turbulent or dynamic underwater environments.

Notable examples of torpedo-shaped AUVs include the *REMUS* family, such as REMUS 100 and REMUS 600, developed by Hydroid [15], widely used in hydrographic surveying and mine countermeasure operations. The *HUGIN* series from Kongsberg [16], including HUGIN 3000 and HUGIN 4500, are designed for deep-sea missions, offering high-resolution seabed mapping capabilities at depths up to 4500 meters. The *Bluefin* AUVs, including the Bluefin-9 and Bluefin-21, developed by Bluefin Robotics (now part of General Dynamics) [17], are recognized for search and recovery applications, most notably in the search for the missing Malaysian Airlines Flight MH370 [18].

**AUV Modules**

The internal system layout of the Flight-Style Autonomous Underwater Vehicle (FSAUV), developed by the ARMs Laboratory of the School of Naval Architecture and Ocean Engineering (SNAOE) at Huazhong University of Science and Technology (HUST), Wuhan, China, is depicted in Fig. 1.2 [21]. This reference model has been adopted to describe the major onboard functional modules. The overall architecture is categorized into four primary subsystems: actuators, sensors, control units, and power sources.

The actuator configuration includes bow and stern control fins that enable pitch adjustments, along with stern-mounted rudders responsible for yaw control. Propulsion is achieved through an aft-mounted thruster. The integrated sensor suite comprises an inertial navigation unit, a Doppler Velocity Log (DVL), a GPS module for surface localization, a forward-facing altimeter, and a depth sensor for precise vertical positioning.

To ensure reliable operation and guidance, the control system incorporates both data acquisition and command execution modules. It features an interface for communication and a layered control framework comprising five distributed node controllers and a central supervisory controller. Power for the onboard systems is supplied by two separate battery packs: a 24V unit dedicated to electronic and control modules, and a 48V unit allocated for driving the propulsion and actuation mechanisms. The

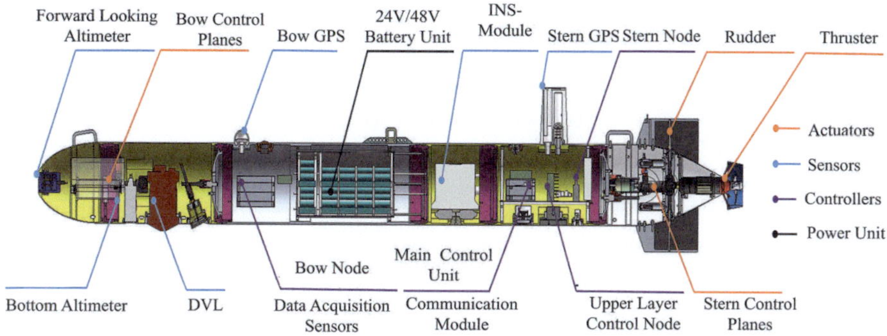


**Fig. 1.2** Subsections and integral modules of FSAUV [22]

spatial arrangement of these subsystems within the vehicle's pressure hull is also illustrated in Fig. 1.2.

### *1.2.2 Complex-Shaped and Open-Frame AUVs*

Complex-shaped Unmanned Underwater Vehicles (UUVs) exhibit streamlined or enclosed configurations with multiple appendages and structural elements optimized for specialized tasks. These designs enhance protection of internal modules and enable high-performance operations in missions such as underwater construction, scientific exploration, and habitat mapping. However, their intricate architecture generally necessitates more demanding maintenance routines. Representative examples of complex-shaped and open-frame UUVs are presented in Fig. 1.3.

One notable example is the Double Eagle Semi-Autonomous Remotely Operated Vehicle (SAROV), shown in Fig. 1.3a [23]. Designed for dual operational modes, SAROV can function autonomously for detection, classification, and identification missions, or as a tethered ROV for mine disposal. Its compact, enclosed configuration supports modular mission adaptability, offering excellent endurance and reliability for applications such as search and rescue, environmental surveys, and Rapid Environmental Assessment (REA). When operated as an ROV, SAROV can be deployed via a thin fiber-optic tether for extended-range operations exceeding 3 km using onboard batteries, or through a power-and-data combined tether for endurance missions up to 1,000 m. It also supports untethered operation, enabling true hybrid deployment capabilities.

Another prominent example, illustrated in Fig. 1.3b, is the AUV *Sentry*, developed under the National Deep Submergence Facility (NDSF). Engineered for deep-sea exploration down to 6,000 m, Sentry combines high maneuverability with a hydrodynamic profile that facilitates rapid ascent and descent. It is equipped with a comprehensive suite of oceanographic sensors and can carry substantial scientific payloads for mid-water and near-seafloor investigations. Data products generated include bathymetry, sidescan sonar images, sub-bottom profiles, magnetic field measurements, and high-resolution seafloor imagery. Sentry is routinely deployed in challenging underwater environments such as volcanic calderas and submarine escarpments. For accurate navigation and positioning, it employs a combination of Doppler Velocity Log (DVL), Inertial Navigation System (INS), and acoustic localization (USBL or LBL). The platform also accommodates third-party scientific instrumentation, including the Nakamura redox probe, ACFR 3D imaging system, and Tethys in-situ mass spectrometer.

In contrast, open-frame UUVs feature a skeletal structure that provides accessibility and ease of reconfiguration, making them ideal for experimental research, underwater inspections, and survey applications. While these platforms offer excellent modularity, they are generally less hydrodynamically efficient and afford limited protection to internal components. Their open architecture facilitates the integration of diverse sensors and payloads, although it introduces vulnerabilities to external environmental hazards and complicates accurate hydrodynamic modeling [24]. Examples of open-frame UUVs are shown in Fig. 1.3c, d.

Figure 1.3c shows the Jason–Medea ROV system, developed by the Deep Submergence Laboratory at the Woods Hole Oceanographic Institution (WHOI) and supported by the National Science Foundation [25]. This two-body configuration allows extended seafloor exploration from a surface vessel via a 10-kilometer fiber-optic cable. Medea stabilizes the system and provides overhead illumination, while Jason performs close-up investigations using imaging systems, sonars, lights, and manipulators. It is capable of collecting geological, biological, and sediment samples using robotic arms, storing them onboard or transferring them via elevator systems. Jason's deployments can last from several hours to multiple days and have included archaeological missions such as surveying the RMS Titanic and exploring a Roman-era shipwreck.

The open-frame Deep Discoverer ROV, illustrated in Fig. 1.3d, is operated by NOAA Ocean Exploration and maintained by the Global Foundation for Ocean Exploration (GFOE). It is deployed from the NOAA Ship *Okeanos Explorer*, often in tandem with its companion vehicle, *Seirios*. Capable of descending to 6,000 meters, Deep Discoverer provides real-time high-definition video of the deep ocean. Its main camera can zoom in on small biological specimens from several meters away, supported by 28 high-intensity LED lights. The ROV is equipped with manipulator arms, rock and biological sample boxes, rotary suction samplers, and Niskin bottles for water collection. It also carries multiple sensors to record salinity, temperature, depth, and dissolved oxygen, making it an invaluable tool for multidisciplinary deep-sea research.

(a) (b)

(c) (d)

**Fig. 1.3** Non-Torpedo-Shaped UUVs **a** SAROV [23]. **b** Sentry AUV [23]. **c** Jason and medea ROV—A part of the NDSF project—WHOI's deep submergence laboratory [25]. **d** Deep discoverer ROV—NOAA ocean exploration [26]

### *1.2.3 Bio-Inspired or Biomimetic AUVs*

Recent research increasingly focuses on developing bio-inspired or biomimetic UUVs, which replicate or draw inspiration from biological systems found in nature to enhance their performance and adaptability in underwater environments. Fish-inspired robotic development initiated with the groundbreaking RoboTuna project at MIT [27], and since then, considerable advancements have been made in the field of bio-inspired underwater vehicles.

Oceanic organisms thrive at extreme depths and demonstrate exceptional pressure resilience, mobility, and sensory capabilities. For instance, snailfish (Fig. 1.4b)[28, 29] exhibit remarkable adaptability and survivability under the harsh deep-sea conditions found at depths of around 8,000 m. The distribution of skulls and muscle actuation in snailfish provides abundant bio-inspiration for designing multifunctional deep-sea soft robots. Inspired by such remarkable organisms, soft robots are designed to mimic muscle-like movements, offering theoretically unlimited degrees of freedom. Constructed entirely from flexible materials and highly deformable components, these soft structures enable gentle interaction with delicate specimens and adaptability in unpredictable environments (Fig. 1.4c)[29, 30].

Moreover, the principle of morphological intelligence–exemplified by the adaptive locomotion and flexibility of deep-sea organisms such as octopuses–has significantly shaped the design of modern soft robotic systems. These biologically inspired robots leverage passive mechanical properties and body morphology to simplify control strategies, reduce algorithmic complexity, and lessen reliance on high-end computational resources. Such features are particularly advantageous in deep-sea environments, where traditional rigid systems face operational and environmental limitations. Technological advancements have led to the development of soft actuators that emulate muscular hydrostats, fluidic systems inspired by hydrostatic skeletons, and dielectric elastomer-based actuators integrated with distributed electronic components. These innovations demonstrate the vital role of bioinspired design in engineering soft robotic platforms capable of reliable, adaptive performance in extreme underwater conditions. Examples include a dexterous soft manipulator that integrates bending, rotary, and grasping units for deep-sea manipulation (Fig. 1.4d) [29, 31], as well as soft robotic grippers used for the delicate collection of fragile deep-sea specimens at depths of 800 m, 843 m, and 1800 m, as shown in Fig. 1.4e[32], Fig. 1.4f [29, 33], and Fig. 1.4g [31], respectively. Furthermore, a soft jamming gripper was field-tested at a depth of 1200 m (Fig. 1.4h) [29, 34], a deep-sea soft gripper integrated with a waveguide-based tactile sensor was tested (Fig. 1.4i) [29, 35], and a bio-inspired soft robot capable of operating at a depth of 10,900 m was developed (Fig. 1.4j) [29, 36].

Overall, Fig. 1.4 provides the principles of designing bio-inspired deep-sea soft robots, covering their applications in actuation, perception, and pressure resilience. It highlights advances in delicate manipulation and untethered movement and suggests future directions, including improved locomotion, sensing capabilities, and sustainable development [29].

Recently developed biomimetic underwater vehicles [37–40] are shown in Fig. 1.5a to d. All of these AUVs emulate natural designs such as the streamlined shapes of fish and the efficient propulsion mechanisms of marine mammals, aiming for superior maneuverability, energy efficiency, and environmental adaptability compared to conventional designs. They incorporate biomimetic propulsion systems, like undulating fins or oscillating tails that mimic natural behaviors [41–43], and utilize advanced control algorithms [44, 45].

The 470 kg Manta Ray-shaped biomimetic soft robot prototype [37], developed by Northwestern Polytechnical University, China, shown in Fig. 1.5a, can dive up to 1,025 m, as demonstrated during sea trials. It has been used for observing the ocean environment and conducting submarine scientific investigations in the Xisha Islands' major coral reef [37]. Multiple variants have completed 60-day underwater glides. The RoboFish [38], developed by York University, UK, shown in Fig. 1.5b, can reach depths of 100 meters, operate for 3 h, weigh 30 kg, measure 1.9 m, and run at 0.5 knots with a 75% duty cycle. It features a modular design for flexibility and maintenance [38]. A biomimetic UUV[39] developed by Poland and Germany under the European Defence Agency (EDA) project 'A swarm of biomimetic underwater vehicles for underwater intelligence, surveillance, and reconnaissance (SABUVIS II)' is shown in Fig. 1.5c. The SABUVIS II project involves a swarm of biomimetic under-

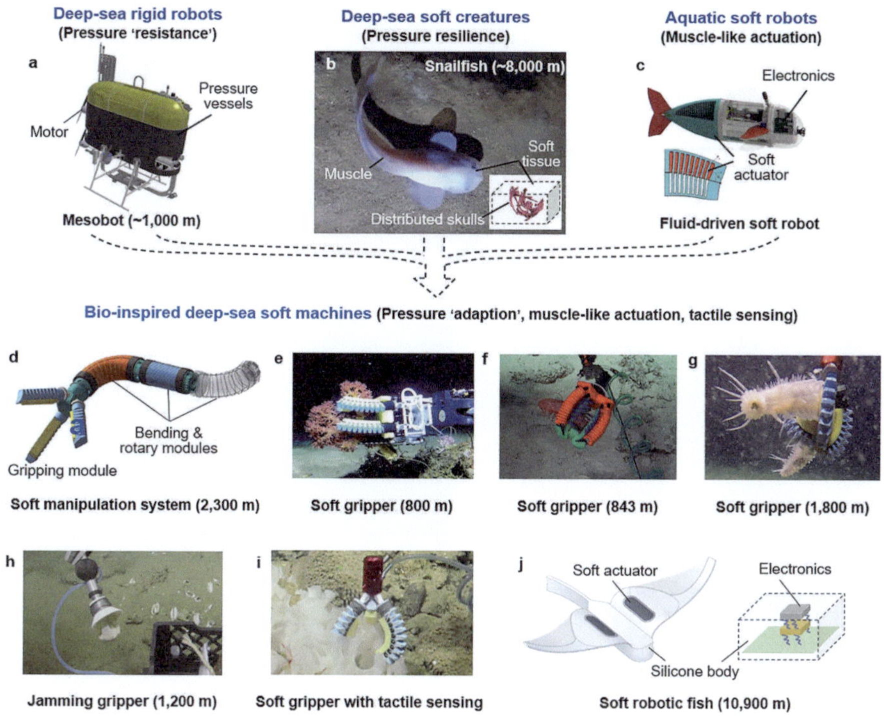


**Fig. 1.4** Deep-Sea soft robots: emerging concepts for ocean exploration [29]

water vehicles designed for intelligence, surveillance, and reconnaissance missions. Key benefits include reduced energy consumption through undulating propulsion and lower noise levels due to varied hydroacoustic signatures. The swarm's reliability is enhanced by incorporating redundant elements, ensuring mission continuity despite individual vehicle loss. The distributed sensors and devices simplify vehicle construction. The project also focuses on navigation in GPS-denied areas, optical coastal navigation systems, and new biomimetic drives [39]. ROBO-SHARK [40], shown in Fig. 1.5d, features dimensions of 2.2 m in length, 0.93 m in width, and 0.85 m in height, a weight of 75 kg, a 24Ah lithium battery, a carry-on capacity of 20 kg, and adjustable 4500LM (lumens) lights. This high-speed, low-noise bionic underwater robotic platform is designed for ocean missions. Modeled after a real shark, it uses a three-joint caudal fin instead of a propeller to minimize operational noise and power consumption. Its sound-absorbing shell enhances camouflage, making it capable of rapid target tracking and excelling in close-up and high-mobility cruising missions, with speeds reaching up to 10 knots [40].

**Fig. 1.5** Bio–Inspired UUVs **a** Manta ray shaped biomimetic robot [37]—NWPU, China **b** RoboFish Prototype—York University, UK [38] **c** Swarming biomimetic UUV [39] **d** Robo-Shark underwater robot AUV [40]

## *1.2.4 Latest Bio-Inspired and Hybrid-Shaped AUVs*

**Manta Ray UUV**

The Manta Ray prototype unmanned underwater vehicle, recently developed by NGC in partnership with DARPA, completed full-scale underwater trials in February and March 2024 [46]. These trials validated the vehicle's at-sea hydrodynamic performance, including operations using its buoyancy-driven gliding, propellers, and control surfaces for propulsion and steering. Assembled rapidly from modular subsections in the field, Manta Ray features multiple payload bays of various sizes and types, enabling versatility across naval mission sets. The latest extra-large UUV aims to establish a new standard for long-duration, long-range UUVs capable of persistent operations in dynamic maritime environments.

**HUGIN Edge AUV—Novel Lozenge Shape**

Recently, Kongsberg[47] unveiled a notable addition to its renowned HUGIN family of AUVs at Oceanology International 2022: the **HUGIN Edge**. This novel AUV immediately stood out due to its distinctive **lozenge shape**, a significant departure from the traditional torpedo-shaped designs that have long dominated the field. This innovative form factor, as depicted in Fig. 1.7, is not merely aesthetic; it's engineered to optimize **hydrodynamic efficiency**, allowing the HUGIN Edge to move through water with less resistance and greater agility.

**Fig. 1.6** Manta ray UUV [46]

**Fig. 1.7** HUGIN Edge AUV—Novel lozenge shape [47]

A key innovation lies in how the HUGIN Edge integrates its sensor suite. Unlike older models where sensors might be externally mounted, creating drag and potential points of vulnerability, the Edge seamlessly incorporates its sensors within its **flat surfaces**. This sleek integration minimizes protrusions, further enhancing its hydrodynamic profile and protecting sensitive equipment.

The HUGIN family of AUVs boasts a thirty-year legacy of successful undersea operations, pushing the boundaries of depth and endurance. The HUGIN Edge, while smaller than many of its predecessors, represents a leap forward in data collection capabilities. Measuring approximately **4 m in length** and weighing around **300 kg**, it's designed for agile and efficient missions. It can operate effectively at depths of up to **1,000 m for 24 h** at a speed of **3.8 knots**, making it ideal for a variety of oceanographic surveys and inspections.

Beyond its physical design, the HUGIN Edge is equipped with cutting-edge internal systems. Its advanced **artificial intelligence-driven mission planning algorithms** allow for more autonomous and optimized operations. This includes features like **3D sensing with a forward-looking sonar**, which is crucial for real-time path planning and robust collision avoidance in complex underwater environments. The HUGIN Edge's ability to "see" and adapt to its surroundings in three dimensions marks a substantial improvement in AUV autonomy and safety.

The HUGIN Edge signifies a pivotal advancement in AUV technology for oceanographic and subsea applications. Its unique shape, coupled with integrated sensors and intelligent navigation systems, positions it as a highly capable platform for researchers and industry professionals seeking to explore and map the underwater world with unprecedented efficiency and precision. This innovative design not only enhances performance but also opens new avenues for how AUVs can be deployed and utilized in the challenging marine environment.

Overall, the continuous development and deployment of AUVs are transforming underwater exploration and operational capabilities, making them indispensable tools for scientific research, environmental monitoring, defense, and industrial applications. Their ability to operate autonomously in challenging underwater environments ensures their growing importance and potential for future innovations in marine technology.

### *1.2.5 AUVs for Submarine Cables and Pipeline Detections and Inspections*

AUV designs have advanced significantly in their applications for detecting subsea cables and pipelines, with a notable evolution from non-torpedo-shaped to torpedo-shaped configurations. To achieve robust and consistent detection and tracking of subsea buried cables, which emit a relatively weak magnetic field, remains challenging with single electromagnetic detection methods. This requires AUVs, equipped with onboard detection equipment, to perform multiple zigzag maneuvers for successful detection and tracking. Moreover, placement of the magnetic sensors is critical, allowing them to acquire near-bottom magnetic data while minimizing electromagnetic interference from batteries, motors, and other sources onboard UUVs. Consequently, the transition from complex open frame ROVs to streamlined AUVs has been driven by the need for improved detection and tracking capabilities near the seabed. The shift from non-torpedo-shaped to torpedo-shaped UUV designs represents a significant advancement, optimizing AUVs for subsea cable detection by enhancing their maneuverability and better placement sensor integration capabilities.

The notable examples of UUVs for seafloor cable and pipeline detection and inspection include MARCAS-V ROVs [48], Qianlong AUVs, AE-2000 AUVs, Freedom AUV, and REMUS 600 AUV. For instance, the MARCAS-V[48] ROV, depicted in Fig. 1.8a, is an open-frame, complex-shaped ROV equipped with TSS-440 and TSS-350 magnetometers for subsea pipeline and cable detection operations[48, 49]. The MT-98 AUV [50], shown in Fig. 1.8c, enhances cable detection capabilities with its onboard VIC and EMS systems [49, 50]. Qianlong II & III (Fig. 1.8b) [49, 51], non-torpedo-shaped AUVs designed for cable detection, utilize a three-component fluxgate magnetometer mounted on their stern to acquire near-bottom magnetic data while minimizing electromagnetic interference. Their unique shape and actuator configuration improve near-bottom maneuverability for effective magnetic-based sensing[49]. The Aqua Explorer (AE) family prototypes [49, 52], shown in Fig. 1.8e, demonstrate further innovations in AUV design. These AUVs, from AE-1000 to AE-2000, underwent significant improvements in shape and actuator configuration to enhance maneuverability near the seabed, improving electromagnetic field detection accuracy and reducing reliance on surface vessels and ROV navigators [49]. Recently, the streamlined, non-torpedo-shaped 'Freedom AUV'[53], shown in Fig. 1.8d, was introduced for pipeline inspection applications. It inspects pipelines at low altitudes (3–5 m from the seabed) for high-resolution data and at 8 m for reconnaissance and seabed mapping. Equipped with advanced obstacle detection, autonomous avoidance capabilities, and high-spec instruments like INS, LSS, and Multibeam Sonar, it ensures safety and efficient pipeline tracking [53]. Very recently, the torpedo-shaped REMUS 600 AUV [54], shown in Fig. 1.8f, developed by WHOI and equipped with a Self-Compensating Magnetometer (SCM), has been deployed to perform the localization of seafloor cables [54].

## 1.3 Merits and Demerits of AUV Designs

A summary of the merits and demerits of torpedo-shaped, non-torpedo-shaped, and bioinspired AUVs is as follows:

**(1) Classic-Myring AUVs**

**Merits**

- Hydrodynamically efficient for high speeds and long-range missions
- Hermetically sealed hull for deep-sea pressure resilience

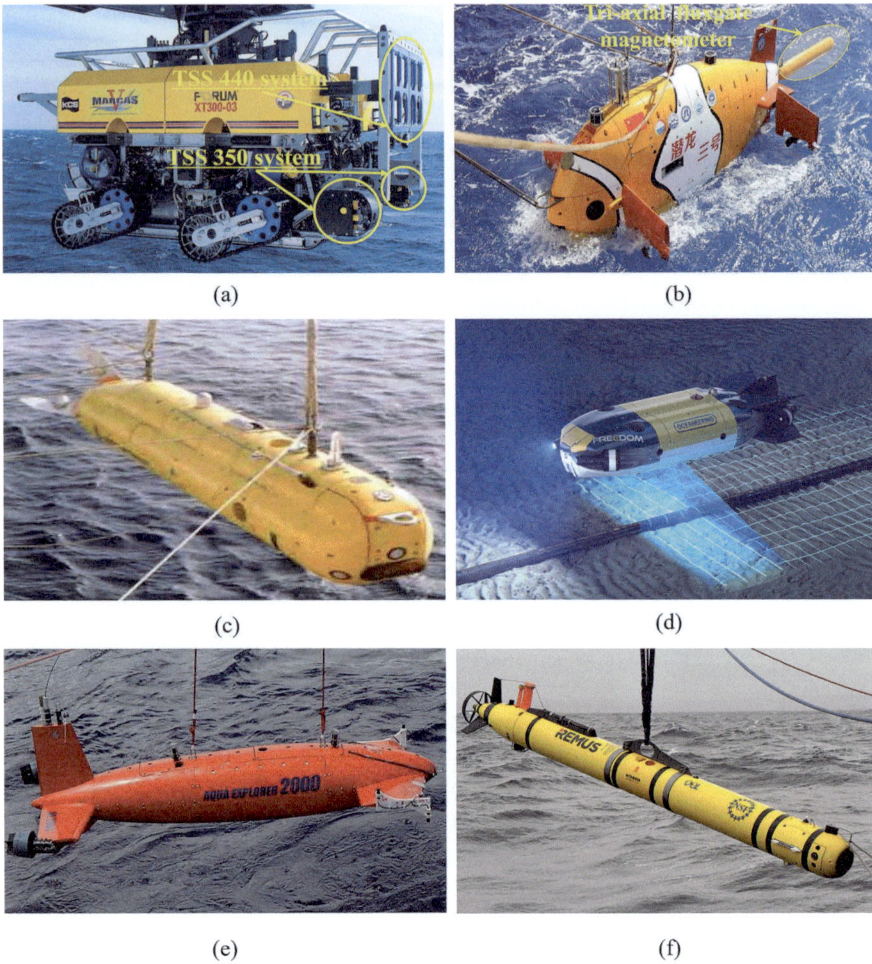


**Fig. 1.8** Submarine cables and pipeline inspection AUVs **a** MARCAS-V ROVs [48] **b** Qianlong II and III[51] **c** MT-98 AUV[50] **d** Freedom AUV [53] **e** Aqua explorer (AE)-2000 [52] **f** REMUS 600 AUV [54]

- Maneuverability with fins and IMU for precise navigation
- Streamlined design minimizes drag, enhancing energy efficiency
- High reliability and robustness in extreme underwater conditions

**Demerits**:

- Limited payload capacity due to compact design
- Challenges in stable control under certain conditions
- Less adaptable to complex payload configurations and specialized equipment requirements

- Reduced versatility in accommodating non-standard mission profiles
- Higher noise levels generated at high speeds, making detection more likely
- Difficulties in modification or retrofit for changing operational needs

**(2) Complex-Shaped and Open Frame AUVs**

**Merits**:

- Capability to accommodate diverse payloads and equipment configurations
- Modular design for easier system reconfiguration
- Superior stability for operations requiring stationary tasks or slow movement
- Better suited for scientific missions, such as seabed mapping and sample collection
- Greater capacity for complex sensor arrays and multi-functional equipment

**Demerits**:

- Lower hydrodynamic efficiency compared to streamlined classical myring AUVs
- Increased maintenance complexity due to intricate designs and varied system configurations
- Limited speed and maneuverability in some operational scenarios
- Larger cross-sectional area increases drag, impacting energy consumption
- Bulkier design may limit access to tight or confined underwater spaces
- Potentially higher production costs due to specialized components and design

**(3) Bioinspired AUVs**

**Merits**:

- Enhanced maneuverability and energy efficiency inspired by biological models
- Quieter operation for reduced detection risks
- Improved adaptability to harsh underwater environments
- Greater agility allows for operations in complex or cluttered environments
- Biomimetic propulsion systems reduce environmental impact and noise pollution
- Superior performance in tasks requiring precision, such as monitoring marine wildlife

**Demerits**:

- Technical challenges and high development costs
- Complex integration and validation of biomimetic technologies
- Limited operational data and reliability in diverse underwater conditions
- Maintenance and repair can be difficult due to intricate, non-traditional components
- Biomimetic designs may be less efficient at high speeds compared to streamlined shapes
- Research and development require significant investment in advanced material science and control algorithms.

## 1.4 Summary

The chapter provides an overview of the evolution of oceanography and highlights the role of underwater vehicles in advancing marine exploration. It covers various Autonomous Underwater Vehicle (AUV) designs, from streamlined torpedo-shaped models to complex and bio-inspired shapes, discussing their specific applications in seabed mapping, environmental monitoring, and deep-sea exploration. Recent advancements, particularly in bioinspired designs that enhance maneuverability, energy efficiency, and operational performance, are also addressed. The chapter concludes by examining the merits and limitations of different AUV designs, offering valuable insights for scientists, engineers, and academics.

## References

1. Ahmed, F., Xiang, X., Jiang, C., Xiang, G., Yang, S.: Survey on traditional and AI based estimation techniques for hydrodynamic coefficients of autonomous underwater vehicle. Ocean Eng. **268**, 113300 (2023)
2. Sivčev, S., Coleman, J., Omerdić, E., Dooly, G., Toal, D.: Underwater manipulators: a review. Ocean Eng. **163**, 431–450 (2018)
3. Shang, D., Li, X., Yin, M., Zhou, S.: Dynamic modeling and rotation control for flexible single-link underwater manipulator considering flowing water environment based on modified morison equation. Ocean Eng. **291**, 116427 (2024)
4. Hu, X., Chen, J., Zhou, H., Ren, Z.: Development of underwater electric manipulator based on interventional autonomous underwater vehicle (AUV). J. Zhejiang Univ.-Sci. A **25**(3), 238–250 (2024)
5. Xiong, X., Xiang, X., Wang, Z., Yang, S.: On dynamic coupling effects of underwater vehicle-dual-manipulator system. Ocean Eng. **258**, 111699 (2022)
6. Von Alt, C.: Autonomous underwater vehicles. In: Autonomous Underwater Lagrangian Platforms and Sensors Workshop, vol. 3, p. 2 (2003)
7. Gafurov, S.A., Klochkov, E.V.: Autonomous unmanned underwater vehicles development tendencies. Procedia Eng. **106**, 141–148 (2015)
8. Sahoo, A., Dwivedy, S.K., Robi, P.: Advancements in the field of autonomous underwater vehicle. Ocean Eng. **181**, 145–160 (2019)
9. Widditsch, H.: Spurv-the first decade. Washington UNIV Seattle Applied Physics LAB, Technical report (1973)
10. Nodland, W., Ewart, T., Bendiner, W., Miller, J., Aagaard, E.: Spurv ii-an unmanned, free-swimming submersible developed for oceanographic research. In: OCEANS 81, pp. 92–98. IEEE (1981)
11. McPhail, S.: Autosub6000: A deep diving long range AUV. J. Bionic Eng. **6**(1), 55–62 (2009). https://doi.org/10.1016/S1672-6529(08)60095-5. https://www.sciencedirect.com/science/article/pii/S1672652908600955
12. Furlong, M.E., Paxton, D., Stevenson, P., Pebody, M., McPhail, S.D., Perrett, J.: Autosub long range: A long range deep diving AUV for ocean monitoring. In: 2012 IEEE/OES Autonomous Underwater Vehicles (AUV), pp. 1–7 (2012). https://doi.org/10.1109/AUV.2012.6380737
13. Yang, Y., Xiao, Y., Li, T.: A survey of autonomous underwater vehicle formation: performance, formation control, and communication capability. IEEE Commun. Surv. Tutor. **23**(2), 815–841 (2021)
14. Liu, G., Chen, L., Liu, K., Luo, Y.: A swarm of unmanned vehicles in the shallow ocean: a survey. Neurocomputing **531**, 74–86 (2023)

15. WHOI (2024). https://www2.whoi.edu/site/osl/vehicles/
16. Kongsberg (2024). https://www.kongsberg.com/discovery/autonomous-and-uncrewed-solutions/auv/hugin/
17. NavalTechnology. https://www.naval-technology.com/projects/bluefin-21-autonomous-underwater-vehicle-auv/
18. MITNews2014 (2024). https://news.mit.edu/2014/robot-dives-search-malaysian-airlines-flight
19. Underwood, A., Murphy, C.: Design of a micro-AUV for autonomy development and multi-vehicle systems. In: OCEANS 2017-Aberdeen, pp. 1–6. IEEE (2017)
20. AtlasElektronik (2024). https://www.atlas-elektronik.com/solutions/mine-warfare-systems/seacat.html
21. Zhang, J., Xiang, X., Li, W., Zhang, Q.: Adaptive neural control of flight-style AUV for subsea cable tracking under electromagnetic localization guidance. IEEE/ASME Trans. Mechatron. (2023)
22. Ahmed, F., Xiang, X., Wang, H., Zhang, J., Xiang, G., Yang, S.: Nonlinear dynamics of novel flight-style autonomous underwater vehicle with bow wings, part i: ase and cfd based estimations of hydrodynamic coefficients, part ii: nonlinear dynamic modeling and experimental validations. Appl. Ocean Res. **141**, 103739 (2023)
23. SAAB (2024). https://www.saab.com/products/double-eagle
24. Hong, L., Wang, X., Zhang, D.S.: Cfd-based hydrodynamic performance investigation of autonomous underwater vehicles: a survey. Ocean Eng. **305**, 117911 (2024)
25. WHOI (2024). https://www.whoi.edu/what-we-do/explore/underwater-vehicles/ndsf-jason/
26. NOAA-OCEAN-EXPLORER (2024). https://oceanexplorer.noaa.gov/technology/subs/deep-discoverer/deep-discoverer.html
27. Tolkoff, S.W.: Robotics and power measurements of the robotuna. Ph.D. thesis, Massachusetts Institute of Technology (1999)
28. Wang, K., Shen, Y., Yang, Y., Gan, X., Liu, G., Hu, K., Li, Y., Gao, Z., Zhu, L., Yan, G., et al.: Morphology and genome of a snailfish from the Mariana trench provide insights into deep-sea adaptation. Nat. Ecol. Evol. **3**(5), 823–833 (2019)
29. Li, G., Wong, T.W., Shih, B., Guo, C., Wang, L., Liu, J., Wang, T., Liu, X., Yan, J., Wu, B., et al.: Bioinspired soft robots for deep-sea exploration. Nat. Commun. **14**(1), 7097 (2023)
30. Katzschmann, R.K., DelPreto, J., MacCurdy, R., Rus, D.: Exploration of underwater life with an acoustically controlled soft robotic fish. Sci. Robot. **3**(16), eaar3449 (2018)
31. Phillips, B.T., Becker, K.P., Kurumaya, S., Galloway, K.C., Whittredge, G., Vogt, D.M., Teeple, C.B., Rosen, M.H., Pieribone, V.A., Gruber, D.F., et al.: A dexterous, glove-based teleoperable low-power soft robotic arm for delicate deep-sea biological exploration. Sci. Rep. **8**(1), 14779 (2018)
32. Galloway, K.C., Becker, K.P., Phillips, B., Kirby, J., Licht, S., Tchernov, D., Wood, R.J., Gruber, D.F.: Soft robotic grippers for biological sampling on deep reefs. Soft Rob. **3**(1), 23–33 (2016)
33. Vogt, D.M., Becker, K.P., Phillips, B.T., Graule, M.A., Rotjan, R.D., Shank, T.M., Cordes, E.E., Wood, R.J., Gruber, D.F.: Shipboard design and fabrication of custom 3d-printed soft robotic manipulators for the investigation of delicate deep-sea organisms. PLoS ONE **13**(8), e0200386 (2018)
34. Licht, S., Collins, E., Mendes, M.L., Baxter, C.: Stronger at depth: jamming grippers as deep sea sampling tools. Soft Rob. **4**(4), 305–316 (2017)
35. Teeple, C.B., Becker, K.P., Wood, R.J.: Soft curvature and contact force sensors for deep-sea grasping via soft optical waveguides. In: 2018 IEEE/RSJ International Conference on Intelligent Robots and Systems (IROS), pp. 1621–1627. IEEE (2018)
36. Laschi, C., Calisti, M.: Soft robot reaches the deepest part of the ocean (2021)
37. NPUGazette (2021). https://en.nwpu.edu.cn/info/1175/3801.htm
38. Gorma, W., Post, M.A., White, J., Gardner, J., Luo, Y., Kim, J., Mitchell, P.D., Morozs, N., Wright, M., Xiao, Q.: Development of modular bio-inspired autonomous underwater vehicle for close subsea asset inspection. Appl. Sci. **11**(12), 5401 (2021)

39. Nathan, G.: (NavalNews2019). https://www.navalnews.com/naval-news/2019/10/eda-expands-swarming-biomimetic-uuv-development-program/
40. ROBOSEA (2024). http://www.robosea.org/sanguanjie.html
41. Randeni, S., Mellin, E.M., Sacarny, M., Cheung, S., Benjamin, M., Triantafyllou, M.: Bioinspired morphing fins to provide optimal maneuverability, stability, and response to turbulence in rigid hull auvs. Bioinspir. Biomimetics **17**(3), 036012 (2022)
42. Li, J., Li, W., Liu, Q., Luo, B., Cui, W.: Current status and technical challenges in the development of biomimetic robotic fish-type submersible. Ocean-Land-Atmosph. Res. **3**, 0036 (2024)
43. Gan, W., Zhuang, J., Zhang, Y., Zuo, Z., Xiang, J.: Numerical investigation of the water-entry impact performance of a bionic unmanned aerial-underwater vehicle. Ocean Eng. **303**, 117458 (2024)
44. Xiong, X., Xiang, X., Duan, Y., Yang, S.: Adaptive sndo-stsm hierarchical robust control of autonomous underwater vehicle: theory and experimental validation. IEEE Trans. Ind. Electron. (2024)
45. Cui, Z., Li, L., Wang, Y., Zhong, Z., Li, J.: Review of research and control technology of underwater bionic robots. Intell. Marine Technol. Syst. **1**(1), 7 (2023)
46. DARPA (2024). https://www.darpa.mil/news-events/2024-05-01
47. Kongsberg (2022). https://www.kongsberg.com/maritime/the-full-picture-magazine/2022/7/pushing-the-edge-of-auv-design/
48. KCS (2024). https://www.k-kcs.co.jp/english/cableship/marcas5.html
49. Zhang, J., Xiang, X., Li, W.: Advances in marine intelligent electromagnetic detection system, technology and applications: a review. IEEE Sens. J. (2021)
50. Inzartsev, A., Pavin, A.: Auv application for inspection of underwater communications. Underwater Vehicles (December) (2009)
51. Wu, T., Tao, C., Zhang, J., Wang, A., Zhang, G., Zhou, J., Deng, X.: A hydrothermal investigation system for the qianlong-ii autonomous underwater vehicle. Acta Oceanol. Sin. **38**, 159–165 (2019)
52. Kojima, J.: Cable tracking of autonomous underwater vehicle aqua explorer 1000. Proc. Underwater Invention'94 pp. 349–356 (1994)
53. Oceaneering (2022). https://www.oceaneering.com/oceaneering-announces-freedom-auv-achieves-trl-6-for-pipeline-inspection/
54. Littlefield, R.H., Soenen, K., Packard, G., Kaeli, J.: Seafloor cable based navigation and monitoring with autonomous underwater vehicles. In: OCEANS 2019 MTS/IEEE SEATTLE, pp. 1–5. IEEE (2019)

# Chapter 2
# Principles of Autonomous Underwater Vehicle Dynamics

## 2.1 Fundamentals of AUV Dynamics

The fundamentals of AUV dynamics modeling involve physical principles and mathematical formulations required to describe and predict the AUV's motion in three-dimensional (3D) space under various operational and environmental conditions. It is divided into kinematics and kinetics. Together, kinematics and kinetics provide a comprehensive framework for modeling AUV motion, capturing both trajectory and the governing forces. Kinematics focuses on the transformation of linear and angular velocities, describing how the position, orientation, and velocity of the vehicle change over time. It deals only geometrical aspects of motion without considering forces, using a three-dimensional coordinate system (e.g., North-East-Down frame) and Euler angles (roll, pitch, yaw) or quaternions for orientation. The AUV's motion is further described by linear and angular velocities, which are transformed between the body-fixed and earth-fixed reference frames using rotation matrices.

Kinetics, on the other hand, deals with the forces and moments acting on the vehicle, including those from hydrodynamic interactions and external influences, and their effect on motion. Kinetics focuses on the forces and moments driving the AUV's motion, governed by Newton's Second Law. Translational motion is described by the equation

$$m\,\frac{d}{dt}\left(\boldsymbol{\nu}_{G/n}\right) = \mathbf{F}_{\text{ext}} + \mathbf{F}_{\text{hydro}},$$

where $m$ is the AUV's mass, $\boldsymbol{\nu}_G$ is the velocity of the AUV's rigid body center of mass in the inertial frame. $\mathbf{F}_{\text{ext}}$ and $\mathbf{F}_{\text{hydro}}$ represent external forces and hydrodynamic forces, respectively. Rotational motion is described by the moment equation

$$\mathbf{I}\dot{\boldsymbol{\omega}} + \boldsymbol{\omega} \times (\mathbf{I}\boldsymbol{\omega}) = \mathbf{M}_{\text{ext}} + \mathbf{M}_{\text{hydro}},$$

where $\mathbf{I}$ is the inertia matrix, $\boldsymbol{\omega}$ is the angular velocity, and $\mathbf{M}_{\text{ext}}$ and $\mathbf{M}_{\text{hydro}}$ represent external and hydrodynamic moments, respectively.

 
X. Xiang et al., *Dynamics Modeling and Maneuvering of Autonomous Underwater Vehicles*, https://doi.org/10.1007/978-981-95-1521-9_2

The dynamics of an AUV are significantly influenced by **hydrodynamic forces and moments**. These forces mainly include lift and drag, resulting from the interaction between the vehicle and the surrounding fluid. Lift is generated by the AUV's wings or control surfaces, while drag represents the resistance encountered as the vehicle moves through the water. Moments, such as pitching, rolling, and yawing, are induced by hydrodynamic forces acting on the vehicle's body and appendages. Additionally, added mass and damping effects must be considered, particularly for vehicles operating at high speeds or in transient conditions, as these induce extra forces due to the fluid's inertia and viscosity.

The dynamic behavior of the AUV is typically described using **dynamic models** that represent the equations of motion. These models integrate the forces and moments acting on the vehicle to predict its position, velocity, and orientation over time. In addition to modeling the forces, it is essential to account for **control inputs and actuators**, such as thrusters and control surfaces. These actuators alter the forces and moments in the equations of motion, enabling the AUV to maneuver. Thrusters generate thrust forces in the direction of their orientation, while control surfaces, such as rudders or wings, produce forces and moments that change the vehicle's orientation.

Finally, **environmental effects** play a critical role in shaping the AUV's motion. Ocean currents, waves, tides, and even vehicle-acoustic interactions must be considered, as they can introduce additional forces and moments that affect the AUV's trajectory and stability. These effects become particularly pronounced in deep or expansive underwater environments. The inherent **non-linearities and complexities** of AUV dynamics, such as those caused by large angles of attack, hydrodynamic interference, and variable depths or speeds, require detailed modeling techniques to accurately predict the vehicle's behavior in diverse operational conditions. Therefore, a comprehensive understanding of both kinematics and kinetics is essential for the precise modeling and control of AUVs in real-world environments.

## 2.2 Degrees of Freedom and AUV Motion

AUVs underwater motion is described in six degrees of freedom (DOFs), which define the independent displacements and rotations required to fully describe the vehicle's position and orientation, as shown in Fig. 2.1. The translational motions are **surge**, which refers to forward and backward motion, **sway**, which represents sideways motion, and **heave**, which represents vertical motion. The rotational motions are **roll**, which refers to rotation about the vehicle's longitudinal axis, **pitch**, which refers to rotation about the transverse axis, and **yaw**, which refers to rotation about the vertical axis that defines the vehicle's heading. These six DOFs provide a comprehensive description of the vehicle's motion and are essential for modeling its dynamics and maneuvering behavior.

The maneuvering dynamics models can be 1DOF, 3DOF, 4DOF or 6DOF models.

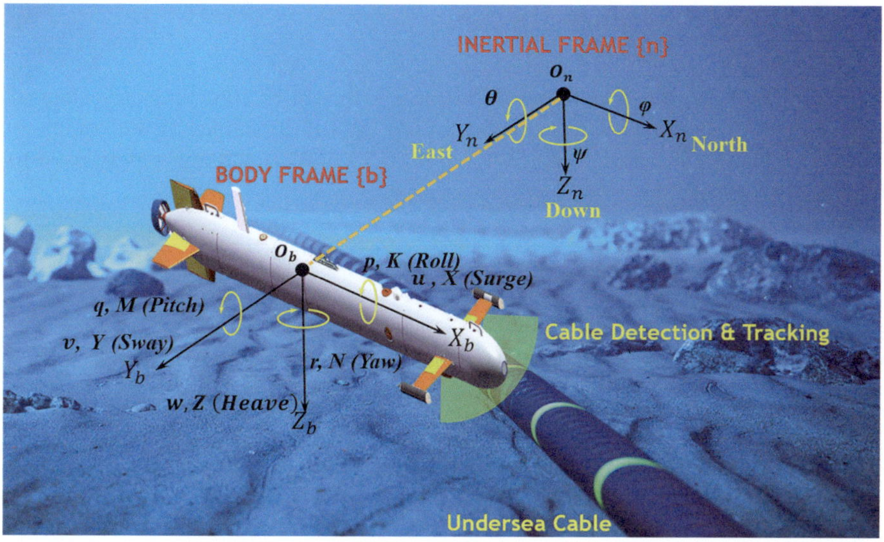


**Fig. 2.1** Earth-Fixed and body-fixed coordinate systems [1]

### *2.2.1 1 DOF Dynamics Modeling*

1 DOF dynamics modeling refers to modeling a system in a single direction or rotational axis. In the context of AUVs, it focuses on a specific type of motion, such as forward speed control (surge), heading control (yaw), or roll damping. For example:

- **Surge**: Describes the forward and backward motion of the AUV along its longitudinal axis. This model is useful for designing controllers that regulate the vehicle's speed, such as speed controllers or autopilots focused on longitudinal motion.
- **Yaw**: Involves rotation about the vertical axis, controlling the vehicle's heading. Yaw control is typically used in navigation systems and heading autopilots.
- **Roll**: Describes the rotation about the vehicle's longitudinal axis. Roll damping systems focus on reducing excessive roll movements that could affect stability or human comfort in some cases.

1 DOF models are useful when the motion of the AUV can be simplified to one key direction or axis, reducing computational complexity and focusing on specific control tasks.

### 2.2.2 3 DOF Dynamics Modeling

In 3 DOF models, the dynamics are typically decoupled into three translational and rotational motions. These models simplify the full dynamics of the vehicle by focusing on a specific plane (either horizontal or vertical) and are widely used for AUV motion control systems.

**(1) Horizontal Plane (Surge, Sway, Yaw)**

- **Surge**: Forward/backward motion along the longitudinal axis.
- **Sway**: Side-to-side motion along the lateral axis.
- **Yaw**: Rotation about the vertical axis, determining the vehicle's heading.

Horizontal plane 3 DOF models are often used in dynamic positioning systems, trajectory tracking, and path-following applications, where the focus is on controlling the vehicle's motion in the horizontal plane, such as maintaining a steady course or following a specific path.

**(2) Vertical Plane (Surge, Heave, Pitch)**

- **Surge**: Forward/backward motion along the longitudinal axis.
- **Heave**: Vertical motion (up and down).
- **Pitch**: Rotation about the transverse axis, affecting the vehicle's angle of ascent or descent.

Vertical plane 3 DOF models are primarily applied to control depth, diving operations, and pitch stability, which are important for AUVs performing underwater missions.

**(3) 4 DOF Dynamics Modeling**

4 DOF models focus on surge, sway, roll, and yaw. These models are used when the roll motion is significant, especially in situations where it is necessary to reduce roll through active control systems such as fins, rudders, or stabilizing liquid tanks. By incorporating the roll dynamics, these models allow for better control of the vehicle's stability and orientation, particularly in maneuvering operations or in environments where roll motion can significantly affect the performance or safety of the AUV.

**(4) 6 DOF Dynamics Modeling**

6 DOF dynamics modeling is the most comprehensive model, involving all six independent motions: three translational motions (surge, sway, heave) and three rotational motions (roll, pitch, yaw). This model is fully coupled, meaning that all motion axes interact with each other, providing a complete description of the AUV's movement in 3D space.

- **Surge**: Forward/backward motion.
- **Sway**: Side-to-side motion.
- **Heave**: Vertical motion.
- **Roll**: Rotation about the longitudinal axis.
- **Pitch**: Rotation about the transverse axis.
- **Yaw**: Rotation about the vertical axis.

6 DOF models are used for simulation, prediction, and control of the full range of AUV motion. They are essential for advanced control systems where all axes are actuated, such as in high-precision tasks that require the vehicle to move freely and independently in all directions, such as navigation in complex environments or when performing multi-axis maneuvers.

### 2.2.3 *Summary*

- **1 DOF models**: Simplified models for a single direction or rotational motion (e.g., surge, yaw, roll).
- **3 DOF models**: Models for horizontal or vertical planes (surge, sway, yaw for horizontal; surge, heave, pitch for vertical).
- **4 DOF models**: Surge, sway, roll, and yaw models used when roll motion is important, particularly for active roll control systems.
- **6 DOF models**: Fully coupled models capturing all independent translational and rotational motions, used for comprehensive vehicle behavior simulation and control.

Each of these models is used depending on the complexity of the task and the type of control required for the AUV's motion.

## 2.3 Nonlinear Dynamics Modeling of AUV

The dynamic modeling of the vehicle is categorized into kinematics and kinetics. Kinematics describes the geometric aspects of motion, such as position, velocity, and orientation, without considering the forces involved. In contrast, kinetics focuses on the modeling of hydrodynamic forces and moments acting on the vehicle. The mathematical formulations for both kinematics and kinetics in vector form are presented in Eqs. (2.1) and (2.2), respectively [2].

$$\dot{\eta} = \boldsymbol{J}_{\Theta}(\eta)\boldsymbol{\nu} \tag{2.1}$$

$$\boldsymbol{M}\dot{\boldsymbol{\nu}} + \boldsymbol{C}(\boldsymbol{\nu})\boldsymbol{\nu} + \boldsymbol{D}(\boldsymbol{\nu})\boldsymbol{\nu} + \boldsymbol{g}(\eta) = \boldsymbol{\tau} \tag{2.2}$$

### 2.3.1 Modeling Assumptions and Simplifications

In order to simplify the dynamic modeling of an AUV, a set of standard assumptions is typically adopted. First, the AUV is treated as a rigid body, implying that deformations of the structure during motion are negligible. The vehicle's geometry is assumed to be symmetric with respect to both the horizontal (top/bottom) and vertical (port/starboard) planes, which simplifies the formulation of hydrodynamic forces and moments. Furthermore, the AUV is considered neutrally buoyant, meaning the net buoyant force is equal to its weight, resulting in stable submerged operation without requiring additional trimming forces. The origin of the body-fixed coordinate system is positioned at the center of gravity of the vehicle to streamline the derivation of motion equations. Finally, the AUV is assumed to remain fully submerged throughout its operation, thereby allowing the influence of free-surface and wave effects to be neglected. These assumptions enable a more tractable and analytically manageable dynamic model for control and simulation purposes.

### 2.3.2 Kinematics Modeling

Kinematics modeling focuses on mathematically representing an AUV's position, orientation, velocity, and acceleration within a specified reference frame, as described in Eq. (2.1), without considering the forces and moments that cause the motion. This framework is essential for understanding and predicting the vehicle's states.

**(1) Coordinate Frames**

To investigate the 6-DOF motion of underwater vehicles, two orthogonal coordinate systems are required: one is the earth-fixed (inertial frame) and the other is the body-fixed (body-frame) coordinate system, as shown in Fig. 2.2. In the context of dynamics and control of AUVs, these reference frames are essential to describe the motion of the vehicle.

The Body-Fixed Frame is a coordinate system that moves with the AUV, typically denoted by $X_b$, $Y_b$, $Z_b$. The origin of this frame is often located at the center of mass of the AUV or at a point that simplifies the mathematical modeling of its dynamics. The axes are aligned with the principal directions of the vehicle: $X_b$ usually points forward, $Y_b$ points to the right, and $Z_b$ points downward (assuming a right-handed coordinate system). This frame is used to describe the local motion of the AUV, including its linear and angular velocities. Equations of motion, forces, and moments acting on the vehicle are often formulated in this frame, making it essential for understanding and analysing the AUV's dynamic behavior.

The Earth-Fixed Frame (Inertial Frame) is a stationary reference frame that is fixed relative to the Earth, typically denoted by $X_n$, $Y_n$, $Z_n$. The origin of this frame can be chosen arbitrarily, often at a specific location on the Earth's surface or in the water, such as the initial position of the AUV. The axes are typically aligned with geographic or geocentric coordinates: $X_n$ points towards the North direction, $Y_n$ points towards the East direction, and $Z_n$ points downward towards, the center of

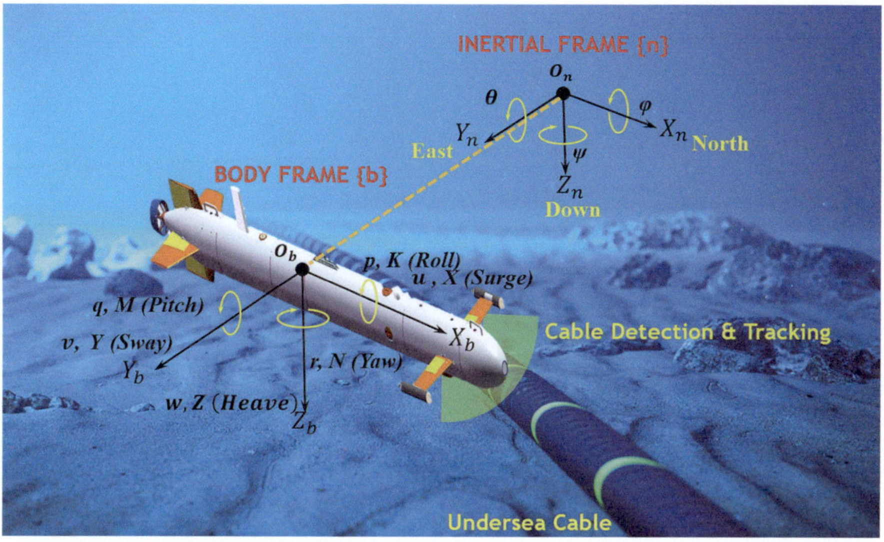


**Fig. 2.2** Earth-fixed and body-fixed coordinate systems [1]

the Earth. This frame is used to describe the global position and orientation of the AUV, providing a fixed reference point that allows for the description of the vehicle's trajectory and overall movement relative to the Earth.

### (2) Positions and Orientations

The positions and orientations of the vehicle with respect to inertial frame $\{n\}$ are represented by vector $\boldsymbol{\eta}$ in Eq. (2.1) is given as follows:

$$\boldsymbol{\eta} = \left[\, \boldsymbol{p}^{n}_{b/n}, \boldsymbol{\Theta}_{nb} \right]^{\top}$$

where,

$\boldsymbol{p}^{n}_{b/n} = [\, x, y, z]^{\top} \in \mathbb{R}^3$ represents the NED position,

$\boldsymbol{\Theta}_{nb} = [\, \phi, \theta, \psi]^{\top} \in \mathcal{S}^3$ represents the orientation (Euler angles).

### (3) Translational and Angular Velocities

The translational and angular velocities of the vehicle are represented by the vector $\nu$ in Eq. (2.1) is given as follows:

$$\boldsymbol{\nu} = \left[\, \boldsymbol{v}^{b}_{b/n}, \boldsymbol{\omega}^{b}_{b/n} \right]^{\top}$$

where,

$\boldsymbol{v}^{b}_{b/n} = [\, u, v, w]^{\top} \in \mathbb{R}^3$ represents linear velocities (surge, sway & heave) in {b},

$\boldsymbol{\omega}^{b}_{b/n} = [\, p, q, r]^{\top} \in \mathbb{R}^3$ represents angular velocities (roll, pitch & yaw rates) in {b}.

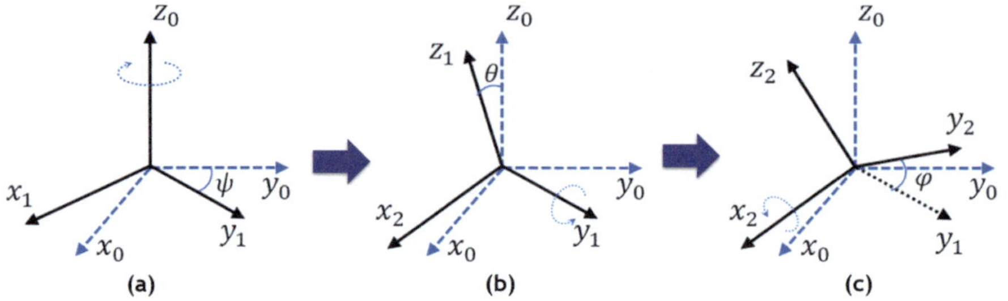


**Fig. 2.3** Sequence of three rotations following $z-y-x$ Euler convention

### (4) Transformation Matrices

In AUV dynamics, transformation matrices and Euler angle transformations are essential for describing the vehicle's orientation and motion between body-fixed and earth-fixed frames. Euler angles (yaw, pitch, roll) define the AUV's orientation through sequential rotations, crucial for accurate motion modeling in navigation, control, and stability. They represent the orientation of the body-fixed frame relative to the inertial frame, describing the motion of a 3D rigid body through a sequence of rotations. Euler angle transformation involves rotating one coordinate system with respect to another through a specific sequence of three rotations.

In guidance, navigation, and control applications of AUVs, the z-y-x (zyx) convention is commonly used to derive the rotation matrix formulations. This convention specifies the sequence of Euler angles $\psi$, $\theta$, and $\phi$ for the rotations from frame {b} to frame {n}. In this zyx Euler convention, the body-fixed frame {b} is first rotated around the z-axis (yaw, $\psi$), followed by the y-axis (pitch, $\theta$), and finally around the x-axis (roll, $\phi$). The order of these rotations is important and is illustrated in Fig. 2.3. The sequential rotations in 3D space about the principal axes $z$, $y$, and $x$ are mathematically represented by the rotation matrices $\boldsymbol{R}_{z,\psi}$ , $\boldsymbol{R}_{y,\theta}$, and $\boldsymbol{R}_{x,\phi}$, given in Eq. (2.3).

$$\boldsymbol{R}_{z,\psi}=\begin{bmatrix}\cos\psi & -\sin\psi & 0\\ \sin\psi & \cos\psi & 0\\ 0 & 0 & 1\end{bmatrix},\quad \boldsymbol{R}_{y,\theta}=\begin{bmatrix}\cos\theta & 0 & \sin\theta\\ 0 & 1 & 0\\ -\sin\theta & 0 & \cos\theta\end{bmatrix},\quad \boldsymbol{R}_{x,\phi}=\begin{bmatrix}1 & 0 & 0\\ 0 & \cos\phi & -\sin\phi\\ 0 & \sin\phi & \cos\phi\end{bmatrix} \tag{2.3}$$

The yaw rotation matrix ($\boldsymbol{R}_{z,\psi}$) represents a rotation about the $z$-axis by the yaw angle $\psi$ (Fig. 2.3a). It rotates the $x$ and $y$ coordinates in the $xy$-plane, while the $z$ coordinate remains unchanged. The rotation matrix $\boldsymbol{R}_{z,\psi}$ is applied to observe the heading of the AUV in the inertial frame $\{n\}$.

The pitch rotation matrix ( $\boldsymbol{R}_{y,\theta}$ ) represents a rotation about the $y$-axis by the pitch angle $\theta$ (Fig. 2.3b). Here, the $x$ and $z$ coordinates are rotated in the $xz$-plane, while the $y$ coordinate remains unchanged. Pitch rotation is typically used to describe the pitching up or down motion of the AUV in inertial frame $\{n\}$.

The roll rotation matrix ( $\boldsymbol{R}_{x,\phi}$ ) represents a rotation about the $x$-axis by the roll angle $\phi$ (Fig. 2.3c). In this case, the $y$ and $z$ coordinates are rotated in the $yz$-plane, while the $x$ coordinate remains unchanged. Roll rotation matrix is used to describe the rotation of an AUV around its forward axis.

**(5) Translational Velocity Transformation**

The transformation matrix, denoted by $\boldsymbol{R}_b^n(\boldsymbol{\Theta}_{nb})$, relates the body-fixed translational velocities $u$, $v$, and $w$ ($\boldsymbol{v}_{b/n}^b = [\ u,\ v,\ w]^\top \in \mathbb{R}^3$ ) to the time derivatives of the inertial frame positions $\dot{x}$, $\dot{y}$, and $\dot{z}$ ($\dot{\boldsymbol{p}}_{b/n}^n = [\ \dot{x},\ \dot{y},\ \dot{z}]^\top \in \mathbb{R}^3$).

The combined transformation matrix $\boldsymbol{R}_b^n(\boldsymbol{\Theta}_{nb})$ to describe the orientation of an AUV body-fixed frame relative to an inertial frame is obtained by multiplying the three matrices $\boldsymbol{R}_{z,\psi}$, $\boldsymbol{R}_{y,\theta}$ and $\boldsymbol{R}_{x,\phi}$. The resulting matrix ($\boldsymbol{R}_b^n(\boldsymbol{\Theta}_{nb})$), in the z-y-x (yaw-pitch-roll) convention can be mathematically written in Eqs. (2.4) and (2.5).

$$\boldsymbol{R}_b^n(\Theta_{nb}) = \boldsymbol{R}_{z,\psi}\boldsymbol{R}_{y,\theta}\boldsymbol{R}_{x,\phi} \tag{2.4}$$

$$\boldsymbol{R}_b^n(\boldsymbol{\Theta}_{nb}) = \begin{bmatrix} c\psi c\theta & -s\psi c\phi + c\psi s\theta s\phi & s\psi s\phi + c\psi c\phi s\theta \\ s\psi c\theta & c\psi c\phi + s\phi s\theta s\psi & -c\psi s\phi + s\theta s\psi c\phi \\ -s\theta & c\theta s\phi & c\theta c\phi \end{bmatrix} \tag{2.5}$$

where, c, s and t, represents circular functions cos, sin and tan, respectively.

The resulting translational velocity transformations from {b} to {n} can be mathematically expressed in Equs. (2.6) and (2.7):

$$\dot{\boldsymbol{p}}_{b/n}^n = \boldsymbol{R}_b^n(\boldsymbol{\Theta}_{nb})\boldsymbol{v}_{b/n}^b \tag{2.6}$$

$$\begin{bmatrix} \dot{x} \\ \dot{y} \\ \dot{z} \end{bmatrix} = \begin{bmatrix} c\psi c\theta & -s\psi c\phi + c\psi s\theta s\phi & s\psi s\phi + c\psi c\phi s\theta \\ s\psi c\theta & c\psi c\phi + s\phi s\theta s\psi & -c\psi s\phi + s\theta s\psi c\phi \\ -s\theta & c\theta s\phi & c\theta c\phi \end{bmatrix} \begin{bmatrix} u \\ v \\ w \end{bmatrix} \tag{2.7}$$

**(6) Angular Velocity Transformation**

The angular velocity vector $\boldsymbol{\omega}_{b/n}^b = [p, q, r]^\top \in \mathbb{R}^3$ in {b} and Euler rate vector $\dot{\boldsymbol{\Theta}}_{nb} = \left[\dot{\phi}, \dot{\theta}, \dot{\psi}\right]^\top \in \mathcal{S}^3$ are related through a transformation matrix $\boldsymbol{T}_\Theta(\boldsymbol{\Theta}_{nb})$ and are mathematically expressed in Eq. 2.8) [2].

$$\dot{\boldsymbol{\Theta}}_{nb} = \boldsymbol{T}_\Theta(\boldsymbol{\Theta}_{nb})\boldsymbol{\omega}_{b/n}^b \tag{2.8}$$

Equation (2.8) can be written as follows:

$$\boldsymbol{\omega}_{b/n}^b = \boldsymbol{T}_\Theta^{-1}(\boldsymbol{\Theta}_{nb})\dot{\boldsymbol{\Theta}}_{nb} \tag{2.9}$$

The transformation matrix $\boldsymbol{T}_{\boldsymbol{\Theta}}(\boldsymbol{\Theta}_{nb})$ can be derived using the following relationship[2].

$$\boldsymbol{\omega}_{b/n}^{b} = \begin{bmatrix} \dot{\phi} \\ 0 \\ 0 \end{bmatrix} + \boldsymbol{R}_{x,\phi}^{\top} \begin{bmatrix} 0 \\ \dot{\theta} \\ 0 \end{bmatrix} + \boldsymbol{R}_{x,\phi}^{\top} \boldsymbol{R}_{y,\theta}^{\top} \begin{bmatrix} 0 \\ 0 \\ \dot{\psi} \end{bmatrix} \tag{2.10}$$

From Eq. (2.10), the transformation matrix can be written in Eq. (2.11).

$$\boldsymbol{T}_{\boldsymbol{\Theta}}^{-1}(\boldsymbol{\Theta}_{nb}) = \begin{bmatrix} 1 & 0 & -s\theta \\ 0 & c\phi & c\theta s\phi \\ 0 & -s\phi & c\theta c\phi \end{bmatrix} \tag{2.11}$$

$$\boldsymbol{T}_{\Theta}(\boldsymbol{\Theta}_{nb}) = \begin{bmatrix} 1 & 0 & -s\theta \\ 0 & c\phi & c\theta s\phi \\ 0 & -s\phi & c\theta c\phi \end{bmatrix}^{-1} = \begin{bmatrix} 1 & s\phi t\theta & c\phi t\theta \\ 0 & c\phi & -s\phi \\ 0 & \frac{s\phi}{c\theta} & \frac{c\phi}{c\theta} \end{bmatrix} \tag{2.12}$$

The transformation matrix $\boldsymbol{T}_{\Theta}(\boldsymbol{\Theta}_{nb})$ relates the angular velocities $p$, $q$, and $r$ to the time derivatives of the Euler angles $\dot{\phi}$, $\dot{\theta}$, and $\dot{\psi}$, yielding the angular velocity transformation from the body-fixed frame to the inertial frame as follows:

$$\begin{bmatrix} \dot{\phi} \\ \dot{\theta} \\ \dot{\psi} \end{bmatrix} = \begin{bmatrix} 1 & s\phi t\theta & c\phi t\theta \\ 0 & c\phi & -s\phi \\ 0 & \frac{s\phi}{c\theta} & \frac{c\phi}{c\theta} \end{bmatrix} \begin{bmatrix} p \\ q \\ r \end{bmatrix} \tag{2.13}$$

**(7) Linear and Angular Velocities: Combined Equations**

Combining linear and angular transformations, the overall vehicle Jacobian matrix $\boldsymbol{J}_{\Theta}$ in Eq. (2.1) is given as follows.

$$\boldsymbol{J}_{\Theta} = \left[\, \boldsymbol{R}_{b}^{n}(\boldsymbol{\Theta}_{nb}), 0_{3\times3}; 0_{3\times3}, \boldsymbol{T}_{\Theta}(\boldsymbol{\Theta}_{nb})\right] \tag{2.14}$$

Solving, Eq. (2.1), final forms of the kinematic equations for translational and angular velocity transformations are given by Eq. (2.15).

$$\begin{cases} \dot{x} = u\cos\theta\cos\psi + v\sin\phi\sin\theta\cos\psi - v\cos\phi\sin\psi + w\cos\phi\sin\theta\cos\psi + w\sin\phi\sin\psi \\ \dot{y} = u\cos\theta\sin\psi + v\sin\phi\sin\theta\sin\psi + v\cos\phi\cos\psi + w\cos\phi\sin\theta\sin\psi - w\sin\phi\cos\psi \\ \dot{z} = -u\sin\theta + v\sin\phi\cos\theta + w\cos\phi\cos\theta \\ \dot{\phi} = p + q\sin\phi\tan\theta + r\cos\phi\tan\theta \\ \dot{\theta} = q\cos\phi - r\sin\phi \\ \dot{\psi} = q\frac{\sin\phi}{\cos\theta} + r\frac{\cos\phi}{\cos\theta} \end{cases} \tag{2.15}$$

## 2.3.3 *Kinetics Modeling*

Nonlinear dynamic equations of motion in vector form of an underwater vehicle, given by Fossen [2] in equation (3.1) can be re-written as equation (2.16).

$$\boldsymbol{M}\dot{\boldsymbol{\nu}} + \boldsymbol{C}(\boldsymbol{\nu})\boldsymbol{\nu} + \boldsymbol{D}(\boldsymbol{\nu})\boldsymbol{\nu} + \boldsymbol{g}(\boldsymbol{\eta}) = \boldsymbol{\tau} \tag{2.16}$$

$$\underbrace{(\boldsymbol{M}_{RB} + \boldsymbol{M}_{A})\dot{\boldsymbol{\nu}}}_{\text{1st term}} + \underbrace{(\boldsymbol{C}_{RB}(\boldsymbol{\nu}) + \boldsymbol{C}_{A}(\boldsymbol{\nu}))\boldsymbol{\nu}}_{\text{2nd term}} + \underbrace{\boldsymbol{D}(\boldsymbol{\nu})\boldsymbol{\nu}}_{\text{3rd term}} + \underbrace{\boldsymbol{g}(\boldsymbol{\eta})}_{\text{4th term}} = \underbrace{\boldsymbol{\tau}_{c}}_{\text{5th term}} \tag{2.17}$$

Rearranging the terms in Eq. (2.17).

$$\underbrace{\boldsymbol{M}_{RB}\dot{\boldsymbol{\nu}} + \boldsymbol{C}_{RB}(\boldsymbol{\nu})\boldsymbol{\nu}}_{\text{Rigid Body Dynamics}} + \underbrace{\boldsymbol{M}_{A}\dot{\boldsymbol{\nu}} + \boldsymbol{C}_{A}(\boldsymbol{\nu})\boldsymbol{\nu} + \boldsymbol{D}(\boldsymbol{\nu})\boldsymbol{\nu}}_{\text{Hydrodynamics}} + \underbrace{\boldsymbol{g}(\boldsymbol{\eta})}_{\text{Hydrostatics}} = \boldsymbol{\tau}_{c} \tag{2.18}$$

$$\boldsymbol{\tau}_{RB} + \boldsymbol{\tau}_{hyd} + \boldsymbol{\tau}_{hs} = \boldsymbol{\tau}_{c} \tag{2.19}$$

$$\boldsymbol{\tau}_{RB} = \boldsymbol{\tau}_{c} - \boldsymbol{\tau}_{hyd} - \boldsymbol{\tau}_{hs} \tag{2.20}$$

## 2.4 Summary

This chapter explores the principles of Autonomous Underwater Vehicle (AUV) dynamics, focusing on the fundamental concepts of kinematics and kinetics. Kinematics describes the geometric aspects of AUV motion, such as position, orientation, and velocity, using coordinate systems (e.g., North-East-Down frame) and Euler angles or quaternions. Kinetics deals with the forces and moments acting on the AUV, including hydrodynamic forces (lift, drag, and moments), external forces, and environmental effects like ocean currents and waves. The chapter introduces the six degrees of freedom (DOF) that define AUV motion—surge, sway, heave, roll, pitch, and yaw—and discusses various dynamic models (1DOF, 3DOF, 4DOF, and 6DOF) used to simplify or fully capture AUV behavior. It also emphasizes the importance of coordinate systems (body-fixed and earth-fixed frames) and provides a foundation for understanding the nonlinear dynamics of AUVs, leading into the detailed mathematical derivations of 6DOF rigid body dynamics in the next chapter.

## References

1. Ahmed, F., Xiang, X., Wang, H., Zhang, J., Xiang, G., Yang, S.: Investigating wing-body lift interference effects on the dynamics of a novel flight-style AUV with bow-wings: maneuvering simulations and experimental validations. Ocean Eng. **326**, 120778 (2025)
2. Fossen, T.I.: Handbook of Marine Craft Hydrodynamics and Motion Control. Wiley (2011)

# Chapter 3
# Dynamics Modeling of Autonomous Underwater Vehicles

## 3.1 Derivation of 6-DOF Dynamics Equations of Motion

Nonlinear dynamic equations of motion in vector form of an underwater vehicle, given by Fossen [1] in Eq. (3.1) can be re-written as equation (3.2).

$$M\dot{\nu} + C(\nu)\,\nu + D(\nu)\,\nu + g(\eta) = \tau \tag{3.1}$$

$$\underbrace{(M_{RB} + M_A)\dot{\nu}}_{\text{1st term}} + \underbrace{(C_{RB}(\nu) + C_A(\nu))\nu}_{\text{2nd term}} + \underbrace{D(\nu)\nu}_{\text{3rd term}} + \underbrace{g(\eta)}_{\text{4th term}} = \underbrace{\tau_c}_{\text{5th term}} \tag{3.2}$$

Rearranging the terms in equation (3.2).

$$\underbrace{M_{RB}\dot{\nu} + C_{RB}(\nu)\,\nu}_{Rigid\ Body\ Dynamics} + \underbrace{M_A\dot{\nu} + C_A(\nu)\nu + D(\nu)\,\nu}_{Hydrodynamics} + \underbrace{g(\eta)}_{Hydrostatics} = \tau_c \tag{3.3}$$

$$\tau_{RB} + \tau_{hyd} + \tau_{hs} = \tau_c \tag{3.4}$$

$$\tau_{RB} = \tau_c - \tau_{hyd} - \tau_{hs} \tag{3.5}$$

### 3.1.1 Rigid Body AUV Dynamics ($\tau_{RB}$): Mathematical Derivation of 6-DOF Equations of Motion for AUV

The rigid body equations of motion for AUV have been derived by applying the Euler's first and second axioms [1]. These equations of motion are derived in the body-fixed coordinate system specifying the forces and moments acting on the AUV. The coordinate system's origin located arbitrarily on the AUV and the location of

 
X. Xiang et al., *Dynamics Modeling and Maneuvering of Autonomous Underwater Vehicles*, https://doi.org/10.1007/978-981-95-1521-9_3

CG and CB in body-fixed coordinate systems are defined as $r_G$ and $r_B$ respectively and given in equation (3.6).

$$r_G = \left[x_G\ y_G\ z_G\right]^\top, \quad r_B = \left[x_B\ y_B\ z_B\right]^\top \tag{3.6}$$

In case the weight distribution of the AUV is adjusted such that the CG with reference to the vehicle origin is given as $r_G = \left[0, 0, z_g\right]^\top$ and $z_g > 0$ to ensure roll stability of the vehicle. Accordingly, the CB is fixed at the origin of the body-fixed frame {b} resulting $r_B = [0, 0, 0]^\top$ for the practice FSAUV.

#### Linear Momentum: Force Equations for AUV Dynamics

Consider body-fixed frame {b} is rotating with an angular velocity $\omega_{b/n}$, about inertial frame {n}. The translational momentum equation for the AUV can be written as follows:

$$\mathbf{F} = m\,\frac{d}{dt}\left(\boldsymbol{v}_{G/n}\right) \tag{3.7}$$

where $\boldsymbol{v}_G$ is the velocity of the AUV's rigid body center of mass in the inertial frame and expressed as:

$$\boldsymbol{v}_{G/n} = \boldsymbol{v}_{b/n} + \boldsymbol{\omega}_{b/n} \times \mathbf{r}_G \tag{3.8}$$

where $\boldsymbol{v}_{b/n}$ and $\boldsymbol{\omega}_{b/n}$ are the translational and angular velocity vectors of the $O_b$ with respect to {n}.

Combining Eqs. (3.7) and (3.8).

$$\mathbf{F} = m\,\frac{d}{dt}\left(\boldsymbol{v}_{b/n} + \boldsymbol{\omega}_{b/n} \times \mathbf{r}_G\right) \tag{3.9}$$

$$\mathbf{F} = m\frac{\partial \boldsymbol{v}_{b/n}}{\partial t} + m\frac{d}{dt}\left(\boldsymbol{\omega}_{b/n} \times \mathbf{r}_G\right) \tag{3.10}$$

Expanding the time derivative of the cross product in the equation:

$$\frac{d}{dt}(\boldsymbol{\omega}_{b/n} \times \mathbf{r}_G) = \frac{d\boldsymbol{\omega}_{b/n}}{dt} \times \mathbf{r}_G + \boldsymbol{\omega}_{b/n} \times \frac{d\mathbf{r}_G}{dt}$$

where, $\frac{d\mathbf{r}_G}{dt} = \boldsymbol{v}_{b/n}$

Equation (3.10) can be written as follows:

$$\mathbf{F} = m\frac{\partial \boldsymbol{v}_{b/n}}{\partial t} + m\left(\frac{d\boldsymbol{\omega}_{b/n}}{dt} \times \mathbf{r}_G + \boldsymbol{\omega}_{b/n} \times \boldsymbol{v}_{b/n}\right). \tag{3.11}$$

The expanded form of the equation is:

$$\mathbf{F} = m\left(\frac{\partial \boldsymbol{\nu}_{b/n}}{\partial t} + \boldsymbol{\omega}_{b/n} \times \boldsymbol{\nu}_{b/n} + \frac{d\boldsymbol{\omega}_{b/n}}{dt} \times \mathbf{r}_G\right) \tag{3.12}$$

To account for the rotational effect the term $\boldsymbol{\omega}_{b/n} \times (\boldsymbol{\omega}_{b/n} \times \mathbf{r}_G)$ has been added in the Eq. (3.12) by applying the vector triple product identity rule as follows:

$$\boldsymbol{\omega}_{b/n} \times (\boldsymbol{\omega}_{b/n} \times \mathbf{r}_G) = (\boldsymbol{\omega}_{b/n} \cdot \mathbf{r}_G)\boldsymbol{\omega}_{b/n} - (\boldsymbol{\omega}_{b/n} \cdot \boldsymbol{\omega}_{b/n})\mathbf{r}_G,$$

The final form of the equation is as follows:

$$\mathbf{F} = m\left(\frac{\partial \boldsymbol{\nu}_{b/n}}{\partial t} + \boldsymbol{\omega}_{b/n} \times \boldsymbol{\nu}_{b/n} + \frac{d\boldsymbol{\omega}_{b/n}}{dt} \times \mathbf{r}_G + \boldsymbol{\omega}_{b/n} \times (\boldsymbol{\omega}_{b/n} \times \mathbf{r}_G)\right) \tag{3.13}$$

where, $\mathbf{F} = [X, Y, Z]^T$, $\boldsymbol{\nu}_{b/n} = [u, v, w]^T$, $\boldsymbol{\omega}_{b/n} = [p, q, r]^T$, and $\mathbf{r}_G = [x_G, y_G, z_G]^T$. Substituting these into Eq. (3.13), the Surge (X), Sway (Y), and Heave(Z) forces equations for the underwater vehicle can be written as follows:

$$X = m\left[\dot{u} - vr + wq - x_G\left(q^2 + r^2\right) + y_G\left(pq - \dot{r}\right) + z_G\left(pr + \dot{q}\right)\right] \tag{3.14}$$

$$Y = m\left[\dot{v} - wp + ur - y_G\left(r^2 + p^2\right) + z_G\left(qr - \dot{p}\right) + x_G\left(qp + \dot{r}\right)\right] \tag{3.15}$$

$$Z = m\left[\dot{w} - uq + vp - z_G\left(p^2 + q^2\right) + x_G\left(rp - \dot{q}\right) + y_G\left(rq + \dot{p}\right)\right] \tag{3.16}$$

Applying the simplifications on the AUV dynamics modeling, where $x_G = 0$ and $y_G = 0$, the surge, sway, and heave force equations are reduced as follows:

$$X = m\left[\dot{u} - vr + wq + z_G\left(pr + \dot{q}\right)\right] \tag{3.17}$$

$$Y = m\left[\dot{v} - wp + ur + z_G\left(qr - \dot{p}\right)\right] \tag{3.18}$$

$$Z = m\left[\dot{w} - uq + vp - z_G\left(p^2 + q^2\right)\right] \tag{3.19}$$

### Angular Momentum: Moment Equations for AUV Dynamics

The total angular momentum $\mathbf{M}$ acting on the AUV can be expressed as a sum of the angular momentum $\mathbf{M}_G$ at the center of mass of the AUV and the angular momentum generated by the external force $\mathbf{F}$ applied at a distance $\mathbf{r}_G$ from the center of mass. This relationship is given by the Eq. (3.20).

$$\mathbf{M} = \mathbf{M}_G + \mathbf{r}_G \times \mathbf{F} \tag{3.20}$$

$$\mathbf{M}_G = \frac{d}{dt}(I_G \boldsymbol{\omega}_{b/n}) \tag{3.21}$$

Equation (3.20) can be written as:

$$\mathbf{M} = \mathbf{r}_G \times \frac{d}{dt}\left(m \boldsymbol{v}_{G/n}\right) \tag{3.22}$$

$$\mathbf{M} = m\mathbf{r}_G \times \left(\frac{\partial \boldsymbol{v}_{b/n}}{\partial t} + \boldsymbol{\omega}_{b/n} \times \boldsymbol{v}_{b/n}\right) + m\mathbf{r}_G \times \left(\frac{d\boldsymbol{\omega}_{b/n}}{dt} \times \mathbf{r}_G\right) + m\mathbf{r}_G \times \left(\boldsymbol{\omega}_{b/n} \times (\boldsymbol{\omega}_{b/n} \times \mathbf{r}_G)\right) \tag{3.23}$$

The inertia tensor in vectorial form is given in equation (3.25).

$$(I_G \boldsymbol{\omega}_{b/n}) = \int_V \mathbf{r}_G \times (\boldsymbol{\omega}_{b/n} \times \mathbf{r}_G)\, \rho\, dV \tag{3.24}$$

$$I_G \boldsymbol{\omega}_{b/n} = \int_V \mathbf{r}_G \times (\boldsymbol{\omega}_{b/n} \times \mathbf{r}_G)\, \rho\, dV \Rightarrow I_G \boldsymbol{\omega}_{b/n} = m\left(\mathbf{r}_G \times (\boldsymbol{\omega}_{b/n} \times \mathbf{r}_G)\right) \tag{3.25}$$

where $\rho$ and V are the mass density and volume of the rigid-body respectively.

The inertia matrix $I_G$ about the center of gravity (CG) is defined in equation (3.26).

$$I_G = \begin{bmatrix} I_x & -I_{xy} & -I_{xz} \\ -I_{yx} & I_y & -I_{yz} \\ -I_{zx} & -I_{zy} & I_z \end{bmatrix} \tag{3.26}$$

where, $I_x$, $I_y$, and $I_z$ represent the moments of inertia about the $X_b$, $Y_b$, and $Z_b$ axes, respectively. The terms $I_{xy} = I_{yx}$, $I_{xz} = I_{zx}$, and $I_{yz} = I_{zy}$ denote the products of inertia, which describe the coupling between different axes of rotation.

Equation (3.27) provides the definitions in terms of the mass distribution and geometry of the AUV, for both the diagonal moments of inertia and the products of inertia about the center of gravity (CG).

$$\begin{cases} I_x = \int_V \rho\left(y^2 + z^2\right) dV \Rightarrow I_{x,G} = m\left(y_G^2 + z_G^2\right), \\ I_y = \int_V \rho\left(x^2 + z^2\right) dV \Rightarrow I_{y,G} = m\left(x_G^2 + z_G^2\right), \\ I_z = \int_V \rho\left(x^2 + y^2\right) dV \Rightarrow I_{z,G} = m\left(x_G^2 + y_G^2\right), \\ I_{xy} = \int_V \rho\, xy\, dV \Rightarrow I_{xy,G} = m\left(x_G y_G\right), \\ I_{xz} = \int_V \rho\, xz\, dV \Rightarrow I_{xz,G} = m\left(x_G z_G\right), \\ I_{yz} = \int_V \rho\, yz\, dV \Rightarrow I_{yz,G} = m\left(y_G z_G\right). \end{cases} \tag{3.27}$$

Finally, expanding the second term using the triple product identity in Eq. (3.23), employing the moment of inertia definitions from equations (3.25) and (3.27), and substituting $\mathbf{M} = [K, L, M]^T$, $\boldsymbol{v}_{b/n} = [u, v, w]^T$, $\boldsymbol{\omega}_{b/n} = [p, q, r]^T$, and $\mathbf{r}_G = [x_G, y_G, z_G]^T$ into Eq. (3.13), the Roll (K), Pitch (M), and Yaw (N) moment equations for the underwater vehicle can be written as follows:

$$K = I_x\dot{p} + (I_z - I_y)qr - (\dot{r} + pq)I_{xz} + (r^2 - q^2)I_{yz} + (pr - \dot{q})I_{xy} + m\left[y_G(\dot{w} - uq + vp) - z_G(\dot{v} - wp + ur)\right] \tag{3.28}$$

$$M = I_y\dot{q} + (I_x - I_z)rp - (\dot{p} + qr)I_{xy} + (p^2 - r^2)I_{zx} + (qp - \dot{r})I_{yz} + m\left[z_G(\dot{u} - vr + wq) - x_G(\dot{w} - uq + vp)\right] \tag{3.29}$$

$$N = I_z\dot{r} + (I_y - I_x)pq - (\dot{q} + rp)I_{yz} + (q^2 - p^2)I_{xy} + (rq - \dot{p})I_{zx} + m\left[x_G(\dot{v} - wp + ur) - y_G(\dot{u} - vr + wq)\right] \tag{3.30}$$

By applying the simplifications for the AUV dynamics modeling such that $x_G = 0$ and $y_G = 0$, and choosing the origin of the body-fixed coordinate system at the CG, while considering the top/bottom and port/starboard symmetry of the vehicle, the inertia matrix is reduced to a diagonal matrix. The off-diagonal elements become negligible due to their small values, resulting in the inertia tensor $I_G = \text{diag}\{I_x, I_y, I_z\}$. Consequently, Eqs. (3.28), (3.29), and (3.30) are simplified and used to model the rotational moments in the rigid body dynamics of the AUV.

$$K = I_x\dot{p} + (I_z - I_y)qr - m\left[z_G(\dot{v} - wp + ur)\right] \tag{3.31}$$

$$M = I_y\dot{q} + (I_x - I_z)rp + m\left[z_G(\dot{u} - vr + wq)\right] \tag{3.32}$$

$$N = I_z\dot{r} + (I_y - I_x)pq \tag{3.33}$$

### Rigid Body Dynamics ($\tau_{RB}$): Vectorial Form

The derived rigid body equations of motion in vectorial form for AUV is given as $\tau_{RB} = M_{RB}\dot{\nu} + C_{RB}(\nu)\,\nu$ . The simplified rigid body mass matrix ($M_{RB}$) and Coriolis matrix ($C_{RB}(\nu)$) are given in Eqs. (3.34) and (3.35) respectively.

$$M_{RB} = \begin{bmatrix} m & 0 & 0 & 0 & mz_G & 0 \\ 0 & m & 0 & -mz_G & 0 & 0 \\ 0 & 0 & m & 0 & 0 & 0 \\ 0 & -mz_G & 0 & I_x & 0 & 0 \\ mz_G & 0 & 0 & 0 & I_y & 0 \\ 0 & 0 & 0 & 0 & 0 & I_z \end{bmatrix} \tag{3.34}$$

$$C_{RB}(\nu) = \begin{bmatrix} 0 & 0 & 0 & mz_G r & mw & -mv \\ 0 & 0 & 0 & -mw & mz_G r & mu \\ 0 & 0 & 0 & -m(z_G p - v) & -m(z_G q + u) & 0 \\ -mz_G r & mw & m(z_G p - v) & 0 & I_z r & -I_y q \\ -mw & -mz_G r & m(z_G q + u) & -I_z r & 0 & I_x p \\ mv & -mu & 0 & I_y q & -I_x p & 0 \end{bmatrix} \tag{3.35}$$

## 3.2 Modeling Hydrodynamic Forces and Moments ($\tau_{hyd}$)

The hydrodynamic forces and moments acting on the AUV, arising from added mass effects, hydrodynamic drag, and lift, can be expressed in vectorial form are give as: $\tau_{hyd} = M_A\dot{\nu} + C_A(\nu)\nu + D(\nu)\nu$ (Refer Eq. (3.3). These components collectively contribute to the overall kinetics of the vehicle and are fundamental to accurately representing its motion in a fluid environment.

### 3.2.1 Modeling Added Mass ($\tau^A = M_A\dot{\nu} + C_A(\nu)\nu$)

The added mass represents a hypothetical volume of fluid that accelerates along with the body, rather than a discrete mass of fluid moving at a specific acceleration. When an AUV accelerates in a fluid, it disturbs and accelerates the surrounding fluid, thereby imparting kinetic energy to it. This interaction requires additional force to account for the increased inertia of the system, known as 'added mass' [2, 3]. These pressure-induced forces and moments, resulting from the body's acceleration, are represented by added mass coefficients and are used to develop mathematical formulations to model the AUV dynamics associated with the increased inertial effects. The mathematical derivation is based on assumptions of potential flow considerations with an inviscid, irrotational, frictionless fluid. The mass matrix of the surrounding fluid is symmetric, such that $M_A = M_A^T$.

The fluid kinetic energy $T_A$ in quadratic form can be written in equation (3.36) [4]:

$$T_A = \frac{1}{2}\nu^\top M_A \nu \tag{3.36}$$

The fluid kinetic energy can be related to the added mass associated force vector $\tau_1^A = [X_A, Y_A, Z_A]^\top$ and moment vector $\tau_2^A = [K_A, M_A, N_A]^\top$ using Kirchhoff's equations [1, 5]:

$$\tau_1^A = \frac{d}{dt}\left(\frac{\partial T_A}{\partial \nu_1}\right) + \nu_2 \times \left(\frac{\partial T_A}{\partial \nu_1}\right) \tag{3.37}$$

$$\tau_2^A = \frac{d}{dt}\left(\frac{\partial T_A}{\partial \nu_2}\right) + \nu_2 \times \left(\frac{\partial T_A}{\partial \nu_2}\right) + \nu_1 \times \left(\frac{\partial T_A}{\partial \nu_1}\right) \tag{3.38}$$

The $6 \times 6$ added mass matrix $M_A = M_A^T \geq 0$ is defined in equation (3.39) [1].

$$M_A = - \begin{bmatrix} X_{\dot{u}} & X_{\dot{v}} & X_{\dot{w}} & X_{\dot{p}} & X_{\dot{q}} & X_{\dot{r}} \\ Y_{\dot{u}} & Y_{\dot{v}} & Y_{\dot{w}} & Y_{\dot{p}} & Y_{\dot{q}} & Y_{\dot{r}} \\ Z_{\dot{u}} & Z_{\dot{v}} & Z_{\dot{w}} & Z_{\dot{p}} & Z_{\dot{q}} & Z_{\dot{r}} \\ K_{\dot{u}} & K_{\dot{v}} & K_{\dot{w}} & K_{\dot{p}} & K_{\dot{q}} & K_{\dot{r}} \\ M_{\dot{u}} & M_{\dot{v}} & M_{\dot{w}} & M_{\dot{p}} & M_{\dot{q}} & M_{\dot{r}} \\ N_{\dot{u}} & N_{\dot{v}} & N_{\dot{w}} & N_{\dot{p}} & N_{\dot{q}} & N_{\dot{r}} \end{bmatrix} \tag{3.39}$$

If an underwater vehicle exhibits symmetry across three planes (fore-aft, port-starboard, and top-bottom) the off-diagonal elements of the added mass matrix can be disregarded, as they would be negligible. However, in practice, most AUV designs do not possess all three symmetry planes. For a streamlined AUV that is symmetric in both the vertical (top-bottom) and lateral (port-starboard) planes, the added mass matrix in Eq. (3.39) can be simplified to the form shown in Eq. (3.40).

$$M_A = - \begin{bmatrix} X_{\dot{u}} & 0 & 0 & 0 & 0 & 0 \\ 0 & Y_{\dot{v}} & 0 & 0 & 0 & Y_{\dot{r}} \\ 0 & 0 & Z_{\dot{w}} & 0 & Z_{\dot{q}} & 0 \\ 0 & 0 & 0 & K_{\dot{p}} & 0 & 0 \\ 0 & 0 & M_{\dot{w}} & 0 & M_{\dot{q}} & 0 \\ 0 & N_{\dot{v}} & 0 & 0 & 0 & N_{\dot{r}} \end{bmatrix} \tag{3.40}$$

The Coriolis–Centripetal forces, resulting from the contributions of the added mass, are represented by the reduced matrix $C_A(\nu)$ for the AUV, as given in Eq. (3.41).

$$C_A(\nu) = - \begin{bmatrix} 0 & 0 & 0 & 0 & Z_{\dot{w}}w + Z_{\dot{q}}q & -(Y_{\dot{v}}v + Y_{\dot{r}}r) \\ 0 & 0 & 0 & -(Z_{\dot{w}}w + Z_{\dot{q}}q) & 0 & X_{\dot{u}}u \\ 0 & 0 & 0 & Y_{\dot{v}}v + Y_{\dot{r}}r & -X_{\dot{u}}u & 0 \\ 0 & Z_{\dot{w}}w + Z_{\dot{q}}q & -(Y_{\dot{v}}v + Y_{\dot{r}}r) & 0 & Y_{\dot{r}}v + N_{\dot{r}}r & -(Z_{\dot{q}}w + M_{\dot{q}}q) \\ -(Z_{\dot{w}}w + Z_{\dot{q}}q) & 0 & X_{\dot{u}}u & -(Y_{\dot{r}}v + N_{\dot{r}}r) & 0 & K_{\dot{p}}p \\ Y_{\dot{v}}v + Y_{\dot{r}}r & -X_{\dot{u}}u & 0 & Z_{\dot{q}}w + M_{\dot{q}}q & -K_{\dot{p}}p & 0 \end{bmatrix} \tag{3.41}$$

## 3.2.2 *Linear and Nonlinear Hydrodynamic Damping* ($D(\nu)$)

Modeling hydrodynamic damping involves both linear and nonlinear components. The total hydrodynamic damping matrix $D(\nu)$ is the sum of the linear $D_l$ and nonlinear $D_n(\nu)$ damping matrices given in Eq. (3.42) [1]. The linear damping matrix includes first-order linear coefficients, while the nonlinear matrix incorporates higher-order terms.

For AUV modeling, first-order linear damping terms have been omitted to reduce coefficient estimations complexity and computational costs. In contrast, second-order nonlinear terms are retained, offering a more accurate representation of the AUV's behavior under real-world conditions. Unlike linear damping, which simplifies interactions, nonlinear damping accounts for varying flow conditions, vehicle speed, and complex hydrodynamic forces. The proposed model is also suitable to simulate 3DOF and 6DOF maneuvers to investigate AUV motion response [3, 6].

$$D(\nu) = D_l(\nu) + D_n(\nu) \tag{3.42}$$

Further, applying AUV modeling assumptions and simplifications, the reduced nonlinear damping matrix is given in Eq. (3.43).

$$D(\nu) = -\begin{bmatrix} X_{u|u|}\,|u| & 0 & 0 & 0 & 0 & 0 \\ 0 & Y_{v|v|}\,|v| + Y_{uv}u & 0 & 0 & 0 & Y_{r|r|}\,|r| + Y_{ur}u \\ 0 & 0 & Z_{w|w|}\,|w| + Z_{uw}u & 0 & Z_{q|q|}\,|q| + Z_{uq}u & 0 \\ 0 & 0 & 0 & K_{p|p|}\,|p| & 0 & 0 \\ 0 & 0 & M_{w|w|}\,|w| + M_{uw}u & 0 & M_{q|q|}\,|q| + M_{uq}u & 0 \\ 0 & N_{v|v|}\,|v| + N_{uv}u & 0 & 0 & 0 & N_{r|r|}\,|r| + N_{ur}u \end{bmatrix} \tag{3.43}$$

## 3.3 Hydrostatic Forces and Moments ($\tau_{hs}$)

The submerged AUV observes the weight $W = mg$ and buoyancy force $B = \rho\nabla g$ and given in inertial plane as $f_g^n = [\,0, 0, W]^\top$ and $f_b^n = -[\,0, 0, B]^\top$ corresponding moments $m_g^n = \mathbf{r}_G \times f_g^n$ and $m_b^n = \mathbf{r}_B \times f_b^n$ respectively. These forces and moments in body-fixed frame are expressed by multiplying the inverse of the transformation matrix $R_b^n(\Theta_{nb})^{-1}$ and are given as follows:

$$g(\eta) = -\begin{bmatrix} R_b^n(\Theta_{nb})^{-1} f_g^n + R_b^n(\Theta_{nb})^{-1} f_b^n \\ \mathbf{r}_G \times R_b^n(\Theta_{nb})^{-1} f_g^n + \mathbf{r}_B \times R_b^n(\Theta_{nb})^{-1} f_b^n \end{bmatrix} \tag{3.44}$$

By further solving Eq. (3.45), the resulting expressions to calculate the restoring forces and moments for the underwater vehicle are given as follows:

$$g(\eta) = \begin{bmatrix} X_{HS} \\ Y_{HS} \\ Z_{HS} \\ K_{HS} \\ M_{HS} \\ N_{HS} \end{bmatrix} = \begin{bmatrix} (W - B)\sin(\theta) \\ -(W - B)\cos(\theta)\sin(\phi) \\ -(W - B)\cos(\theta)\cos(\phi) \\ -(y_G W - y_B B)\cos(\theta)\cos(\phi) + (z_G W - z_B B)\cos(\theta)\sin(\phi) \\ (z_G W - z_B B)\sin(\theta) + (x_G W - x_B B)\cos(\theta)\cos(\phi) \\ -(x_G W - x_B B)\cos(\theta)\sin(\phi) - (y_G W - y_B B)\sin(\theta) \end{bmatrix} \tag{3.45}$$

In case the AUV is neutrally buoyant such that $W = B$, and the weight distribution ensures that the center of gravity (CG) is located at $\mathbf{r}_G = [0, 0, z_G]^\top$ with $z_G > 0$, meaning the CG is below the vehicle's origin. The center of buoyancy (CB) is fixed at the origin, $\mathbf{r}_B = [0, 0, 0]^\top$. This configuration provides roll stability due to the vertical separation between the CG and CB, creating a restoring moment to maintain upright orientation, allowing the AUV to be both neutrally buoyant and stable. Accordingly, Eq. (3.45) is further simplified and expressed in Eq. (3.46).

$$\tau_{hs} = g(\eta) = \begin{bmatrix} 0 \; 0 \; 0 \; z_G W\cos(\theta)\sin(\phi) \; z_G W\sin(\theta) \; 0 \end{bmatrix}^\top \tag{3.46}$$

## 3.4 Vector of Control Inputs ($\tau_c$)

Vector of control input is given in the Eq. (3.47) for standard configuration of AUV having only moving fins at the stern end only [7].

$$\tau_c = \begin{bmatrix} 1 & 0 & 0 & 0 \\ 0 & Y_{uu\delta_r} u^2 & 0 & 0 \\ 0 & 0 & Z_{uu\delta_s} u^2 & 0 \\ 0 & 0 & 0 & 1 \\ 0 & 0 & M_{uu\delta_s} u^2 & 0 \\ 0 & N_{uu\delta_r} u^2 & 0 & 0 \end{bmatrix} \begin{bmatrix} X_{prop} \\ \delta_r \\ \delta_s \\ K_{prop} \end{bmatrix} \tag{3.47}$$

In case the AUV is equipped with the bow fins in addition to the stern fins, the vector of control input is modeled as follows:

$$\tau_c = \begin{bmatrix} 1 & 0 & 0 & 0 & 0 \\ 0 & Y_{uu\delta_r} u^2 & 0 & 0 & 0 \\ 0 & 0 & Z_{uu\delta_s} u^2 & Z_{uu\delta_b} u^2 & 0 \\ 0 & 0 & 0 & 0 & 1 \\ 0 & 0 & M_{uu\delta_s} u^2 & M_{uu\delta_b} u^2 & 0 \\ 0 & N_{uu\delta_r} u^2 & 0 & 0 & 0 \end{bmatrix} \begin{bmatrix} X_{prop} \\ \delta_r \\ \delta_s \\ \delta_b \\ K_{prop} \end{bmatrix} \tag{3.48}$$

## 3.5 Linear and Angular Accelerations: Combined Equations

Considering equation (3.2), the first term $(M_{RB} + M_A)\dot{\nu}$ can be written by combining Eqs. (3.34) and (3.40) as follows:

$$(M_{RB} + M_A)\,\dot{\nu} = \begin{bmatrix} m - X_{\dot{u}} & 0 & 0 & 0 & mz_G & 0 \\ 0 & m - Y_{\dot{v}} & 0 & -mz_G & 0 & -Y_{\dot{r}} \\ 0 & 0 & m - Z_{\dot{w}} & 0 & -Z_{\dot{q}} & 0 \\ 0 & -mz_G & 0 & I_x - K_{\dot{p}} & 0 & 0 \\ mz_G & 0 & -M_{\dot{w}} & 0 & I_y - M_{\dot{q}} & 0 \\ 0 & -N_{\dot{v}} & 0 & 0 & 0 & I_z - N_{\dot{r}} \end{bmatrix} \begin{bmatrix} \dot{u} \\ \dot{v} \\ \dot{w} \\ \dot{p} \\ \dot{q} \\ \dot{r} \end{bmatrix} \tag{3.49}$$

Similarly, the second term $(C_{RB}(\nu) + C_A(\nu))\nu$ in equation (3.2) can be written by combining the equations (3.35) and (3.41) as follows:

$$(C_{RB}(\nu) + C_A(\nu))\,\nu = \begin{bmatrix} m(z_G rp + wq - vr) - Z_{\dot{w}} wq - Z_{\dot{q}} qq + -Y_{\dot{v}} vr + Y_{\dot{r}} rr \\ -m(wp - ur - z_G qr) + Z_{\dot{w}} wp + Z_{\dot{q}} pq - X_{\dot{u}} ur \\ -m(uq - vp) - mz_G(p^2 + q^2) - Y_{\dot{v}} vp - Y_{\dot{r}} rp + X_{\dot{u}} uq \\ -mz_G(ur - wp) + (I_z - I_y)qr + (Y_{\dot{v}} - Z_{\dot{w}})vw - (Y_{\dot{r}} + Z_{\dot{q}})vq + (Y_{\dot{r}} + Z_{\dot{q}})rw + (M_{\dot{q}} - N_{\dot{r}})qr \\ mz_G(wq - vr) + (I_x - I_z)rp - (X_{\dot{u}} - Z_{\dot{w}})uw + Z_{\dot{q}} uq + Y_{\dot{r}} vp + (N_{\dot{r}} - K_{\dot{p}})rp \\ (I_y - I_x)pq + (X_{\dot{u}} - Y_{\dot{v}})uv - Y_{\dot{r}} ur - Z_{\dot{q}} wp + (K_{\dot{p}} - M_{\dot{q}})pq \end{bmatrix} \tag{3.50}$$

**Table 3.1** Added mass cross-terms coefficients [6]

| $X_{wq} = Z_{\dot{w}}$ | $X_{qq} = Z_{\dot{q}}$ | $X_{vr} = -Y_{\dot{v}}$ | $X_{rr} = -Y_{\dot{r}}$ |
|---|---|---|---|
| $Y_{ur_a} = X_{\dot{u}}$ | $Y_{wp} = -Z_{\dot{w}}$ | $Y_{pq} = -Z_{\dot{q}}$ | |
| $Z_{uq_a} = -X_{\dot{u}}$ | $Z_{vp} = Y_{\dot{v}}$ | $Z_{rp} = Y_{\dot{r}}$ | |
| $M_{uw_a} = -(Z_{\dot{w}} - X_{\dot{u}})$ | $M_{vp} = -Y_{\dot{r}}$ | $M_{rp} = (K_{\dot{p}} - N_{\dot{r}})$ | $M_{uq_a} = -Z_{\dot{q}}$ |
| $N_{uv_a} = -(X_{\dot{u}} - Y_{\dot{v}})$ | $N_{wp} = Z_{\dot{q}}$ | $N_{pq} = -(K_{\dot{p}} - M_{\dot{q}})$ | $N_{ur_a} = Y_{\dot{r}}$ |

Neglecting the terms $(Y_{\dot{v}} - Z_{\dot{w}})\ vw - (Y_{\dot{r}} + Z_{\dot{q}})\ vq + (Y_{\dot{r}} + Z_{\dot{q}})\ rw + (M_{\dot{q}} - N_{\dot{r}})\ qr$ is technically justified for roll accelerations in a torpedo-shaped AUV, when operates primarily in a forward motion with minimal sway, heave, or pitching. In such cases, these terms can be considered small enough to be neglected. Additionally, many of these terms cancel each other out, as seen in the Coriolis-centripetal matrix, where terms like $(Y_{\dot{v}} - Z_{\dot{w}})$tend to cancel due to the vehicle's symmetric design.

In case when the AUV is equipped with bow-wings such as Flight-Style AUV, the horizontal bow wings contribute to the vertical-plane-related hydrodynamic coefficients, their impact on roll motion is minimal. This is because these terms involve products of small velocities, which further reduce their magnitudes, making them negligible. Moreover, in low-speed operations, Coriolis and centripetal forces are smaller, especially in the roll motion, allowing further simplification of the dynamics model by neglecting these terms.

The added mass cross terms are defined in Table 3.1. The cross terms in the nonlinear dynamic model, such as $X_{wq}$, $X_{qq}$, $Y_{ura}$, $M_{uwa}$, etc., represents the added mass couplings between the different degrees of freedom, which are important for accurately predicting the AUV's behaviour during 6-DOF maneuvers.

Substituting the added mass cross terms and neglecting the terms $(Y_{\dot{v}} - Z_{\dot{w}})\ vw - (Y_{\dot{r}} + Z_{\dot{q}})\ vq + (Y_{\dot{r}} + Z_{\dot{q}})\ rw + (M_{\dot{q}} - N_{\dot{r}})\ qr$, the resulting Coriolis-Centripetal matrix is given in Eq. (3.51).

$$(C_{RB}(\nu) + C_A(\nu))\,\nu = \begin{bmatrix} m(z_G rp + wq - vr) - X_{wq}wq - X_{qq}qq - X_{vr}vr + X_{rr}rr \\ -m(wp - ur - z_G qr) - Y_{wp}wp - Y_{pq}pq - Y_{ur_a}ur \\ -m(uq - vp) - mz_G(p^2 + q^2) - Z_{vp}vp - Z_{rp}rp - Z_{uq_a}uq \\ -mz_G(ur - wp) + (I_z - I_y)qr \\ mz_G(wq - vr) + (I_x - I_z)rp - M_{uw_a}uw - M_{uq_a}uq - M_{vp}vp - (M_{rp})rp \\ (I_y - I_x)pq - N_{uv_a}uv - N_{ur_a}ur - N_{wp}wp - N_{pq}pq \end{bmatrix} \tag{3.51}$$

The third term $D(\nu)\nu$ in Eq. (3.2) can be written as follows:

$$D(\nu)\cdot\nu=-\begin{bmatrix} X_{u|u|}|u|u \\ Y_{v|v|}|v|v+Y_{uv}uv+Y_{r|r|}|r|r+Y_{ur}ur \\ Z_{w|w|}|w|w+Z_{uw}uw+Z_{q|q|}|q|q+Z_{uq}uq \\ K_{p|p|}|p|p \\ M_{w|w|}|w|w+M_{uw}uw+M_{q|q|}|q|q+M_{uq}uq \\ N_{v|v|}|v|v+N_{uv}uv+N_{r|r|}|r|r+N_{ur}ur \end{bmatrix} \tag{3.52}$$

Further, 4th and 5th terms of Eq. (3.2), are given in Eqs. (3.53) and (3.54) respectively. However, for AUV equipped with bow fins in addition to the stern fins, Eq. (3.54) can be written as equation (3.55):

$$\tau_{hs}=g\left(\eta\right)=\left[0\ 0\ 0\ z_G W\cos(\theta)\sin(\phi)\ z_G W\sin(\theta)\ 0\right]^\top \tag{3.53}$$

$$\tau_c=\begin{bmatrix} X_{prop} \\ Y_{uu\delta_r}u^2\cdot\delta_r \\ Z_{uu\delta_s}u^2\cdot\delta_s \\ K_{prop} \\ M_{uu\delta_s}u^2\cdot\delta_s \\ N_{uu\delta_r}u^2\cdot\delta_r \end{bmatrix} \tag{3.54}$$

$$\tau_c=\begin{bmatrix} X_{prop} \\ Y_{uu\delta_r}u^2\cdot\delta_r \\ Z_{uu\delta_s}u^2\cdot\delta_s+Z_{uu\delta_b}u^2\cdot\delta_b \\ K_{prop} \\ M_{uu\delta_s}u^2\cdot\delta_s+M_{uu\delta_b}u^2\cdot\delta_b \\ N_{uu\delta_r}u^2\cdot\delta_r \end{bmatrix} \tag{3.55}$$

By substituting Eqs. (3.49), (3.51), (3.52), (3.53), and (3.54) into Eq. (3.2), the final form of the kinetic equations used to solve the linear and angular accelerations of the AUV is given by Eq. (3.56).

Similarly, by substituting Eqs. (3.49), (3.51), (3.52), (3.53), and (3.55) into equation (3.2), the final form of the kinetic equations used to solve the linear and angular accelerations of the AUV with bow wings is given by Eq. (3.57).

$$
\begin{Bmatrix} \dot{u} \\ \dot{v} \\ \dot{w} \\ \dot{p} \\ \dot{q} \\ \dot{r} \end{Bmatrix} =
\begin{bmatrix}
m - X_{\dot{u}} & 0 & 0 & 0 & m z_G & 0 \\
0 & m - Y_{\dot{v}} & 0 & -m z_G & 0 & -Y_{\dot{r}} \\
0 & 0 & m - Z_{\dot{w}} & 0 & -Z_{\dot{q}} & 0 \\
0 & -m z_G & 0 & I_x - K_{\dot{p}} & 0 & 0 \\
m z_G & 0 & -M_{\dot{w}} & 0 & I_y - M_{\dot{q}} & 0 \\
0 & -N_{\dot{v}} & 0 & 0 & 0 & I_z - N_{\dot{r}}
\end{bmatrix}^{-1}
\begin{bmatrix}
m\left(vr - wq - z_G rp\right) + X_{u|u|} u\,|u| + X_{wq} wq + X_{qq} qq + X_{vr} vr + X_{rr} rr + X_{prop} \\
m\left(wp - ur - z_G qr\right) + Y_{v|v|} v\,|v| + Y_{r|r|} r\,|r| + Y_{ur} ur + Y_{wp} wp + Y_{pq} pq + Y_{uv} uv + Y_{uu\delta_r} u^2 \delta_r \\
m\left(uq - vp\right) + m z_G\left(p^2 + q^2\right) + Z_{w|w|} w\,|w| + Z_{q|q|}\, q\,|q| + Z_{uq} uq + Z_{vp} vp + Z_{rp} rp + Z_{uw} uw + Z_{uu\delta_s} u^2 \delta_s \\
-z_G W \cos\theta \sin\phi + m z_G\left(ur - wp\right) + \left(I_y - I_z\right) qr + K_{p|p|} p\,|p| + K_{prop} \\
-z_G W \sin\theta + m z_G\left(vr - wq\right) + \left(I_z - I_x\right) rp + M_{w|w|} w\,|w| + M_{q|q|} q\,|q| + M_{uq} uq + M_{uw} uw + M_{vp} vp + M_{rp}\, rp + M_{uu\delta_s}\, u^2 \delta_s \\
\left(I_x - I_y\right) pq + N_{v|v|} v\,|v| + N_{r|r|} r\,|r| + N_{ur} ur + N_{wp} wp + N_{pq} pq + N_{uv} uv + N_{uu\delta_r} u^2 \delta_r
\end{bmatrix}
\tag{3.56}
$$

$$
\begin{Bmatrix} \dot{u} \\ \dot{v} \\ \dot{w} \\ \dot{p} \\ \dot{q} \\ \dot{r} \end{Bmatrix} = \begin{bmatrix} m - X_{\dot{u}} & 0 & 0 & 0 & mz_G & 0 \\ 0 & m - Y_{\dot{v}} & 0 & -mz_G & 0 & -Y_{\dot{r}} \\ 0 & 0 & m - Z_{\dot{w}} & 0 & -Z_{\dot{q}} & 0 \\ 0 & -mz_G & 0 & I_x - K_{\dot{p}} & 0 & 0 \\ mz_G & 0 & -M_{\dot{w}} & 0 & I_y - M_{\dot{q}} & 0 \\ 0 & -N_{\dot{v}} & 0 & 0 & 0 & I_z - N_{\dot{r}} \end{bmatrix}^{-1}
\begin{bmatrix} m\left(vr - wq - z_G rp\right) + X_{u|u|}u\left|u\right| + X_{wq}wq + X_{qq}qq + X_{vr}vr + X_{rr}rr + X_{prop} \\ m\left(wp - ur - z_G qr\right) + Y_{v|v|}v\left|v\right| + Y_{r|r|}r\left|r\right| + Y_{ur}ur + Y_{wp}wp + Y_{pq}pq + Y_{uv}uv + Y_{uu\delta_r}u^2\delta_r \\ m\left(uq - vp\right) + mz_G\left(p^2 + q^2\right) + Z_{w|w|}w\left|w\right| + Z_{q|q|}q\left|q\right| + Z_{uq}uq + Z_{vp}vp + Z_{rp}rp + Z_{uw}uw + Z_{uu\delta_s}u^2\delta_s + Z_{uu\delta_b}u^2\delta_b \\ -z_G W\cos\theta\sin\phi + mz_G\left(ur - wp\right) + \left(I_y - I_z\right)qr + K_{p|p|}p\left|p\right| + K_{prop} \\ -z_G W\sin\theta + mz_G\left(vr - wq\right) + \left(I_z - I_x\right)rp + M_{w|w|}w\left|w\right| + M_{q|q|}q\left|q\right| + M_{uq}uq + M_{uw}uw + M_{vp}vp + M_{rp}rp + M_{uu\delta_s}u^2\delta_s + M_{uu\delta_b}u^2\delta_b \\ \left(I_x - I_y\right)pq + N_{v|v|}v\left|v\right| + N_{r|r|}r\left|r\right| + N_{ur}ur + N_{wp}wp + N_{pq}pq + N_{uv}uv + N_{uu\delta_r}u^2\delta_r \end{bmatrix}
\tag{3.57}
$$

## 3.6 Thrust and Propulsion Modeling

### 3.6.1 Propeller Thrust Force and Moment Coefficients

The control forces acting on the AUV's hull are generated by the steering and propulsion mechanisms, specifically the cross-shaped rudder and the rear propeller, which produces steering force and thrust.

The hydrodynamic performance of a propeller is evaluated by obtaining the Propeller Open-Water (POW) characteristic curves, which comprehensively represent the propeller's behavior under various operating conditions. The performance of a screw propeller is typically described using several non-dimensional coefficients that depend on parameters such as the advance ratio $J = \frac{U}{nD_p}$, where $U$ is the advance velocity, $n$ is the propeller's rotational speed in revolutions per second, $D_p$ is the propeller diameter, and $\rho$ is the water density [8, 9]. These non-dimensional coefficients are derived from POW test results and are essential for estimating thrust and torque at given rotational speeds and inflow velocities [7, 10]. From the open-water characteristic curves, the thrust coefficient $K_T$ and torque coefficient $K_Q$ can be determined. Using these coefficients, the propeller thrust $T$ and torque $Q$ can be computed using equations (3.58) and (3.59) [11, 12].

$$T = K_T \rho n^2 D_p^4 \tag{3.58}$$

$$Q = K_Q \rho n^2 D_p^5 \tag{3.59}$$

### 3.6.2 Propeller Thrust Mooring Test

To satisfy the thrust and propulsion requirements of the AUV, particularly for the case of the FSAUV, a marine thruster known as the *Whale 1214* has been selected. This thruster, with a diameter of 140 mm, is illustrated in Fig. 3.1. It is capable of generating a maximum thrust of 14.8 kg, which provides sufficient force to propel the FSAUV efficiently through the water to achieve the desired speed. In addition to its peak performance, the thruster offers a rated mooring thrust of 12.5 kg, ensuring stable and continuous thrust during low-speed or stationary operations—such as position holding or heading stabilization—as shown in Fig. 3.2. The rotational speed (RPM) and thrust data obtained from mooring thrust and fatigue tests are presented in Table 3.2.

**Note:** The selection of a thruster for specific underwater applications should be carried out in accordance with established marine engineering standards and performance requirements [13, 14]. Factors such as required thrust, operational endurance, environmental conditions, power consumption, and system integration must be thoroughly considered to ensure reliable and efficient propulsion performance.

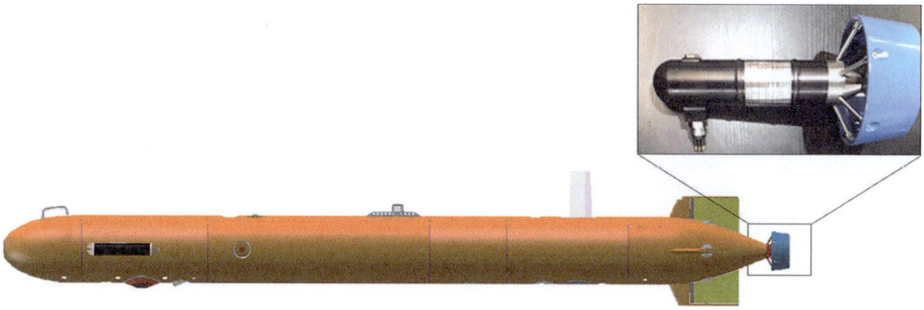

**Fig. 3.1** Thruster 'Whale 1214' [15]

**Table 3.2** Propeller thrust at different RPMs [15]

| RPM | 1100 | 1300 | 1500 | 1700 | 1900 | 2100 | 2300 | 2500 |
|---|---|---|---|---|---|---|---|---|
| Thrust (N) | 25 | 40 | 55 | 70 | 88 | 105 | 125 | 135 |

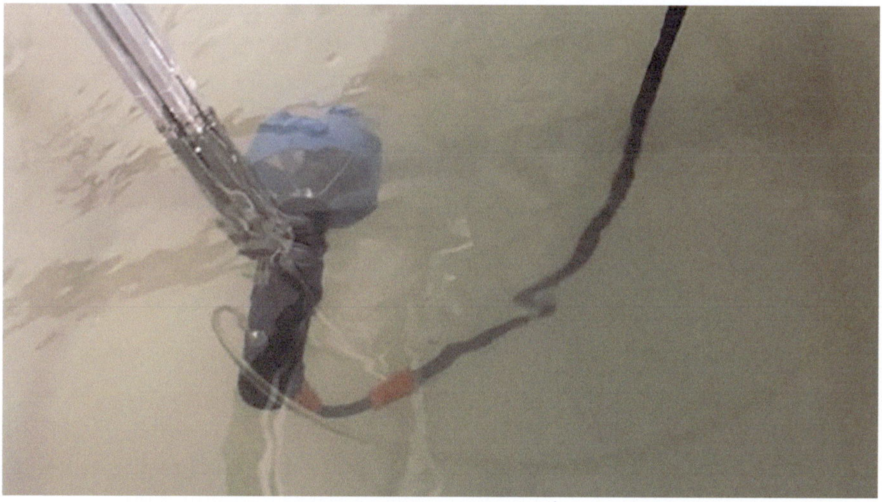

**Fig. 3.2** Mooring thrust and fatigue test [15]

### *3.6.3 Vehicle Thrust and Drag Relationship*

The efficiency of an underwater vehicle is significantly impacted by the interplay between its hull and the propulsion system. Specifically, the drag experienced by the vehicle directly relates to the reduced thrust available from the propeller. When the propeller is positioned at the aft (rear) section of an Autonomous Underwater Vehicle (AUV), it operates within the wake generated by the hull. This interaction leads to a phenomenon known as thrust deduction, where the propeller's performance is diminished.

This reduction in thrust is quantified by the thrust reduction factor, denoted as t. The value of t typically falls within the range of 0.25–0.4, as supported by research from [16, 17]. A higher thrust reduction factor indicates a greater loss in propulsive efficiency due to the hull's influence. This factor is crucial for accurately predicting the net thrust available for propulsion and, consequently, the vehicle's speed and endurance.

The fundamental relationship between the effective thrust generated by the propeller and the drag encountered by the vehicle can be expressed as follows, drawing upon the principles of marine hydrodynamics outlined by Lewis (1988) [11]:

$$R_T = (1 - t)T \tag{3.60}$$

$$R_T = \frac{C_{D_T}}{2}\rho S U^2 \tag{3.61}$$

$$\frac{C_{D_T}}{2}\rho S U^2 = (1 - t)K_T \rho n^2 D_p^4 \tag{3.62}$$

In the above equations, $T$ represents the propeller thrust, $\rho$ denotes the water density, $n$ is the propeller's rotational speed in revolutions per second, and $d$ is the propeller diameter. The hull resistance or drag is indicated by $R_T$, with its corresponding drag coefficient $C_{D_T}$. Additionally, $K_T$ stands for the thrust coefficient, $S$ refers to the wetted surface area of the AUV hull, and $U$ denotes the velocity of the AUV.

Accordingly, the vector of control input in Eq. (3.55) can be re-written as follows:

$$\tau_c = \begin{bmatrix} X_{prop} \\ Y_{uu\delta_r}u^2\delta_r \\ Z_{uu\delta_s}u^2\delta_s + Z_{uu\delta_b}u^2\delta_b \\ K_{prop} \\ M_{uu\delta_s}u^2\delta_s + M_{uu\delta_b}u^2\delta_b \\ N_{uu\delta_r}u^2\delta_r \end{bmatrix} = \begin{bmatrix} K_T\rho n^2 D_p^4 \\ \rho A_{f_1} C_{L\alpha_{f_1}} u^2\delta_r \\ -\rho A_{f_2} C_{L\alpha_{f_2}} u^2\delta_s - \rho A_{f_3} C_{L\alpha_{f_3}} u^2\delta_b \\ K_Q\rho n^2 D_p^5 \\ -\rho A_{f_2} C_{L\alpha_{f_2}} x_{f_2} u^2\delta_s + \rho A_{f_3} C_{L\alpha_{f3}} x_{f_3} u^2\delta_b \\ \rho A_{f_1} C_{L\alpha_{f_1}} x_{f_1} u^2\delta_r \end{bmatrix} \tag{3.63}$$

As practical example, the velocity and propeller rotational speed curves recorded during the free-running experiments of the FSAUV are shown in Fig. 3.3a, b, respectively. The actual vehicle drag can be estimated by correlating the free-running experimental data and propeller rotational speed with the data recorded during the POW mooring thrust tests, as presented in Table 3.2. A thrust reduction factor of 0.4 can be applied [16, 17].

Given that the FSAUV is intended to operate at a cruising speed of 3 knots [18], free-running experimental data corresponding to a steady translational speed of approximately 3 knots ($\approx$ 1.5 m/s) were employed to estimate the thrust coefficient. Accordingly, the thrust force coefficient is approximated by the product of the axial

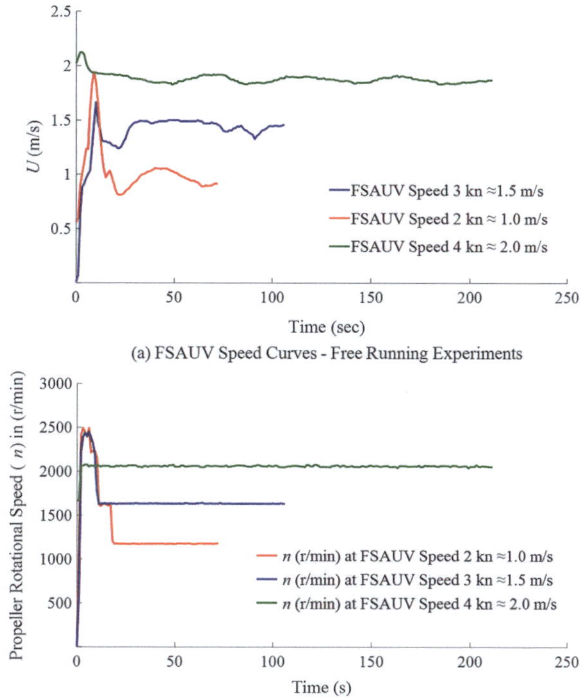


(a) FSAUV Speed Curves - Free Running Experiments

(b) FSAUV Propeller Rotational Speed Curves - Free Running Experiments

**Fig. 3.3** Free running underwater experimental data of FSAUV [15]

drag coefficient and the square of the translational velocity, expressed as:

$$X_{\text{prop}} = -X_{u|u|}\, u|u|$$

Furthermore, under minimum roll conditions, the torque generated by the AUV's propeller counterbalances the hydrostatic roll moment. This equilibrium condition is represented as:

$$K_{\text{prop}} = K_{\text{HS}} = z_G W \cos(\theta)\sin(\phi)$$

## 3.7 Summary

This chapter focuses on the dynamics modeling of AUVs, providing a detailed derivation of 6-DOF equations of motion. The dynamics are divided into rigid body dynamics, hydrodynamic forces, and hydrostatic forces. Rigid body dynamics are derived using Euler's first and second axioms, resulting in equations for translational and rotational motion. Hydrodynamic forces, including added mass and damping effects, are modeled to account for the interaction between the AUV and the surrounding fluid. Hydrostatic forces, arising from buoyancy and weight, are also incorporated to ensure stability and equilibrium. The chapter concludes with a discussion on thrust and propulsion modeling, including the relationship between propeller thrust and vehicle drag, and provides practical examples from experimental data. The comprehensive 6-DOF model integrates these components to accurately predict AUV behavior in various operational conditions.

## References


1. Fossen, T.I.: Handbook of Marine Craft Hydrodynamics and Motion Control. Wiley (2011)
2. Severholt, J.: Generic 6-dof added mass formulation for arbitrary underwater vehicles based on existing semi-empirical methods (2017)
3. Kepler Jr, M.E.: Dynamics of a small autonomous underwater vehicle that tows a large payload. Ph.D. thesis, Virginia Tech (2018)
4. Lamb, H.: Hydrodynamics. Cambridge University Press, pp. 134–139 (1932)
5. Kirchhoff, G.: Ueber die bewegung eines rotationskörpers in einer flüssigkeit. J. für die reine und angewandte Mathematik (Crelles Journal) **1870**(71), 237–262 (1870)
6. Prestero, T.T.J.: Verification of a six-degree of freedom simulation model for the remus autonomous underwater vehicle (2001)
7. Ahmed, F., Xiang, X., Wang, H., Zhang, J., Xiang, G., Yang, S.: Investigating wing-body lift interference effects on the dynamics of a novel flight-style AUV with bow-wings: maneuvering simulations and experimental validations. Ocean Eng. **326**, 120778 (2025)
8. Newman, J.N.: Marine Hydrodynamics. The MIT Press (2018)
9. Carlton, J.: Marine Propellers and Propulsion. Butterworth-Heinemann (2018)
10. Lee, C.M., Choi, H.T., Kim, K.: A study on the method of estimation of thrust performance of AUVs. In: The Abstracts of the International Conference on Advanced Mechatronics: Toward Evolutionary Fusion of IT and Mechatronics: ICAM 2010.5, pp. 98–102. The Japan Society of Mechanical Engineers (2010)
11. Lewis, E.V.: Principles of naval architecture second revision. Jersey: Sname **2** (1988)
12. ITTC: Recommended procedures and guidelines-UV full scale manoeuvring trials, 7.5-04-02-02 (2021)
13. Shipping, A.B.: Rules for building and classing underwater vehicles, systems, and hyperbaric facilities. Am. Bureau Ship. (2002)
14. Veritas, D.N.: Chapter 2: Propulsion, power generation and auxiliary systems. Technical report, DNV-RU-SHIP Pt. 6 Chap. 2) (2023). https://standards.dnv.com/explorer/document
15. Ahmed, F., Xiang, X., Wang, H., Xiang, G., Yang, S.: Cfd-based lift and drag estimations of a novel flight-style AUV with bow-wings: insights from drag polar curves and thrust estimations. J. Mar. Sci. Appl. **23**(2), 352–365 (2024)
16. Pivano, L.: Thrust estimation and control of marine propellers in four-quadrant operations (2008)
17. Min, F., Pan, G., Xu, X.: Modeling of autonomous underwater vehicles with multi-propellers based on maximum likelihood method. J. Marine Sci. Eng. **8**(6), 407 (2020)
18. Ahmed, F., Xiang, X., Wang, H., Zhang, J., Xiang, G., Yang, S.: Nonlinear dynamics of novel flight-style autonomous underwater vehicle with bow wings, part i: ase and cfd based estimations of hydrodynamic coefficients, part ii: nonlinear dynamic modeling and experimental validations. Appl. Ocean Res. **141**, 103739 (2023)

# Chapter 4
# Analytical and Semi-Empirical Methods for Hydrodynamic Coefficients Estimation

## 4.1 Introduction

The accurate prediction of hydrodynamic coefficients is crucial for understanding and modeling the behavior of underwater vehicles. Historically, methods developed for estimating the aerodynamic coefficients of aircraft have been adapted and applied to submerged vehicles. This cross-pollination of methodologies reflects the fundamental similarities in fluid dynamics principles, even across different operating environments.

Early advancements in this field include Strumpf's semi-empirical formula from the 1960s [1]. Derived from curve-fitting data from torpedo tests conducted at the Stevens Institute of Technology, this method provided an early framework for drag estimation. Subsequently, the USAF Datcom method, introduced by Finck in 1976 [2] for aerodynamic coefficient estimation, proved adaptable for submerged, torpedo-shaped underwater vehicles [3–5].

Hoerner's extensive theoretical and experimental work on fluid dynamic drag [6] and lift [7] for aerial vehicles has been particularly influential in computing the damping coefficients of AUVs [8–13]. AUVs typically operate in transitional flow regimes, often with Reynolds numbers exceeding $Re > 106$. For these conditions, Hoerner [6] (Page 6–18) provided valuable relationships for calculating the axial flow drag coefficient.

Hoerner also offered insights into cross-flow drag coefficients for cylindrical shapes, which can be effectively approximated for torpedo-shaped AUV hulls exhibiting two-plane symmetry (top-bottom and port-starboard). For the cross-flow drag forces on the fins, Hoerner [6] further derived the drag coefficient for a square flat plate, providing a useful basis for estimating the coefficients of the AUV's control surfaces. Complementing this, Whicker and Fehlner [14] also proposed a relationship for computing drag coefficients specific to fins.

Rolling drag in AUVs primarily arises from the lateral movement of the vehicle, with the fins acting as the primary components providing resistance during roll.



X. Xiang et al., *Dynamics Modeling and Maneuvering of Autonomous Underwater Vehicles*, https://doi.org/10.1007/978-981-95-1521-9_4

Therefore, when computing rolling drag, it's essential to consider the empirically derived drag coefficients used for determining the sway damping coefficient of the fins. For estimating lift force coefficients, Hoerner [7] provided separate empirical relationships applicable to both AUV hulls and their fins.

Various researchers have applied and refined these methodologies. For instance, Prestero [8] calculated the axial flow drag coefficient for the REMUS 100 AUV using Triantafyllou's relationship and Schoenherr's constant [15], while deriving cross-flow drag and lift coefficients from Hoerner's empirical relationships [6]. Kepler [16] applied Hoerner's methodology to determine the damping coefficient of a torpedo-shaped AUV, and Watt [17] utilized ASE methods for the Dorado class remote mine-hunting vehicle. Significant advancements in ASE methods for underwater vehicles have continued with contributions from de-Barros et al. [18–21], Kepler [16], and others [22, 23], continually refining our ability to predict the complex hydrodynamic behavior of these autonomous platforms.

In addition to hydrodynamic drag and lift, added mass is vital for modeling AUV dynamics. As an AUV moves underwater, it disturbs the surrounding water, causing the fluid to accelerate with the vehicle. This interaction increases the propulsion force needed compared to a medium like a vacuum, where no added mass effect exists. Consequently, the additional force acting on the hull highlights the importance of AUV geometry in estimating added mass coefficients [23, 24]. For torpedo-shaped AUVs, analytical methods rely on strip theory and ellipsoid approximations, which depend on the vehicle's geometry. Strip theory simplifies calculations by dividing the AUV into infinitesimal 2D slices, integrating each slice's contributions along the vehicle's length. This method, based on potential flow theory, was first approximated in 2D by Korvin-Kroukovsky and Jacobs [25, 26] and detailed by Newman [27]. In 1970, Salvesen et al. [28] extended this theory to predict ship motions and loads, including pitch, sway, heave, roll, and yaw, as well as wave-induced forces and moments. Later, Prestero [8], Milgram [29], and Ferreira et al. [13] applied strip theory to torpedo-shaped AUVs. For AUVs approximated as ellipsoids, as shown in Fig. 4.1, added mass coefficients are calculated analytically by solving Laplace's equations for velocity potential, excluding viscous effects [11].

Lamb in 1945 [31] provided the foundations for estimation of added mass on prolate spheroid, by deriving an expression for kinetic energy in an inviscid, circulation-free fluid. The method was later applied to underwater vehicles by Imlay in 1961 [32], and other marine vehicles by Fossen [33]. Humphreys and Watkinson [34] used this method to predict acceleration hydrodynamic coefficients for defense applications,

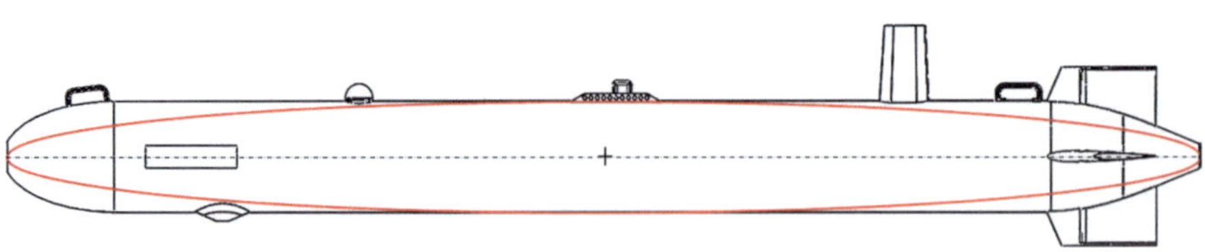

**Fig. 4.1** Ellipsoid mapped to Torpedo-Shaped AUV [30]

and Watt [35] extended it to multi-component submerged vehicles. Lamb's method remains widely used due to its applicability to prolate spheroids, which approximate many slender underwater vehicles. Researchers such as Doherty [36], Humphreys and Watkinson [34], Lee et al. [37], Prestero [8], Severholt [23], and Kepler [16] have employed it effectively on Torpedo-Shaped AUVs. Newman [27] offered a slender body theory method for more accurate shape modeling for better accuracy. Added mass estimations for wings and fins using ASE methods approximate them as flat plates, employing established aerodynamic formulations. Munk in 1934 developed the foundation for estimating added mass for control surfaces [38], while Gracey in 1941 [24] conducted experimental analyses. Humphreys and Watkinson later provided approximations for flat plates in relation to underwater control surfaces [34]. The ASE method evolution over the period of last many years is shown in the Fig. 4.2.

## 4.2 Fundamental Theories for ASE-Based Estimations of Hydrodynamic Coefficients

The estimation of hydrodynamic forces including added mass and damping forces coefficients of underwater vehicles relies on several fundamental theories. These theories offer mathematical frameworks to accurately model the interaction between the vehicle and the surrounding fluid. The three primary theories used are Strip Theory, Potential Flow Theory, and Slender Body Theory. These theories are often used in combination to estimate the hydrodynamic coefficients (e.g., added mass, damping) required for AUV dynamics modeling. For example, Strip Theory and Slender Body Theory are used for preliminary estimates of added mass and damping, while Potential Flow Theory is applied for detailed analysis of complex geometries or unsteady flows. The choice of theory depends on the body's geometry, the flow conditions, and the required level of accuracy. By leveraging these fundamental theories, accurate estimates of ASE can be obtained, enabling the design and control of efficient and stable underwater vehicles.

### 4.2.1 *Strip Theory*

Strip Theory is a simplified method for estimating hydrodynamic forces on slender bodies, such as torpedoes or submarines. The body is divided into thin strips (sections) along its length, and the hydrodynamic forces on each strip are calculated independently. The total hydrodynamic forces are obtained by integrating the contributions from all strips. Mathematically, this is expressed as:

$$F_{\text{strip}} = \int_L f(x)\,dx$$

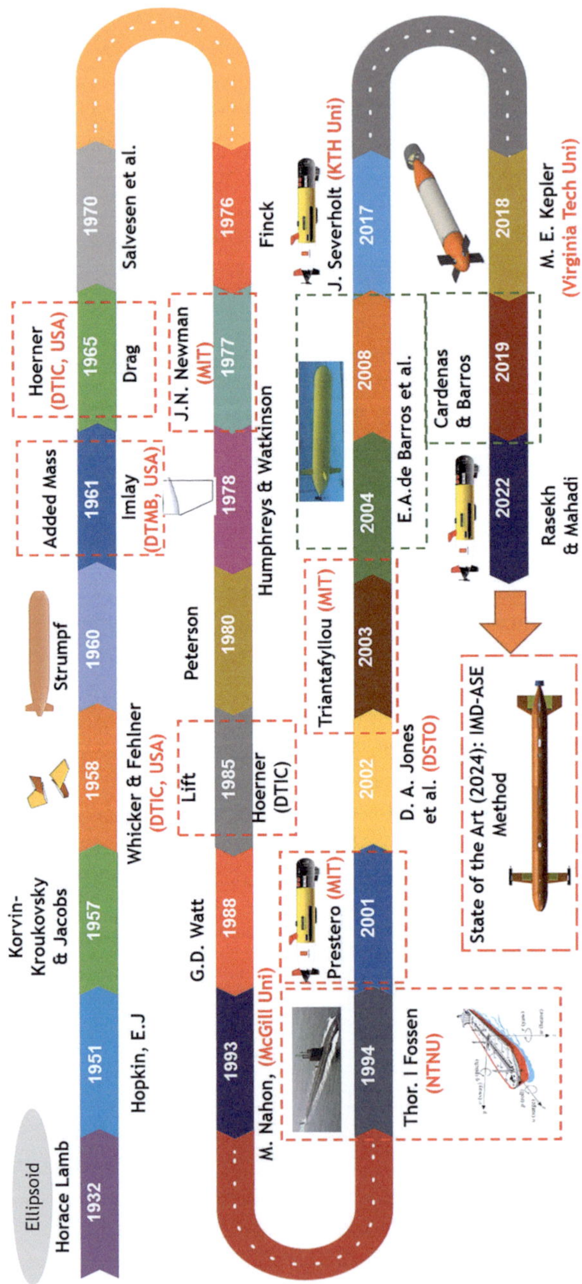


Fig. 4.2 State-Of-The-Art

where $f(x)$ is the force per unit length on a strip at position $x$. This theory is particularly suitable for long, slender bodies with a high length-to-diameter ratio and is commonly used for estimating added mass and damping coefficients. One of its key advantages is its computational efficiency, making it a practical choice for preliminary analyses. However, Strip Theory assumes two-dimensional flow around each strip and neglects three-dimensional effects. This assumption can lead to inaccuracies for bodies with complex geometries or low length-to-diameter ratios.

### 4.2.2 *Potential Flow Theory*

Potential Flow Theory assumes that the fluid is inviscid, incompressible, and irrotational. In this theory, the flow is described by a velocity potential, which satisfies Laplace's equation. Hydrodynamic forces are derived from the pressure distribution on the body surface, calculated using Bernoulli's equation. The governing equation for Potential Flow Theory is:

$$\nabla^2\phi = 0$$

where $\phi$ is the velocity potential. This theory is widely used to estimate added mass and hydrodynamic forces for bodies of arbitrary shape and is suitable for analyzing both steady and unsteady flows. Its primary advantages include the ability to provide analytical solutions for simple geometries and the flexibility to extend to complex shapes using numerical methods, such as the Boundary Element Method. However, Potential Flow Theory neglects viscous effects, such as drag due to fluid viscosity, and assumes small-amplitude motions. These assumptions limit its applicability to scenarios involving highly dynamic or turbulent flows.

### 4.2.3 *Slender Body Theory*

Slender Body Theory is an extension of Strip Theory and is specifically designed for long, slender bodies. Unlike Strip Theory, it accounts for three-dimensional effects by considering the flow around the entire body rather than treating it as a series of independent strips. The theory assumes that the body's cross-sectional dimensions are small compared to its length. The total hydrodynamic force in Slender Body Theory is given by:

$$F_{\text{total}} = \int_L f_{3\text{D}}(x)\, dx$$

where $f_{3\text{D}}(x)$ accounts for three-dimensional flow effects. Slender Body Theory is used to estimate added mass, damping, and hydrodynamic forces for slender underwater vehicles and is particularly suitable for analyzing maneuvering and dynamic stability. Its advantages include greater accuracy compared to Strip Theory for slender bodies and the incorporation of three-dimensional flow effects. However, it is limited to bodies with high length-to-diameter ratios and may be less accurate for bodies with complex geometries or significant cross-sectional variations.

## 4.3 Added Mass Coefficients

The added mass phenomenon experienced by an AUV results from the inertia imparted to the surrounding fluid as the vehicle accelerates. When the AUV moves through still water, it displaces the fluid, requiring additional kinetic energy to accelerate both the vehicle and the displaced fluid. This interaction effectively increases the vehicle's inertia, causing it to behave as though it possesses more mass, commonly known as *added mass*. The pressure distribution created by the moving fluid acts normal to the AUV's surface, with the magnitude of this effect highly dependent on the vehicle's geometry [39]. The estimation of added mass coefficients is primarily based on potential flow theory and strip theory. Potential flow theory assumes that the flow is inviscid, incompressible, and irrotational, allowing the velocity field around the AUV to be described using a scalar potential function. The assumptions inherent in potential flow theory simplify the estimation of added mass coefficients by neglecting viscous effects, making it particularly suitable for preliminary hydrodynamic analyses. In contrast, strip theory divides the AUV's hull into discrete cross-sectional segments (strips), each analysed independently to compute the hydrodynamic forces and added mass. The strip theory approach is well-suited for slender bodies such as torpedo-shaped AUVs, as it provides reasonably accurate approximations of their behavior. The significance of added mass has been recognized since the 19th century [24], and extensive studies have quantified its effects for various underwater vehicle motions. For surge, sway, and heave, added mass is typically estimated using analytical methods such as the ASE approach, which provides reliable hydrodynamic coefficients for accurate modeling of AUV dynamics [16, 23, 32].

To derive the hydrodynamic coefficients using the ASE methods, Flight-Style AUV is taken as a practical example to derive the mathematical relationships. The FSAUV is shown in Fig. 4.3 Corresponding parameters of the FSAUV are given in Table 4.1.

### *4.3.1 Axial Flow (Surge) Added Mass Coefficients*

Approximating the torpedo-shaped AUV as ellipsoid, shown in Fig. 4.4, the added mass $X_{\dot{u}} = m_{11}$ due to surge velocity has been estimated using the expression (4.1) [42].

$$X_{\dot{u}} = -k_1 \, m_f \tag{4.1}$$

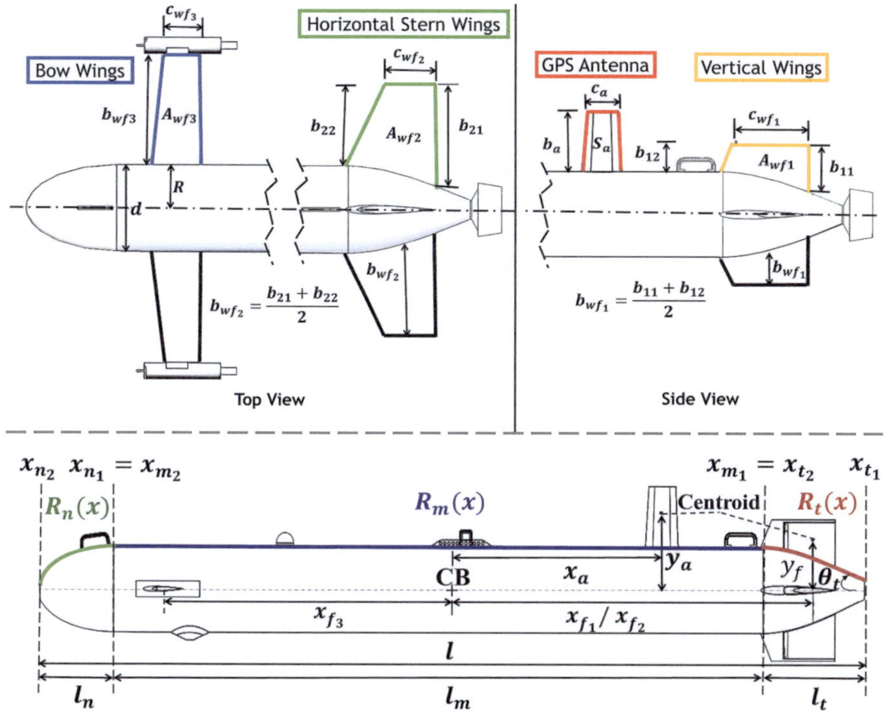


**Fig. 4.3** Geometric parameters of Myring Hull, Wings, Fins and Antenna [40]

**Table 4.1** Geometric parameters of FSAUV hull, wings, fins, and antenna [41]

| Parameters | $d$ | $l$ | $l_n$ | $n_o$ | $l_m$ | $l_t$ | $t_o$ | $n$ | $\theta_t$ |
|---|---|---|---|---|---|---|---|---|---|
| Values | 0.24 m | 2.712 m | 0.25 m | 0.008 m | 2.135 m | 0.4 m | 0.065 m | 2 | 20° |
| Parameters | $l_f$ | $A_{fx}$ | $A_{fy}$ | $A_{fz}$ | $A_p$ | $A_{wf_1}$ | $A_{wf_2}$ | $A_{wf_3}$ | $A_{f_1}$ |
| Values | 2.377 m | 0.07 m$^2$ | 0.69 m$^2$ | 0.8 m$^2$ | 0.62 m$^2$ | 0.02 m$^2$ | 0.04 m$^2$ | 0.05 m$^2$ | 0.015 m$^2$ |
| Parameters | $A_{f_2}$ | $A_{f_3}$ | $S_a$ | $b_{wf_1}$ | $b_{wf_2}$ | $b_{wf_3}$ | $b_{f_1}$ | $b_{f_2}$ | $b_{f_3}$ |
| Values | 0.015 m$^2$ | 0.01 m$^2$ | 0.0164 m$^2$ | 0.1 m | 0.25 m | 0.3 m | 0.103 m | 0.103 m | 0.134 m |
| Parameters | $b_a$ | $x_{f_1}$ | $x_{f_2}$ | $x_{f_3}$ | $x_a$ | $y_f$ | $y_a$ | $c_{wf_1}$ | $c_{wf_2}$ |
| Values | 0.168 m | −1.1 m | −1.1 m | +1.0 m | -0.63 m | 0.14 m | 0.215 m | 0.23 m | 0.20 m |
| Parameters | $c_{wf_3}$ | $c_a$ | $\delta_{max}$ | $m$ | $W$ | $B$ | | | |
| Values | 0.11 m | 0.097 m | 30° | 84.7 kg | 831 N | 831 N | | | |

where, $k_1$ is Lamb's $k$-factor [31], $m_f$ is mass of the fluid and be estimated using Eq. (4.2).

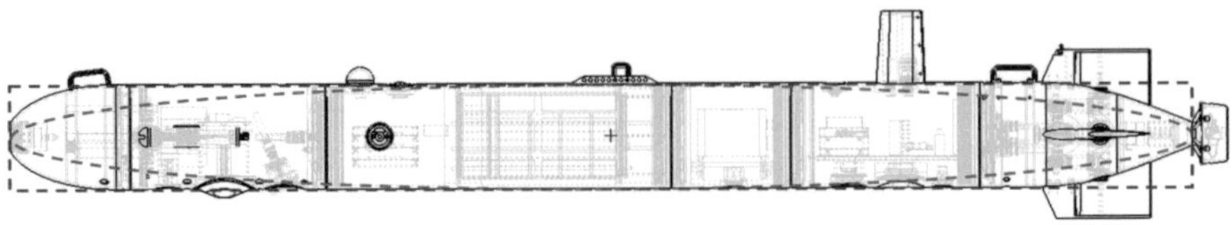

**Fig. 4.4** FSAUV Hull compared to ellipsoid and circular cylinder [41]

$$\begin{cases} k_1 = -\frac{\alpha_0}{2-\alpha_0} \\ m_f = \frac{4}{3}\pi\rho r_1 r_2^2 \\ \alpha_0 = \frac{2(1-e^2)}{e^3}\left(\frac{1}{2}\ln\frac{1+e}{1-e} - e\right) \\ e = \sqrt{1-\left(\frac{r_2}{r_1}\right)^2} \end{cases} \tag{4.2}$$

where, $\rho$ is the density of the fluid and $e$ is the eccentricity of the ellipsoid and $2r_1$ and $2r_2$ in Eq. (4.2) are equivalent to the length and diameter of the vehicle respectively.

### 4.3.2 Cross Flow (Sway and Heave) Added Mass Coefficients

Added mass coefficients due to lateral motion of the vehicle have been calculated separately for the bare-hull [27], wings/fins and antenna [34] using Eqs. (4.3) through (4.8).

$$Y_{\dot{v}} = -\pi\rho\int_L R^2(x)\,dx - 2\left(k_p\frac{1}{4}\pi\rho c_{wf_1}^2 b_{wf_1}\right) - \left(k_p\frac{1}{4}\pi\rho c_a^2 b_a\right) \tag{4.3}$$

$$Z_{\dot{w}} = -\pi\rho\int_L R^2(x)\,dx - 2\left(k_p\frac{1}{4}\pi\rho c_{wf_2}^2 b_{wf_2}\right) - 2\left(k_p\frac{1}{4}\pi\rho c_{wf_3}^2 b_{wf_3}\right) \tag{4.4}$$

$$N_{\dot{v}} = Y_{\dot{r}} = -\pi\rho\int_L R^2(x)\,x\,dx - 2\left(k_p\frac{1}{4}\pi\rho c_{wf_1}^2 b_{wf_1}\right)x_{f_1} - \left(k_p\frac{1}{4}\pi\rho c_a^2 b_a\right)x_a \tag{4.5}$$

$$M_{\dot{w}} = Z_{\dot{q}} = \pi\rho\int_L R^2(x)\,x\,dx - 2\left(k_p\frac{1}{4}\pi\rho c_{wf_2}^2 b_{wf_2}\right)x_{f_2} - 2\left(k_p\frac{1}{4}\pi\rho c_{wf_3}^2 b_{wf_3}\right)x_{f_3} \tag{4.6}$$

$$N_{\dot{r}} = -\pi\rho\int_L R^2(x)\,x^2\,dx - 2\left(k'_p\frac{1}{48}\pi\rho c_{wf_1}^3 b_{wf_1}^2\right) - 2\left(k_p\frac{1}{4}\pi\rho c_{wf_1}^2 b_{wf_1}\right)x_{f_1}^2 - \left(k_p\frac{1}{4}\pi\rho c_a^2 b_a\right)x_a^2 \tag{4.7}$$

$$M_{\dot{q}} = -\pi\rho \int_L R^2(x)\, x^2\, dx - 2\left(k'_p \frac{1}{48}\pi\rho c^3_{wf_2} b^2_{wf_2}\right) - 2\left(k'_p \frac{1}{48}\pi\rho c^3_{wf_3} b^2_{wf_3}\right)$$
$$- 2\left(k_p \frac{1}{4}\pi\rho c^2_{wf_2} b_{wf_2}\right) x^2_{f_2} - 2\left(k_p \frac{1}{4}\pi\rho c^2_{wf3} b_{wf_3}\right) x^2_{f_3} \quad (4.8)$$

where, $k_p$ is coefficient of additional mass for the flat plate given by Humphreys and Watkinson [34] and $k^{'}_p$ is coefficient of additional moment of inertia presented by Gracey [24]. These coefficients are the functions of $\frac{1}{AR}$ [23, 43] of the flat plate. The values of $k_p$ and $k^{'}_p$ approximating the wings and fins to the flat plate are estimated from the graphs in Figs. 14 and 25 of reference [34] respectively. The locations ($x_f$, $y_f$, $x_a$ & $y_a$) of fins and antenna centroids are shown in Fig. 4.3.

### 4.3.3 Rolling Added Mass Coefficients

The rotational motion of an Autonomous Underwater Vehicle (AUV) about its longitudinal axis (x-axis) induces added mass effects. While these effects are typically negligible for the main hull due to its streamlined cylindrical geometry, they can be significant for appendages such as fixed wings, control fins, and antennas. These components, owing to their arbitrary shapes and off-center placements, contribute substantially to the rolling added mass. To accurately estimate the rolling added mass coefficients associated with these appendages, their respective centroid locations must be taken into account. The cumulative rolling added mass contribution from all such components can be determined using the following expressions:

$$K_{\dot{p}} = K_{\dot{p}_{wf}} + K_{\dot{p}_a} \quad (4.9)$$

$$K_{\dot{p}_{wf}} = -2\left[\left(k'_p \frac{1}{48}\pi\rho c^3_{wf_1} b^2_{wf_1}\right) + \left(k'_p \frac{1}{48}\pi\rho c^3_{wf_2} b^2_{wf_2}\right) + \left(k'_p \frac{1}{48}\pi\rho c^3_{wf_3} b^2_{wf_3}\right) - \left(Y_{\dot{v}_{wf}} y^2_f\right)\right] \quad (4.10)$$

$$K_{\dot{p}_a} = -k'_p \frac{1}{48}\pi\rho c^3_a b^2_a + Y_{\dot{v}_a} y^2_a \quad (4.11)$$

where, $K_{\dot{p}}$ represents the rolling added mass due to all the wings, fins, and antennas; $K_{\dot{p}_{wf}}$ denotes the contribution from the wings and fins; and $K_{\dot{p}_a}$ accounts for the contribution from the antennas.

### *4.3.4 Added Mass Cross-Terms*

The cross-coupling terms in the nonlinear dynamic model, such as $X_{wq}$, $X_{qq}$, $Y_{ura}$, $M_{uwa}$, and others, represent the added mass interactions between different degrees of freedom. These terms are essential for accurately capturing the AUV's dynamic behavior during six-degree-of-freedom (6-DOF) maneuvers. The corresponding parameters, expressed in terms of added mass coefficients, are summarized in Table 3.1.

## 4.4 Drag Coefficients

The drag forces acting on an AUV maneuvering in six degrees of freedom can be categorized into axial and lateral components. The axial drag corresponds to the resistance encountered along the longitudinal axis due to forward motion (axial flow), while the lateral drag arises due to side-slip and cross-flow perpendicular to the longitudinal axis. In addition to these, the AUV experiences rolling drag, which is induced by its roll motion around the x-axis. The total drag force on the AUV moving in a fluid medium can be estimated using the general drag equation, as expressed in Eq. (4.12) [6, 8].

$$F_D = \frac{1}{2}\rho A V^2 C_d \tag{4.12}$$

where, $F_D$ is drag force, $\rho$ is density of the fluid, $A$ is effective area and $V$ is the velocity of the vehicle. Whereas, $C_d$ is drag coefficient.

### *4.4.1 Axial Drag Coefficient*

The axial drag force ($X$) and corresponding nonlinear drag coefficient ($X_{u|u|}$) acting on the FSAUV can be estimated using Eq. (4.13).

$$\begin{cases} X = -\left(\frac{1}{2}\rho A_{fx} C_{d_a}\right) u\,|u| \\ X_{u|u|} = -\frac{1}{2}\rho A_{fx} C_{d_a} \end{cases} \tag{4.13}$$

where, $A_f$ is the frontal area as illustrated in Fig. 4.5 and $C_{d_a}$ is the axial drag coefficient of the FSAUV and can be computed using empirical relationship provided by Triantafyllou [8, 44] in Eq. (4.14). Figure 4.5 demonstrates the geometries and objects contributing in frontal area to compute the axial drag force for both the configurations of AUV.

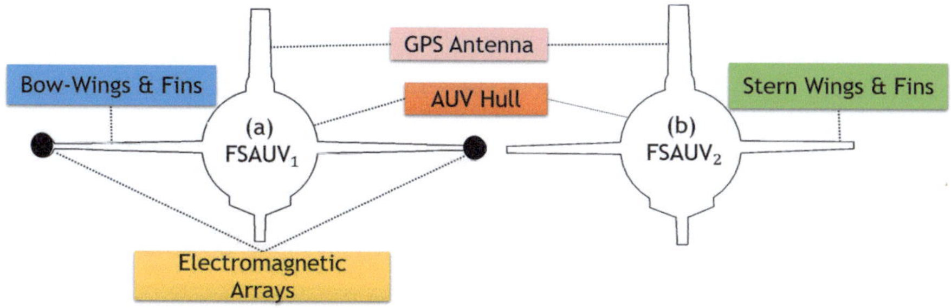


**Fig. 4.5** Projected Area of $FSAUV_1$ and $FSAUV_2$ along $x$-axis [41]

$$C_{d_a} = \frac{C_{ss}\pi A_P}{A_x}\left[1 + 60(\lambda)^{-3} + 0.0025\,(\lambda)\right] \tag{4.14}$$

where, $C_{ss}$ is Schoenherr's value and is estimated as 0.0034. $\lambda$ is fineness ratio $l/d$. $A_p$ is projected area of the hull and $l$ & $d$ are the length and diameter of the vehicle respectively.

Additionally, the axial drag for streamlined bodies given by Hoerner [6] Page 6-18, is given in Eq. (4.15) for the transition flow region such as flow approaching $R_e = 10^6$.

$$C_{d_a} = C_f\left[3\,(\lambda) + 4.5(\lambda)^{-\frac{1}{2}} + 21(\lambda)^2\right] \tag{4.15}$$

where, $C_f$ is the skin friction drag coefficient given by Hoerner [6], (Page 6–18) and can be estimated as follows:

$$C_f = \frac{0.045}{{R_e}^{(1/6)}} \cong 0.004$$

Considering that the FSAUV has a hull with a myring profile and a rounded or streamlined head, can be approximated as an ellipsoid. Accordingly, Hoerner [6] provided empirical relationships specifically for calculating the axial drag coefficients of ellipsoidal shapes, as detailed in Eq. (4.16). These standard formulations are applied to estimate the axial drag coefficient of the FSAUV, given the similarity of its profile to an ellipsoid.

$$C_{da} = C_{f_{turb}}\left[4 + 2(\lambda)\; + 120(\lambda)^{-2}\right] \tag{4.16}$$

where, $C_{f_{turb}}$= 0.005 given by Hoerner [6], Page 3–11 for elliptical shapes having the flow in above critical region approaching Reynold number within range $10^5 \geq R_e \leq 10^6$.

The axial drag coefficients for the given AUV have been estimated using empirical formulations provided in equations (4.14), (4.15), and (4.16). The resulting values are compiled in Table 5.2. Furthermore, for cylindrical bodies featuring rounded or streamlined nose profiles with a fineness ratio of approximately $\left(\frac{l}{d} \cong 11.3\right)$, the axial flow drag coefficient can also be referenced from Hoerner's classical work [6]. Specifically, Fig. 21 on Page 3–12 of [6] provides graphical data applicable to such geometries.

### *4.4.2 Cross-Flow Drag Coefficients: Improved ASE Approach*

The total drag acting on the FSAUV during lateral motion arises from the combined effects of the hull, vertical wings, fins, and antenna. To facilitate the estimation of cross-flow drag, the torpedo-shaped hull of the AUV is idealized as either an ellipsoid or a circular cylinder. For comparative analysis, the projected lateral area of the actual FSAUV hull is approximately $0.62\,\mathrm{m}^2$, while the corresponding projected areas for an ellipsoid and a circular cylinder–both having the same length and diameter as the FSAUV–are $0.51\,\mathrm{m}^2$ and $0.65\,\mathrm{m}^2$, respectively. As illustrated in Fig. 4.4, the geometric configuration of the FSAUV more closely resembles that of a circular cylinder than an ellipsoid. This observation supports the use of circular-cylinder-based hydrodynamic models for improved accuracy in capturing cross-flow drag effects, especially for slender-bodied underwater vehicles like the FSAUV [8, 16].

The cross-flow drag coefficients for both horizontal and vertical plane dynamics include yaw and sway-induced coefficients ($Y_{v|v|}$, $N_{v|v|}$, $Y_{r|r|}$, and $N_{r|r|}$) and pitch and heave-induced coefficients ($Z_{w|w|}$, $M_{w|w|}$, $Z_{q|q|}$, $M_{q|q|}$). The terms $Y_{v|v|}$ and $N_{v|v|}$ represent lateral forces and yaw moments generated by sway motion, improving the prediction of trajectory stability and path-following accuracy. Similarly, $Z_{w|w|}$ and $M_{w|w|}$ correspond to heave-induced vertical forces and pitch moments, capturing the vehicle's depth stability and response during vertical plane motions. The terms $Y_{r|r|}$ and $N_{r|r|}$ describe yaw-induced lateral forces and moments, which are crucial for accurately modeling the turning dynamics and rotational resistance. Meanwhile, $Z_{q|q|}$ and $M_{q|q|}$ represent forces and moments due to pitch motion, ensuring better characterization of pitch stability and depth control.

The ASE formulations to estimate these coefficients depend on the cross-flow drag coefficient ($C_{dc}$). However, in previous studies [8, 16], the drag coefficient ($C_{dc}$) for 2D flow past a circular cylinder was considered as $C_{dc}^{2D}$. In contrast, the present study introduces an improved approach by incorporating the actual 3D effects of the flow, considering cross-flow drag coefficients as $C_{dc}^{3D}$. Moreover, the improved formulations for estimating these coefficients ($Y_{v|v|}$, $N_{v|v|}$, $Y_{r|r|}$, $N_{r|r|}$, $Z_{w|w|}$, $M_{w|w|}$, $Z_{q|q|}$, and $M_{q|q|}$) also account for the novel contributions of wings, fins, and hull geometry of the FSAUV, which significantly affect lateral drag due to their specific shapes and positioning.

To estimate the cross-flow drag coefficient, improved mathematical formulations incorporating $C_{dc}^{3D}$ have been derived, including additional contributions from the wings and fins. Equations (4.17) through (4.24) are utilized to estimate the cross-flow drag coefficients and corresponding moment coefficients for FSAUV motion during sway, heave, pitching, and yawing.

$$Y_{v|v|} = -\frac{1}{2}\rho C_{dc}^{3D} \int_L 2R(x)\,dx - 2\left(\frac{1}{2}\rho C_{d_f} A_{wf_1}\right) - \left(\frac{1}{2}\rho C_{d_f} S_a\right) \tag{4.17}$$

$$Z_{w|w|} = -\frac{1}{2}\rho C_{dc}^{3D} \int_L 2R(x)\,dx - 2\left(\frac{1}{2}\rho C_{d_f} A_{wf_2}\right) - 2\left(\frac{1}{2}\rho C_{d_f} A_{wf_3}\right) \tag{4.18}$$

$$M_{w|w|} = \frac{1}{2}\rho C_{dc}^{3D} \int_L 2xR(x)\,dx + 2\left(\frac{1}{2}\rho C_{d_f} A_{wf_2}\right) x_{f_2} - 2\left(\frac{1}{2}\rho C_{d_f} A_{wf_3}\right) x_{f_3} \tag{4.19}$$

$$N_{v|v|} = -\frac{1}{2}\rho C_{dc}^{3D} \int_L 2xR(x)\,dx - 2\left(\frac{1}{2}\rho C_{d_f} A_{wf_1}\right) x_{f_1} - \left(\frac{1}{2}\rho C_{d_f} S_a\right) x_a \tag{4.20}$$

$$Y_{r|r|} = -\frac{1}{2}\rho C_{dc}^{3D} \int_L 2x\,|x|\,R(x)\,dx - 2\left(\frac{1}{2}\rho C_{d_f} A_{wf_1}\right) x_{f_1}\left|x_{f_1}\right| - \left(\frac{1}{2}\rho C_{d_f} S_a\right) x_a\,|x_a| \tag{4.21}$$

$$Z_{q|q|} = \frac{1}{2}\rho C_{dc}^{3D} \int_L 2x\,|x|\,R(x)\,dx + 2\left(\frac{1}{2}\rho C_{d_f} A_{wf_2}\right) x_{f_2}\left|x_{f_2}\right| + 2\left(\frac{1}{2}\rho C_{d_f} A_{wf_3}\right) x_{f_3}\left|x_{f_3}\right| \tag{4.22}$$

$$M_{q|q|} = -\frac{1}{2}\rho C_{dc}^{3D} \int_L 2x^2\,|x|\,R(x)\,dx - 2\left(\frac{1}{2}\rho C_{d_f} A_{wf_2}\right) x_{f_2}^2\left|x_{f_2}\right| - 2\left(\frac{1}{2}\rho C_{d_f} A_{wf_3}\right) x_{f_3}^2\left|x_{f_3}\right| \tag{4.23}$$

$$N_{r|r|} = -\frac{1}{2}\rho C_{dc}^{3D} \int_L 2x^2\,|x|\,R(x)\,dx - 2\left(\frac{1}{2}\rho C_{d_f} A_{wf_1}\right) x_{f_1}^2\left|x_{f_1}\right| - \left(\frac{1}{2}\rho C_{d_f} S_a\right) x_a^2\,|x_a| \tag{4.24}$$

In Eqs. (4.17) to (4.24), $C_{d_c}$ denotes the cross-flow drag coefficient. Previous research efforts [8, 45] that focused on estimating cross-flow drag coefficients–specifically $Y_{v|v|}$, $Z_{w|w|}$, $M_{w|w|}$, $N_{v|v|}$, $Y_{r|r|}$, $Z_{q|q|}$, $M_{q|q|}$, and $N_{r|r|}$–for torpedo-shaped autonomous underwater vehicles have adopted a representative value of $C_{d_c}^{2D} = 1.2$. This value is based on the experimental data compiled by Hoerner [6], which reflects the drag characteristics for two-dimensional flow around a circular cylinder operating at subcritical Reynolds numbers, as originally established by Wieselsberger [46].

To more accurately capture the actual fluid flow conditions encountered by the FSAUV, it is essential to consider experimental data corresponding to three-dimensional (3D) flow past a circular cylinder with both ends free. Accordingly, this study adopts the results presented by Wieselsberger [47, 48], which report a cross-flow drag coefficient of $C_{d_c}^{3D} \approx 0.84$ for a circular cylinder with a length-to-diameter ratio $l/d = 11.3$, equivalent to that of the FSAUV. Accurate approximation of $C_{d_c}$ is critical when applying the ASE-based method for estimating cross-flow drag force coefficients. This refinement substantially affects the final estimations of drag and moment coefficients using Eqs. (4.17) to (4.24), enhancing the accuracy of the nonlinear dynamic model developed for the FSAUV.

To estimate the drag forces and moments induced by control surfaces such as wings and fins, these components are approximated as flat plates. Based on Hoerner's empirical data [6], the drag coefficient for flat plates ($C_{d_f}$) is taken as 1.17 (refer to page 3-15). This value is employed in the computation of corresponding coefficients in Eqs. (4.17) to (4.24). Overall, incorporation of these refined drag coefficients improves the fidelity of dynamic simulations and enables more reliable predictions of the FSAUV's stability, control, and maneuvering performance in real-world operating environments.

### 4.4.3 Rolling Drag Coefficient

The cross-flow drag of wings/fins creates resistance during the roll moment, which is quantified using Eq. (4.25).

$$K_{p|p|} = \underbrace{-\left(\rho C_{d_f} A_{wf_1}\right)}_{Y_{v|v|f}} y_f^3 \underbrace{-\left(\frac{1}{2}\rho C_{d_f} S_a\right)}_{Y_{v|v|a}} y_a^3 \tag{4.25}$$

where, $K_{p|p|}$ is the rolling drag, $Y_{v|v|_{wf}}$ and $Y_{v|v|_a}$ is the cross flow drag by vertical wings/fins and antenna respectively. The corresponding location of the centroid from the center axis of the AUV for wings/fins and antenna are denoted by $y_f$ and $y_a$. Same is shown in Fig. 4.3.

## 4.5 Lift Coefficients

The lift force acts perpendicular to the relative fluid flow around a body and arises due to the pressure difference between its upper and lower surfaces caused by fluid interaction. In the case of an AUV, the generation of lift is primarily influenced by the vehicle's geometry, the density of the surrounding fluid, the vehicle's velocity relative to the fluid, and its angle of attack or side-slip angle.

For dynamic modeling purposes, the lift force and associated moment coefficients are typically computed separately for individual components of the AUV–namely, the hull, fixed wings, and control fins. Each of these components contributes to the total lift based on its unique geometry and local flow conditions. Once the lift coefficients for the individual elements are determined, their contributions are aggregated to evaluate the net lift force acting on the vehicle. The total lift force $L$ generated by the AUV is generally expressed as:

$$L = \frac{1}{2}\rho V^2 C_L A \tag{4.26}$$

where $\rho$ denotes the fluid density, $V$ represents the relative velocity between the vehicle and the surrounding fluid, $A$ is the reference area–typically the planform area associated with a lifting surface and $C_L$ is the corresponding lift coefficient.

### 4.5.1 Bare-Hull Lift Coefficients

In ASE method, the lift force $L^h$ for the AUV hull/body is typically estimated using empirical relationships, as described by Hoerner (1985) for various geometries of bodies in fluid flow. The lift generated by the body is proportional to the dynamic pressure, the reference area of the hull, and the lift coefficient, as expressed by the following formula:

$$L^h = -\frac{1}{2}\rho\, d^2\, C_L\, u^2 \tag{4.27}$$

where:

- $L^h$ is the lift force generated by the hull,
- $d^2$ is the reference area of the hull, typically taken as the planform area of the vehicle,
- $C_L$ is the lift coefficient of the hull, and
- $u$ is the forward velocity of the vehicle along the longitudinal axis.

**(1) Vertical Plane Lift Coefficients**

When considering the dynamics in the vertical plane and referring to Fig. 4.6, the angle of attack, $\alpha$, is typically defined by the ratio of the vertical velocity component $w$ to the horizontal velocity component $u$. This can be expressed as $\tan\alpha = \frac{w}{u}$, where $w$ and $u$ represent the vertical and horizontal velocity components of the vehicle, respectively.

In many practical cases, the magnitude of the horizontal velocity $u$ is much larger than the vertical component $w$, i.e., $|u| \gg |w|$. This condition allows us to use the small-angle approximation, which simplifies the relationship between the angle of attack $\alpha$ and the ratio of the velocities. Using this approximation, we can express the angle of attack as:

$$\alpha \approx \frac{w}{u}$$

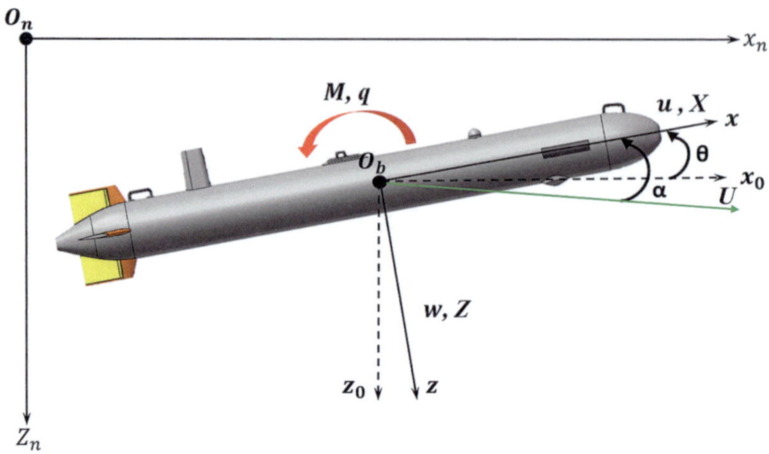


**Fig. 4.6** Vertical plane—coordinate system [40]

From the general equation for the lift force in rigid body dynamics (4.27), the lift coefficient $C_L$ of bodies with rounded shapes, such as the AUVs under consideration, is directly proportional to the square of their characteristic diameter $d$. This relationship can be represented as:

$$C_L = C_{zd} = \frac{L^h}{q} d^2$$

where $q$ denotes the dynamic pressure, and $L^h$ represents the lift force generated by the body.

In the context of vertical plane dynamics, the lift coefficient is denoted by $C_{zd}$, which represents the lift coefficient in the direction normal to the vehicle's motion. This is a key quantity in determining the vertical forces acting on the body, which is crucial for accurate dynamic modeling. Following the empirical formulation from Hoerner [7], the lift coefficient $C_{zd}$ is related to the angle of attack $\alpha$, and can be expressed as:

$$C_{zd}(\alpha) = \frac{dC_{zd}}{d\alpha}\alpha \tag{4.28}$$

In this formulation, the derivative $\frac{dC_{zd}}{d\alpha}$ represents how the lift coefficient changes with respect to the angle of attack $\alpha$, indicating the sensitivity of the lift force to variations in the angle.

According to Hoerner's analysis [7], the derivative of the lift coefficient with respect to the angle of attack increases approximately in direct proportion to the ratio of the length $l$ of the body to its characteristic diameter $d$. This suggests that longer bodies exhibit a higher rate of change of lift with respect to angle of attack, which is a critical consideration for vehicles with elongated shapes, such as AUVs. As the length-to-diameter ratio increases, the lateral force generated by the body also increases, influenced by factors such as wetted area, skin friction, and drag forces.

Hoerner [7] estimated the value of the derivative $\frac{dC_{zd}}{d\alpha}$ based on the body's length-to-diameter ratio, $\frac{l}{d}$, using thc following empirical relation:

$$\frac{dC_{zd}}{d\alpha} = 0.003\left(\frac{l}{d}\right) \tag{4.29}$$

This estimation is valid for bodies with a length-to-diameter ratio between 5 and 10, which is typical for many underwater vehicles. For the AUVs under consideration, the length-to-diameter ratio slightly exceeds the upper bound of this range. Nevertheless, for simplicity and to maintain consistency in the modeling, the length-to-diameter ratio is approximated as:

$$\frac{l}{d} \approx 10 \tag{4.30}$$

This approximation allows for a practical estimate of the lift coefficient's dependence on the angle of attack, even though the exact ratio may vary.

To express the lift coefficient in radians, the lift slope coefficient is given as:

$$C_{zd}(\alpha) = 0.003\left(\frac{l}{d}\right)\left(\frac{180}{\pi}\right) \tag{4.31}$$

where the factor $\left(\frac{180}{\pi}\right)$ converts the lift coefficient derivative from radians to degrees. This provides a more direct application in aerodynamic calculations where angles are often measured in degrees.

The total lift force acting on the body or hull in the vertical plane (the $x - z$ plane) is then expressed as:

$$L^h = -\frac{1}{2}\rho d^2 C_{zd}(\alpha)\, uw \tag{4.32}$$

Here, $L^h$ is the lift force, $\rho$ is the density of the fluid, and $uw$ represents the relative velocity components in the horizontal and vertical directions. The negative sign indicates that the lift force acts in the opposite direction to the motion of the vehicle, in accordance with standard aerodynamic conventions.

Finally, the body or hull lift coefficient in the vertical plane can be written as:

$$Z^h_{uw} = -\frac{1}{2}\rho d^2 C_{zd}(\alpha) \tag{4.33}$$

This equation represents the total vertical force $Z^h_{uw}$ exerted on the body by the surrounding fluid. This force is critical in determining the vertical motion and stability

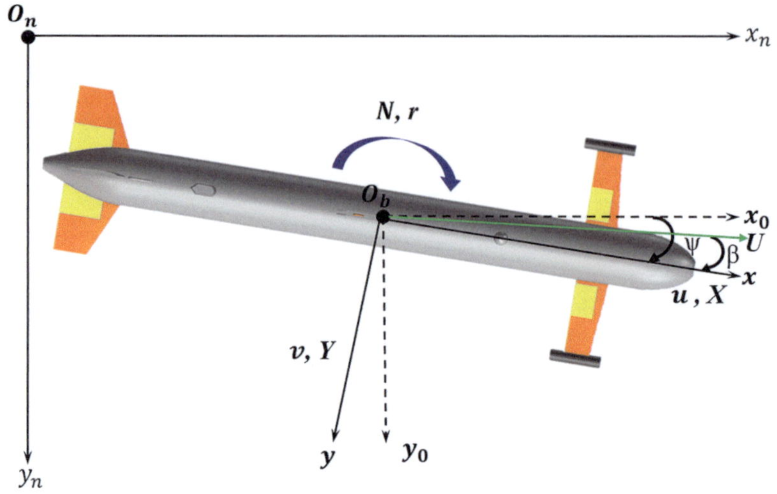


**Fig. 4.7** Horizontal plane—coordinate system [40]

of the vehicle, and is influenced by factors such as the body's size, shape, and speed of travel.

**(2) Horizontal Plane Lift Coefficients**

When considering the dynamics in the horizontal plane and referring to Fig. 4.7, the side-slip angle, $\beta$, is typically defined by the ratio of the lateral velocity component $v$ to the horizontal velocity component $u$. This can be expressed as $\tan\beta = \frac{v}{u}$, where $v$ and $u$ represent the lateral and horizontal velocity components of the vehicle, respectively.

Similar to the vertical plane dynamics, in many practical cases, the magnitude of the horizontal velocity $u$ is much larger than the lateral component $v$, i.e., $|u| \gg |v|$. This condition allows for the small-angle approximation, which simplifies the relationship between the side-slip angle $\beta$ and the velocity ratio. Using this approximation, we can express the side-slip angle as:

$$\beta \approx \frac{v}{u}$$

The lift slope coefficient corresponding to the side-slip angle in the horizontal plane is denoted by $C_{yd}(\beta)$. It can be empirically estimated in radians as follows:

$$C_{yd}(\beta) = 0.003 \left(\frac{l}{d}\right) \left(\frac{180}{\pi}\right) \tag{4.34}$$

Here, $C_{yd}(\beta)$ represents the lift coefficient for the body in the $x - y$ plane, and the factor $\left(\frac{180}{\pi}\right)$ converts the lift slope from radians to degrees for practical aerodynamic calculations.

The total lift force in the horizontal plane can be expressed as:

$$L^h = -\frac{1}{2}\rho d^2 C_{yd}(\beta)\, uv \tag{4.35}$$

In this equation, $L^h$ represents the lift force acting on the hull or body, with $\rho$ being the fluid density, $d$ the characteristic diameter of the body, and $uv$ representing the relative velocity components in the horizontal and lateral directions.

Finally, the total lateral force in the horizontal plane can be written as:

$$Y^h_{uv} = -\frac{1}{2}\rho d^2 C_{yd}(\beta) \tag{4.36}$$

This equation represents the lateral force $Y^h_{uv}$ acting on the body in the horizontal plane, which is essential in understanding the maneuverability and stability of the vehicle.

**(3) Moment Coefficients**

The hull/body moment coefficients corresponding to the lift forces in the vertical and horizontal planes are denoted as $M^h_{uw}$ and $N^h_{uv}$, respectively. These coefficients are estimated using the following equations:

$$M^h_{uw} = -\frac{1}{2}\,\rho\, d^2\, C_{zd}(\alpha)\, x_{cp} \tag{4.37}$$

$$N^h_{uv} = \frac{1}{2}\,\rho\, d^2\, C_{yd}(\beta)\, x_{cp} \tag{4.38}$$

In these equations, $x_{cp}$ represents the distance from the vehicle's center of gravity to the point where the lift force acts, and it is given by:

$$x_{cp} = -0.65l - x_0$$

where $x_0$ is a reference point in the vehicle. When a circular body is subjected to an angle of attack, Hoerner [7] determined that the lift force acts between 0.6 to 0.7 of the total body length from its forward end. To account for this, the mean value of $0.65l$ is used to estimate the location of the center of pressure, $x_{cp}$.

### 4.5.2 *Wings and Fins Lift Coefficients*

The lift force and moment acting on the lifting surfaces of an AUV, specifically the wings and fins, play a critical role in determining its maneuvering and stability characteristics. As illustrated in Fig. 4.8, these lifting surfaces generate forces based on their geometry, angle of attack, and the flow conditions around them.

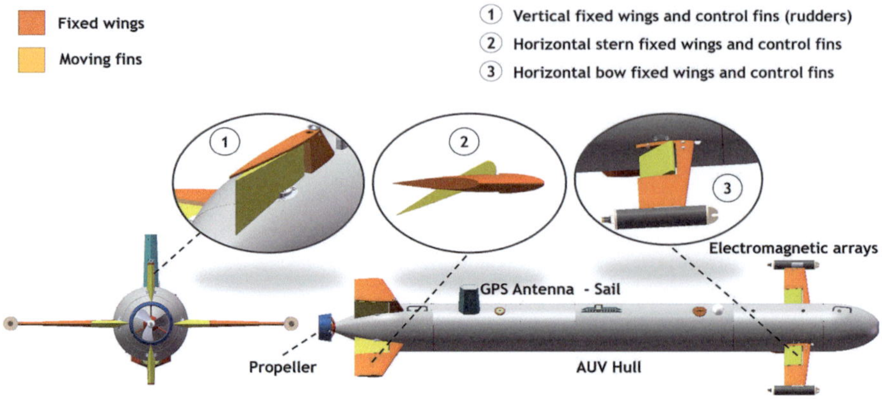


**Fig. 4.8** Hydroplanes configuration of flight-style AUV [40]

The lift force on the fins is estimated using an empirical relationship, which is provided in Eq. (4.39).

$$L^f = -\frac{1}{2}\rho A_f C_L \delta_{fe} u^2 \tag{4.39}$$

where $L^f$ represents the lift force generated by the fins, which is directed perpendicular to the relative flow. $A_f$ is the fin planform area, which refers to the total surface area of the fin as seen from above (or in the plane normal to the flow direction). The effective fin angle, $\delta_{fe}$, is the angle between the fin's chord line and the relative flow direction, which accounts for any geometric modifications or deflections of the fins during operation.

The lift coefficient $C_L(\alpha)$ describes the hydrodynamic efficiency of the fin in generating lift at a given angle of attack. This coefficient is a function of the effective fin attack angle $\alpha$, which is measured in radians. The angle $\alpha$ represents the angle between the direction of the incoming flow and the fin's chord line. As the angle of attack changes, the lift coefficient will vary, influencing the magnitude of the lift force produced by the fins. The empirical formula for $C_{L\alpha}$ is given by Hoerner [7] in Eq. (4.40).

$$C_{L\alpha} = \frac{dC_L}{d\alpha} = \left(\frac{1}{2\bar{a}\pi} + \frac{1}{\pi AR_e}\right)^{-1} \tag{4.40}$$

where $AR_e$ represents the effective fin aspect ratio, which can be estimated as $\frac{b_f^2}{A_f}$, where $b_f$ is the span of the fin. The factor $\bar{a}$ is taken to be 0.9, which is an empirical constant used for estimating the lift coefficient derivative with respect to the angle of attack.

The configuration of lifting surfaces of AUV, including stern fins, bow fins, and fixed wings can be varied based on the AUV's design and operational requirements. These configurations can be categorized into three primary cases: AUVs with only stern fins, AUVs with both stern and bow fins, and AUVs with both stern and bow fins combined with fixed wings, which resemble the aerodynamic surfaces of an airplane.

### (1) Only Stern Fins

In this case, the AUV is equipped solely with stern fins, which are located at the rear of the vehicle. The stern fins are primarily responsible for providing the necessary lift and control for the vehicle's pitch and yaw motions. This configuration is typically used in AUVs where a more compact and streamlined design is needed, with an emphasis on stability and control without the added complexity of additional fins at the bow. The stern fins can generate lift forces that help the AUV resist the downward gravitational forces, enabling the vehicle to maintain desired depths and maneuver efficiently through the water.

The lift coefficients for this configuration are derived based on the effective angles of attack and the hydrodynamic characteristics of the stern fins, which are considered to play a key role in providing the lift and moments required for controlled movements. For an AUV with **only stern fins**, the effective angles for the rudder and stern fin are given by:

$$\delta_{re} = \beta_{re} - \delta_r, \quad \delta_{se} = \alpha_{se} - \delta_s, \tag{4.41}$$

where:

- $\delta_r$ and $\delta_s$ are the angles of the rudder and stern fin relative to the AUV hull.
- $\beta_{re}$ and $\alpha_{se}$ are the effective attack angles of the rudder and stern fin zero plane.

To estimate the effective angles of attack for the rudder and stern fin, we apply the small angle approximation:

$$\beta_{re} = \frac{v + x_{f_1} r}{u}, \quad \alpha_{se} = \frac{w - x_{f_2} q}{u}. \tag{4.42}$$

Here, $x_{f_1}$ and $x_{f_2}$ represent the centroids of the rudder and stern fin, respectively, relative to the body-fixed reference frame.

By solving these equations, we get the effective angles:

$$\delta_{re} = \frac{v + x_{f_1} r - u\delta_r}{u}, \quad \delta_{se} = \frac{w - x_{f_2} q - u\delta_s}{u}. \tag{4.43}$$

Next, the lift forces $Y_r^f$ and $Z_s^f$ generated by the rudder and stern fin are given by:

$$Y_r^f = -\rho A_{f_1} C_{L\alpha_{f_1}} \left( uv + x_{f_1} ur - u^2 \delta_r \right), \tag{4.44}$$

$$Z_s^f = -\rho A_{f_2} C_{L\alpha_{f_2}} \left( uw - x_{f_2} uq - u^2 \delta_s \right), \tag{4.45}$$

where:

- $A_{f_1}$ and $A_{f_2}$ are the reference areas of the rudder and stern fin.
- $C_{L\alpha_{f_1}}$ and $C_{L\alpha_{f_2}}$ are the lift curve slopes for the rudder and stern fin.

The moments $N_r^f$ and $M_s^f$ generated by the rudder and stern fin are:

$$N_r^f = -\rho A_{f_1} C_{L\alpha_{f_1}} x_{f_1} \left(uv + x_{f_1} ur - u^2 \delta_r\right), \tag{4.46}$$

$$M_s^f = \rho A_{f_2} C_{L\alpha_{f_2}} x_{f_2} \left(uw - x_{f_2} uq - u^2 \delta_s\right). \tag{4.47}$$

**(2) Stern and Bow Fins**

In the second configuration, when an AUV is equipped with both stern and bow fins, the addition of horizontal bow fins significantly enhances the AUV's maneuverability, especially in terms of pitch control, while the stern fins provide the necessary stability and lift. This configuration improves the AUV's overall hydrodynamic performance, particularly in terms of stability and maneuverability in both horizontal and vertical planes. The lift forces and moments generated by both the stern and bow fins are computed by considering their effective attack angles and the hydrodynamic coefficients associated with their respective surfaces. In this case, the effective angles of attack for both the stern and bow fins are calculated by considering the relative velocities and motions of the AUV, as well as their geometrical parameters such as the centroid locations.

For an AUV with **stern fins and bow fins**, the effective angles for the rudder, stern fin, and bow fin are given by:

$$\delta_{re} = \beta_{re} - \delta_r, \quad \delta_{se} = \alpha_{se} - \delta_s, \quad \delta_{be} = \alpha_{be} - \delta_b. \tag{4.48}$$

where:

- $\delta_r$, $\delta_s$, and $\delta_b$ are the angles of the rudder, stern fin, and bow fin relative to the AUV hull, respectively.
- $\beta_{re}$, $\alpha_{se}$, and $\alpha_{be}$ are the effective attack angles for the rudder, stern fin, and bow fin zero plane.

The effective angles of attack for the rudder, stern fin, and bow fin are estimated using the small angle approximation:

$$\beta_{re} = \frac{v + x_{f_1} r}{u}, \quad \alpha_{se} = \frac{w - x_{f_2} q}{u}, \quad \alpha_{be} = \frac{w - x_{f_3} q}{u}. \tag{4.49}$$

Here, $x_{f_1}$, $x_{f_2}$, and $x_{f_3}$ represent the centroids of the rudder, stern fin, and bow fin, respectively, relative to the body-fixed reference frame.

By solving these equations, we obtain the effective angles:

$$\delta_{re} = \frac{v + x_{f_1} r - u\delta_r}{u}, \quad \delta_{se} = \frac{w - x_{f_2} q - u\delta_s}{u}, \quad \delta_{be} = \frac{w - x_{f_3} q - u\delta_b}{u}. \tag{4.50}$$

The lift forces for the rudder, stern fin, and bow fin are:

$$Y_r^f = -\rho A_{f_1} C_{L\alpha_{f_1}} \left(uv + x_{f_1} ur - u^2\delta_r\right), \tag{4.51}$$

$$Z_s^f = -\rho A_{f_2} C_{L\alpha_{f_2}} \left(uw - x_{f_2} uq - u^2\delta_s\right), \tag{4.52}$$

$$Z_b^f = -\rho A_{f_3} C_{L\alpha_{f_3}} \left(uw - x_{f_3} uq - u^2\delta_b\right). \tag{4.53}$$

The moments for the rudder, stern fin, and bow fin are:

$$N_r^f = -\rho A_{f_1} C_{L\alpha_{f_1}} x_{f_1} \left(uv + x_{f_1} ur - u^2\delta_r\right), \tag{4.54}$$

$$M_s^f = \rho A_{f_2} C_{L\alpha_{f_2}} x_{f_2} \left(uw - x_{f_2} uq - u^2\delta_s\right), \tag{4.55}$$

$$M_b^f = -\rho A_{f_3} C_{L\alpha_{f_3}} x_{f_3} \left(uw - x_{f_3} uq - u^2\delta_b\right). \tag{4.56}$$

**(3) Stern and Bow Fins and Wings**

The third configuration includes fixed wings, similar to those on airplanes, adding another set of lifting surfaces typically used in Flight-Style AUVs. These wings function as stabilizers, enhancing underwater stability and control. The inclusion of fixed wings increases hydrodynamic complexity but provides greater lift and improved maneuverability, essential for deep or challenging environments. Lift coefficients for this configuration are required to account for the lift generated by hull, wings and fins along with their interaction effects and effective attack angles. Similar to the the moving fins, the fixed wings also generate lift based on their angle relative to the water flow, impacting the AUV's overall dynamics.

The effective angles for the rudder ($\delta_{re}$), stern fins ($\delta_{se}$), and bow fins ($\delta_{be}$), as illustrated in Fig. 4.9, can be estimated as follows:

$$\begin{cases} \delta_{re} = \beta_{re} - \delta_r, \\ \delta_{se} = \alpha_{se} - \delta_s, \\ \delta_{be} = \alpha_{be} - \delta_b, \end{cases} \tag{4.57}$$

where $\delta_r$, $\delta_s$, and $\delta_b$ denote the angles of the rudder, stern fin, and bow fin relative to the AUV hull, respectively. $\beta_{re}$, $\alpha_{se}$, and $\alpha_{be}$ are the effective attack angles of the fin zero plane.

By neglecting velocities that are much smaller compared to the translational velocities and applying small angle approximations, the effective angles of attack can be estimated as follows:

$$\begin{cases} \beta_{re} = \frac{v + x_{f_1} r}{u}, \\ \alpha_{se} = \frac{w - x_{f_2} q}{u}, \\ \alpha_{be} = \frac{w - x_{f_3} q}{u}, \end{cases} \tag{4.58}$$

where $x_f$, $y_f$, and $z_f$ are the fin centroid locations with reference to the origin in the body-fixed frame.

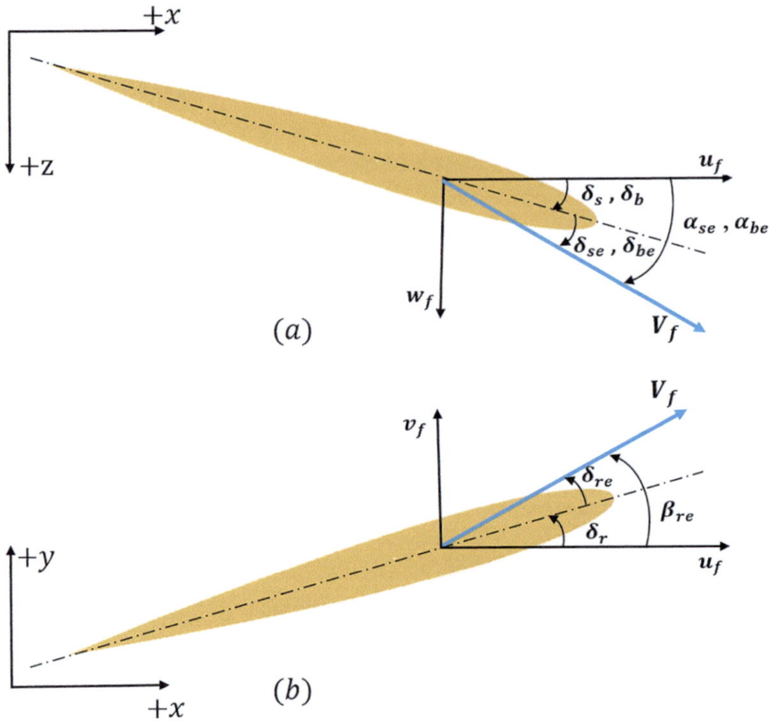


**Fig. 4.9** **a** Effective fin angles, sign convention and fluid velocities in vertical plane **b** Effective fin angles, sign convention and fluid velocities in horizontal plane [40]

Solving Eqs. (4.57) and (4.58), the effective fin angles are given by:

$$\begin{cases} \delta_{re} = \frac{v+x_{f_1}r-u\delta_r}{u}, \\ \delta_{se} = \frac{w-x_{f_2}q-u\delta_s}{u}, \\ \delta_{be} = \frac{w-x_{f_3}q-u\delta_b}{u}, \end{cases} \tag{4.59}$$

Equations (4.39) and (4.59) are combined to provide expressions for the lift forces $Y^f$ and $Z^f$ and the corresponding moments $N^f$ and $M^f$ for the paired fins of the AUV, as presented in Eq. (4.60).

$$\begin{cases} Y_r^f = -\rho A_{f_1} C_{L\alpha_{f_1}} \left(uv + x_{f_1} ur - u^2\delta_r\right), \\ Z_s^f = -\rho A_{f_2} C_{L\alpha_{f_2}} \left(uw - x_{f_2} uq - u^2\delta_s\right), \\ Z_b^f = -\rho A_{f_3} C_{L\alpha_{f_3}} \left(uw - x_{f_3} uq - u^2\delta_b\right), \\ N_r^f = -\rho A_{f_1} C_{L\alpha_{f_1}} x_{f_1} \left(uv + x_{f_1} ur - u^2\delta_r\right), \\ M_s^f = \rho A_{f_2} C_{L\alpha_{f_2}} x_{f_2} \left(uw - x_{f_2} uq - u^2\delta_s\right), \\ M_b^f = -\rho A_{f_3} C_{L\alpha_{f_3}} x_{f_3} \left(uw - x_{f_3} uq - u^2\delta_b\right), \end{cases} \tag{4.60}$$

The fin angles $\delta_r$, $\delta_s$, and $\delta_b$ are assumed to be zero for fixed-wing lift forces and moments. Consequently, Eq. (4.60) is simplified as follows:

$$\begin{cases} Y_r^w = -\rho A_{w_1} C_{L\alpha_{w_1}} \left(uv + x_{f_1} ur\right), \\ Z_s^w = -\rho A_{w_2} C_{L\alpha_{w_2}} \left(uw - x_{f_2} uq\right), \\ Z_b^w = -\rho A_{w_3} C_{L\alpha_{w_3}} \left(uw - x_{f_3} uq\right), \\ N_r^w = -\rho A_{w_1} C_{L\alpha_{w_1}} x_{f_1} \left(uv + x_{f_1} ur\right), \\ M_s^w = \rho A_{w_2} C_{L\alpha_{w_2}} x_{f_2} \left(uw - x_{f_2} uq\right), \\ M_b^w = -\rho A_{w_3} C_{L\alpha_{w_3}} x_{f_3} \left(uw - x_{f_3} uq\right), \end{cases} \tag{4.61}$$

### 4.5.3 *Wing-Body Lift Interference: Insights from Slender Body Theory*

In potential flow theory, the fluid is generally assumed to be inviscid, meaning viscosity is neglected. This assumption simplifies the analysis and is appropriate for idealized flow conditions where viscous effects have minimal influence. Under such circumstances, vortices do not originate from viscous forces but instead arise due to fluid rotation induced by factors like body geometry or flow disturbances. However, when applying slender body theory to analyze flow around elongated bodies, viscosity becomes an important factor, especially in the formation and behavior of vortices.

Although slender body theory primarily treats the flow as inviscid, it incorporates some viscous effects approximately. Viscosity leads to the development of boundary layers near solid surfaces, where fluid particles adhere to the body, creating velocity gradients. These gradients influence how vortices form and shed, particularly along the surfaces of slender bodies. Vortex shedding, caused by the interaction between the fluid and the body geometry, plays a significant role in determining hydrodynamic characteristics such as lift and drag.

Furthermore, viscosity contributes to the gradual dissipation of vortices over time through viscous diffusion and turbulence, thereby affecting the strength and persistence of vortices within the flow field.

The wave equation for the velocity potential governs small disturbances in the fluid flow, especially within the framework of potential flow theory. For slender wing-body configurations, this equation captures the behavior of flow perturbations around the combined geometry, considering factors such as viscosity, compressibility, and shape. Lennertz [49] examined lift distribution between wings and bodies under uniform span loading by representing each side with horseshoe vortices. His analysis showed only minor variations in body lift across different ratios of body radius to vortex semi-span. Since horseshoe vortices usually have shorter spans than wings, this modeling approach aligns well with methods used to determine lift sharing between wing and body.

In estimating wing-body interference effects using slender body theory, the first term of the velocity potential wave equation,

$$(M_{\infty}^2 - 1)\phi_{xx} - \phi_{yy} - \phi_{zz} = 0,$$

can be neglected for slender wing-body combinations. This simplification reduces the equation to Laplace's equation in the $y$-$z$ plane [50, 51], facilitating the derivation of straightforward closed-form expressions for lift-curve slopes. These expressions are instrumental in analyzing hydrodynamic interactions between wings and hulls.

Based on this approach, the wing-body interference factor, $K_c$, which quantifies the modification of lift due to interaction effects, is derived in [50, 52]. This factor depends on the ratio of the vehicle's radius to the wing's semi-span measured from the hull center.

The total lift of the wing-body combination relates to the wing-alone lift through the interference factor $K_c$, defined as the sum of two components:

$$K_c = K_{B(W)} + K_{W(B)}, \tag{4.62}$$

where $K_{B(W)}$ represents the lift interference effect of the wing on the body (or hull), and $K_{W(B)}$ denotes the interference of the body on the wing. These factors are defined under the condition that the angle of attack of the combined system varies while the wing's incidence angle remains zero ($\delta = 0$). They represent the ratios of the combined body and wing lift to the wing lift alone, as expressed in Eq. (4.63).

$$\begin{cases} K_{B(W)} = \frac{L_{B(W)}}{L_W} = \frac{(C_{L\alpha})_{B(W)}}{(C_{L\alpha})_W} \\ \\ K_{W(B)} = \frac{L_{W(B)}}{L_W} = \frac{(C_{L\alpha})_{W(B)}}{(C_{L\alpha})_W} \end{cases} \tag{4.63}$$

Here, $L_{B(W)}$ denotes the lift on the body induced by the presence of the wing, $L_{W(B)}$ represents the lift generated by the wing when influenced by the body, and $L_W$ corresponds to the lift produced by the wing alone. Similarly, the lift curve slope coefficients $(C_{L_\alpha})_{B(W)}$, $(C_{L_\alpha})_{W(B)}$, and $(C_{L_\alpha})_W$ represent the respective lift coefficients associated with the body due to the wing, the wing due to the body, and the wing in isolation.

Following slender-body theory [53, 54], $K_{B(W)}$ and $K_{W(B)}$ can be estimated using the following Eqs. (4.64) and (4.65) respectively.

$$K_{B(W)} = (1+\gamma)^2 - \frac{\frac{2}{\pi}\left\{\left(1+\gamma^4\right)\left[\frac{1}{2}tan^{-1}\frac{1}{2}\left(\gamma^{-1}-\gamma\right)+\frac{\pi}{4}\right]-\gamma^2\left[\left(\gamma^{-1}-\gamma\right)+2\,tan^{-1}\gamma\right]\right\}}{(1-\gamma)^2} \tag{4.64}$$

**Table 4.2** Estimated values of interference factors

| $K_{c_1}$ | $K_{c2}$ | $K_{c3}$ | $K_{c_a}$ |
|---|---|---|---|
| 3.1 | 1.82 | 1.58 | 1.9063 |

$$K_{W(B)} = \frac{\frac{2}{\pi}\left\{(1+\gamma^4)\left[\frac{1}{2}tan^{-1}\frac{1}{2}\left(\gamma^{-1}-\gamma\right)+\frac{\pi}{4}\right]-\gamma^2\left[\left(\gamma^{-1}-\gamma\right)+2\,tan^{-1}\gamma\right]\right\}}{(1-\gamma)^2} \tag{4.65}$$

In Eqs. (4.64) and (4.65), the parameter $\gamma$ represents the ratio of the vehicle radius $R$ to the semi-span of the wing measured from the center of the AUV hull, defined as $\gamma = \frac{R}{S_W}$. The value of $S_W$ is computed separately for the wings, fins, and antenna. Similarly, the expression in Eq. (4.62) is applicable to estimating fin-hull interference factors.

AUVs are often equipped with appendages such as GPS antennas. When the antenna shape can be approximated as a flat plate with defined length and width (chord), the lift interference factor for the antenna–modeled as a rigid sail and considered as an extruded appendage extending in the negative $z$-direction–is estimated using the following relationship. This formula is presented in [19, 55] and was originally derived based on slender-body theory as described in [54].

$$K_{c_a} = \frac{\frac{\pi\rho {S_A}^2}{4}\left\{\left(1+\frac{R^2}{{S_A}^2}\right)\left(-1-\frac{R^2}{{S_A}^2}+2^{1.5}\sqrt{1+\frac{R^4}{{S_A}^4}}\right)\right\}-\pi\rho R^2}{\frac{\pi\rho(S_A-R)^2}{2}} \tag{4.66}$$

Equations (4.62) to (4.66) are applicable for wings and fins mounted on circular cross-sections of the AUV hull or body [52, 54].

In the limited cases studied by Pitts [54], where the hull cross-section varied slightly within the wing region, using the average hull radius for calculations provided satisfactory results. However, for conically tapered submarine sterns with cone angles up to 20°, Lyons and Bisgood [56] proposed an empirical relationship for wing-body interference factors, as expressed in Eq. (4.67) (see pages 57–59 in [52]). They explained that these interference factors account for the lift generated not only by the wing area extending beyond the hull but also by the portion inside the hull up to the hull centerline, as illustrated in Fig. 4.10.

The interference factors are given as a function of the ratio of the hull/fuselage radius at one-third chord, $R_{1/3}$, to one-third of the wing depth measured to the wing outer edge, $S_W$. Consequently, Eq. (4.67) is employed to estimate the wing-body lift interference effects for the stern wings and fins of the FSAUV.

$$[K_{W(B)} + K_{B(W)}]_{Lyons+Bisgood} \approx \frac{1+\frac{R_{1/3}}{S_W}}{1-\frac{R_{1/3}}{S_W}} \tag{4.67}$$

The computed values of lift interference k-factors for FSAUV as a practical case are given in Table 4.2.

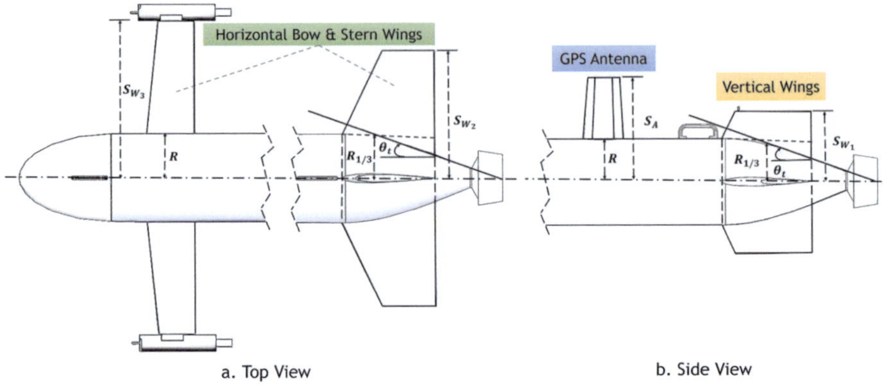


**Fig. 4.10** Bow and stern wing configurations for calculation of lift interference k-factors [40]

### 4.5.4 Wing Body Lift Interference: Vorticity and Horseshoe Vortex Perspectives

Vorticity effects play a fundamental role in determining the lift force on an AUV, as they influence the generation and shedding of vortices, which in turn modify the pressure distribution and consequently the lift production. Specifically, the formation of horseshoe vortices near the solid body of the AUV significantly alters the local pressure field, thereby impacting lift. In the framework of Eqs. (4.65) and (4.66), these vorticity effects are represented by parameters such as $K_c$, $\gamma$, and $K_{c_a}$, which quantify the lift interference between the wings and the hull, as well as the antenna appendage. These parameters provide insight into how the spatial arrangement and interaction of vortices shed from the wings influence the hull and appendages, affecting lift distribution and overall hydrodynamic performance.

A horseshoe vortex is a distinct vortex structure that forms at the junction of a solid body and the fluid flow. When fluid moves around a solid body like an AUV or submarine, flow separation at the leading edges generates vortices that roll up into a horseshoe-shaped pattern. This phenomenon is commonly observed at wing-body or sail-body junctions, as demonstrated in the vortex structures around the DARPA SUBOFF model [57], where regions of high vorticity near the AUV correspond to the presence of horseshoe vortices.

The magnitude of vorticity is typically elevated near horseshoe vortices due to the intense swirling motion of fluid particles. These vortices critically influence flow dynamics around the AUV, impacting key hydrodynamic parameters such as lift, drag, and maneuverability. Thus, understanding the behavior and effects of horseshoe vortices is essential for accurate prediction of AUV dynamics. The terms appearing in Eqs. (4.62) to (4.66) can be interpreted in terms of vorticity effects arising from the flow around the AUV, as detailed below:

- **$K_{W(B)}$ and $K_{B(W)}$ Terms:** These terms relate to the influence of vortices shed from one component on the other. In the context of horseshoe vortices, $K_{W(B)}$ represents the effect of vorticity shed from the wing tips that wraps around and impacts the hull's surface, thereby affecting the hull's hydrodynamics and modifying lift. Conversely, $K_{B(W)}$ quantifies the influence of vortices generated by the hull on the wing's lift characteristics.
- **Parameter $\gamma$**: Defined as the ratio of the vehicle radius to the wing semi-span, $\gamma = \frac{R}{S_W}$, this parameter characterizes the relative positioning of vortices shed from the wing with respect to the hull surface. A higher $\gamma$ indicates closer proximity of these vortices to the hull, which may intensify interference effects and alter lift distribution through vortex interactions.
- **Combined Effect $K_c$**: This term represents the total lift interference factor, encompassing the combined influence of vortices shed from both the hull and the wings on the wing's lift. The magnitude and spatial arrangement of these vortices determine the overall modification in lift distribution and hydrodynamic performance.

### *4.5.5 Lift Coefficients with Interference Factors*

In the ASE approach, lift coefficients for AUV hull, wings, and fins are estimated separately, lacking wing-body interference effects in combined lift formulations given in Eqs. (4.60) and (4.61). Accordingly, the lift force considering the combined wing-body lift interference effects through factor$K_c$ can be defined as follows:

$$L^W = -\frac{1}{2}\rho\, A_W\, K_c\, C_{L_W}\, \delta_{W_e}\, u^2 \tag{4.68}$$

The Eqs. (4.62) to (4.66) are formulated under the assumption that the wing incidence angle $\delta = 0$, focusing on estimating the wing-body interference effects. Consequently, the lift coefficient expressions are unified to encompass both fixed wings and movable fins. In the subsequent equations, the superscript $(W)$ denotes these combined lifting surfaces–fixed wings and moving fins alike.

Incorporating the wing-body interference effects, the final expressions for the lift force and moment coefficients are presented in Eq. (4.69).

$$
\begin{cases}
Y_{uv}^{W} = -\rho A_{W_1} K_{c_1} C_{L\alpha_{W_1}} \\
Y_{ur}^{W} = -\rho A_{W_1} K_{c_1} C_{L\alpha_{W_1}} x_{f_1} \\
N_{uv}^{w} = -\rho A_{W_1} K_{c_1} C_{L\alpha_{W_1}} x_{f_1} \\
N_{ur}^{w} = -\rho A_{W_1} K_{c_1} C_{L\alpha_{W_1}} x_{f_1}^2 \\
Z_{uw}^{W} = -\rho A_{W_2} K_{c_2} C_{L\alpha_{W_2}} - \rho A_{W_3} K_{c_3} C_{L\alpha_{W_3}} \\
Z_{uq}^{W} = \rho A_{W_2} K_{c_2} C_{L\alpha_{W_2}} x_{f_2} + \rho A_{W_3} K_{c_3} C_{L\alpha_{W_3}} x_{f_3} \\
M_{uw}^{W} = \rho A_{W_2} K_{c_2} C_{L\alpha_{W_2}} x_{f_2} + \rho A_{W_3} K_{c_3} C_{L\alpha_{W_3}} x_{f_3} \\
M_{uq}^{W} = -\rho A_{W_2} K_{c_2} C_{L\alpha_{W_2}} x_{f_2}^2 + \rho A_{W_3} K_{c_3} C_{L\alpha_{W_3}} x_{f_3}^2
\end{cases}
\tag{4.69}
$$

Similarly, considering the antenna/sail on the AUV having symmetrical geometry with the flat plate or wings/fins, the lift coefficients for the antenna/sail, incorporating the wing-body lift interference effects between the AUV hull and the antenna/sail can also be accounted for and estimated using the relationships given in Eq. (4.70).

$$
\begin{cases}
Y_{uv}^{a} = -\frac{1}{2}\rho S_A K_{c_a} C_{L\alpha_a} \\
Y_{ur}^{a} = -\frac{1}{2}\rho S_A K_{c_a} C_{L\alpha_a} x_a \\
N_{uv}^{a} = -\frac{1}{2}\rho S_A K_{c_a} C_{L\alpha_a} x_a \\
N_{ur}^{a} = -\frac{1}{2}\rho S_A K_{c_a} C_{L\alpha_a} x_a^2
\end{cases}
\tag{4.70}
$$

The cumulative coefficients, obtained by combining the lift coefficients for fins, wings, and the antenna, are presented in Eq. (4.71).

$$
\begin{cases}
Y_{uv} = Y_{uv}^{h} + Y_{uv}^{W} + Y_{uv}^{a} \\
Y_{ur} = Y_{ur}^{h} + Y_{ur}^{W} + Y_{ur}^{a} \\
Z_{uw} = Z_{uw}^{h} + Z_{uw}^{W} \\
Z_{uq} = Z_{uq}^{h} + Z_{uq}^{W} \\
N_{uv} = N_{uv}^{h} + N_{uv}^{W} + N_{uv}^{a} \\
N_{ur} = N_{ur}^{h} + N_{ur}^{W} + N_{ur}^{a} \\
M_{uw} = M_{uw}^{h} + M_{uw}^{W} \\
M_{uq} = M_{uq}^{h} + M_{uq}^{W}
\end{cases}
\tag{4.71}
$$

### 4.5.6 *Estimating Hydrodynamic Coefficients of FSAUV: A Practical Example*

The complete set of hydrodynamic coefficients taking FSAUV as a practical example, following ASE approach, is given in Table 4.5.

**Table 4.3** Lift coefficients with and without interference effects

| Coefficient | Without interference (A) | With interference (B) | Unit |
|---|---|---|---|
| *Horizontal plane coefficients* | | | |
| $Y_{uv}$ | −122.573 | −234.715 | kg/m |
| $N_{uv}$ | −75.473 | 38.230 | kg |
| $Y_{ur}$ | 61.247 | 174.951 | kg/rad |
| $N_{ur}$ | −64.728 | −183.720 | $\text{kg} \cdot \text{m/rad}$ |
| *Vertical plane coefficients* | | | |
| $Z_{uw}$ | −385.488 | −616.060 | kg/m |
| $M_{uw}$ | −202.323 | −640.260 | kg |
| $Z_{uq}$ | −20.530 | −33.231 | kg/rad |
| $M_{uq}$ | −43.543 | −114.920 | $\text{kg} \cdot \text{m/rad}$ |

**Table 4.4** Nondimensionalized combined lift coefficients ($Y'_{uv}$, $N'_{uv}$, $Z'_{uw}$, & $M'_{uw}$)

| Coefficients | A [41] | B |
|---|---|---|
| *Horizontal plane coefficients* | | |
| $Y'_{uv}$ | $-3.33 \times 10^{-2}$ | $-6.38 \times 10^{-2}$ |
| $N'_{uv}$ | $-7.57 \times 10^{-3}$ | $3.83 \times 10^{-3}$ |
| *Vertical plane coefficients* | | |
| $Z'_{uw}$ | $-1.05 \times 10^{-1}$ | $-1.68 \times 10^{-1}$ |
| $M'_{uw}$ | $-2.03 \times 10^{-2}$ | $-6.42 \times 10^{-2}$ |

### 4.5.7 *Estimating Lift Coefficients of FSAUV: A Practical Example*

The estimated lift coefficients calculated using Eqs. (4.69) to (4.71) are categorized such that the coefficients obtained without accounting for interference effects are labelled as A, while those including interference effects are labelled as B. The corresponding values are summarized in Table 4.3.

The coefficients $Y_{uv}$, $N_{uv}$, $Z_{uw}$&$M_{uw}$ are nondimensionalized following the single prime system (I) and designated as $Y'_{uv}$, $N'_{uv}$, $Z'_{uw}$&$M'_{uw}$. The nondimensionalized values for these coefficients are presented in Table 4.4.

**Table 4.5** ASE estimated hydrodynamic coefficients of flight-style AUV [40, 41]

| IMD-ASE Estimated Hydrodynamic Coefficients of Novel Flight-Style AUV | | | | | | | | | | | |
|---|---|---|---|---|---|---|---|---|---|---|---|
| Added mass coefficients | | | Drag coefficients | | | Added mass cross terms | | | Lift coefficients | | |
| Coefficient | Value | Unit | Coefficient | Value | Unit | Coefficient | Value | Unit | Coefficient | Value | Unit |
| Xudot | -1.3975 | Kg | Xuu | -5.3172 | Kg/m | Xwq | -125.7926 | Kg/rad | Yuv | -122.5729 | Kg/m |
| Yvdot | -119.9478 | Kg | Yvv | -292.0973 | Kg/m | Xvr | 119.9478 | Kg/rad | Zuw | -385.4879 | Kg/m |
| Zwdot | -125.7926 | Kg | Zww | -364.4033 | Kg/m | Yura | -1.3975 | Kg/rad | Yur | 61.2474 | Kg/rad |
| Zqdot | 3.2052 | Kg. m/rad | Nvv | 11.1882 | Kg | Ywp | 125.7926 | Kg/rad | Nuv | -75.4729 | Kg |
| Nvdot | -2.5300 | Kg. m | Mww | 3.0460 | Kg | Zrp | -2.5300 | Kg/rad | Muw | -202.3233 | Kg |
| Yrdot | -2.5300 | Kg. m/rad | Yrr | 5.9378 | Kg. m/rad$^2$ | Zuqa | 1.3975 | Kg/rad | Zuq | -20.5297 | Kg/rad |
| Mwdot | 3.2052 | Kg. m | Zqq | 2.1990 | Kg. m/rad$^2$ | Zvp | -119.9478 | Kg/rad | Nur | -64.7284 | Kg. m/rad |
| Nrdot | -68.1762 | Kg. m$^2$/rad | Nrr | -177.2092 | Kg. m$^2$/rad$^2$ | Xqq | 3.2052 | Kg. m/rad | Muq | -43.5430 | Kg. m/rad |
| Mqdot | -74.9354 | Kg. m$^2$/rad | Mqq | -268.3283 | Kg. m$^2$/rad$^2$ | Xrr | 2.5300 | Kg. m/rad | Yuu$\delta_r$ | 37.3258 | Kg/(m. rad) |
| Kpdot | -0.3138 | Kg. m$^2$/rad | kpp | -0.1596 | Kg. m$^2$/rad$^2$ | Ypq | -3.2052 | Kg. m/rad | Zuu$\delta_s$ | 37.3258 | Kg/(m. rad) |
| | | | | | | Nwp | 3.2052 | Kg. m/rad | Zuu$\delta_b$ | 37.6683 | Kg/(m. rad) |
| | | | **Thrust** | | | Muqa | -3.2052 | Kg. m/rad | Nuu$\delta_r$ | -41.0584 | Kg/rad |
| | | | Xprop | 8.986 | N | Mvp | 2.5300 | Kg. m/rad | Muu$\delta_s$ | 41.0584 | Kg/rad |
| | | | | | | Nura | -2.5300 | Kg. m/rad | Muu$\delta_b$ | 37.6683 | Kg/rad |
| | | | | | | Npq | -74.6216 | Kg. m$^2$/rad$^2$ | | | |
| | | | | | | Mrp | 67.8624 | Kg. m$^2$/rad$^2$ | | | |
| | | | | | | Nuva | -118.5503 | Kg | | | |
| | | | | | | Muwa | 124.3951 | Kg | | | |

**Multiplicative adjustment factors**

Simulation (A): Nrdot (16.5), Nur (5.25), Mqdot (2.0), Muq (0.5), Zuw (0.33), Zuq (0.33), Muw (0.4), Zuuδs (0.08), Zuuδb (0.05), Muuδs (0.08), Muuδb (0.05)

Simulation (B): Nrdot (11.7), Nur (0.515), Mqdot (28), Muq (1.8)

## 4.6 Summary

This chapter explores ASE techniques for estimating hydrodynamic coefficients of underwater vehicles, particularly torpedo-shaped autonomous underwater vehicles (AUVs). The methods, originally derived from aerodynamics, have been adapted for underwater applications, incorporating historical contributions from researchers such as Strumpf [1], Finck [2], and Hoerner [6, 7]. The chapter reviews fundamental theories, including Strip Theory, which divides the AUV into 2D sections for force estimation; Potential Flow Theory, which assumes inviscid, irrotational flow for added mass calculations; and Slender Body Theory, which accounts for 3D effects in elongated bodies.

The discussion then shifts to added mass coefficients, detailing estimation methods for surge (axial flow), sway/heave (cross-flow), and rolling motions. For drag coefficients, the chapter presents empirical formulas for axial drag (Triantafyllou, Hoerner) and introduces an improved ASE approach for cross-flow drag, using 3D coefficients (0.84) instead of traditional 2D values (1.2). Rolling drag, primarily caused by fin resistance, is also examined. Lift coefficients are analyzed for the bare hull, wings, and fins, incorporating wing-body interference effects derived from slender body theory and vortex dynamics.

A practical case study of the FSAUV demonstrates the application of these methods, with computed coefficients validated against established models like the REMUS 100. Key contributions include refined cross-flow drag estimation using 3D coefficients and enhanced lift modeling through interference factor integration. This systematic approach provides a foundation for accurate AUV dynamics modeling, essential for stability, control, and maneuverability analysis in underwater vehicle design.

## References


1. Strumpf, A.: Equations of motion of a submerged body with varying mass. Technical report (1960)
2. Finck, R.: Usaf Stability and Control Data Compendium. Wright Patterson Air Force Base (DATCOM), Air Force Flight Dynamics Laboratory (1976)
3. Nahon, M.: Determination of undersea vehicle hydrodynamic derivatives using the usaf datcom. In: Proceedings of OCEANS'93IEEE, pp. II283–II288 (1993)
4. Miao, T.: Generation of a full-envelope hydrodynamic database for hydrobatic AUVs: Combining numerical, semi-empirical methods to calculate AUV hydrodynamic coefficients (2019)
5. Jones, D.A., Clarke, D.B., Brayshaw, I.B., Barillon, J.L., Anderson, B.: The calculation of hydrodynamic coefficients for underwater vehicles. Technical report, DEFENCE SCIENCE AND TECHNOLOGY ORGANIZATION VICTORIA (AUSTRALIA) PLATFORM (2002)
6. Hoerner, S.F.: Fluid Dynamic Drag, Published by the Author, pp. 16–35. Midland Park, NJ (1965)
7. Hoerner, S.: Fluid-dynamic lift. Hoerner Fluid Dyn. (1985)
8. Prestero, T.T.J.: Verification of a six-degree of freedom simulation model for the remus autonomous underwater vehicle (2001)

9. Javanmard, E., Mansoorzadeh, S., Pishevar, A., Mehr, J.: Determination of drag and lift related coefficients of an AUV using computational and experimental fluid dynamics methods. Int. J. Maritime Eng. **162**(A2) (2020)
10. Tang, S.C.: Modeling and simulation of the autonomous underwater vehicle, autolycus. Ph.D. thesis, Massachusetts Institute of Technology (1999)
11. Javanmard, E., Mansoorzadeh, S., Mehr, J.A.: A new CFD method for determination of translational added mass coefficients of an underwater vehicle. Ocean Eng. **215**, 107857 (2020)
12. Renilson, M.: Submarine Hydrodynamics, vol. 31. Springer (2015)
13. Ferreira, B., Pinto, M., Matos, A., Cruz, N.: Hydrodynamic modeling and motion limits of AUV mares. In: 2009 35th Annual Conference of IEEE Industrial Electronics, pp. 2241–2246. IEEE (2009)
14. Whicker, L.F., Fehlner, L.F.: Free-stream characteristics of a family of low-aspect-ratio, all-movable control surfaces for application to ship design. Technical report, David Taylor Model Basin Washington DC (1958)
15. Lewis, E.V.: Principles of naval architecture second revision. Jersey: Sname **2** (1988)
16. Kepler Jr, M.E.: Dynamics of a small autonomous underwater vehicle that tows a large payload. Ph.D. thesis, Virginia Tech (2018)
17. Watt, G.D.: Estimating the hydrodynamic characteristics of the dorado remote minehunting vehicle. Technical report, Defence Research and Development Canada-Atlantic (2002)
18. Barros, E., Pascoal, A., Sa, E.: Investigation of a method for predicting AUV derivatives. Ocean Eng. **35**(16), 1627–1636 (2008)
19. Cardenas, P., Barros, E.A.: Estimation of AUV hydrodynamic coefficients using analytical and system identification approaches. IEEE J. Oceanic Eng. **45**(4), 1157–1176 (2019)
20. Barros, E., Pascoal, A., Sa, E.: AUV dynamics: modelling and parameter estimation using analytical, semi-empirical, and CFD methods. IFAC Proc. Vol. **37**(10), 369–376 (2004)
21. Dantas, J.L., Barros, E.A., Cruz, J.J.: AUV control in the diving plane subject to waves. IFAC Proc. Vol. **45**(27), 319–324 (2012)
22. Gafurov, S.A., Klochkov, E.V.: Autonomous unmanned underwater vehicles development tendencies. Procedia Eng. **106**, 141–148 (2015)
23. Severholt, J.: Generic 6-dof added mass formulation for arbitrary underwater vehicles based on existing semi-empirical methods (2017)
24. Gracey, W.: The additional-mass effect of plates as determined by experiments. Ann. Rep.-Nat. Advisory Committee Aeron. **27**, 81 (1941)
25. Korvin-Kroukovsky, B.V., Jacobs, W.R.: Pitching and heaving motions of a ship in regular waves. Technical report, Stevens Inst of Tech Hoboken NJ Experimental Towing TANK (1957)
26. Kara, F.: Application of time-domain methods for marine hydrodynamic and hydroelasticity analyses of floating systems. Ships Offshore Struct. **17**(7), 1628–1645 (2022)
27. Newman, J.N.: Marine Hydrodynamics. The MIT Press (2018)
28. Salvesen, N., Tuck, E., Faltinsen, O.: Ship Motions and Sea Loads (1970)
29. Milgram, J.H.: Strip theory for underwater vehicles in water of finite depth. J. Eng. Math. **58**(1), 31–50 (2007)
30. Ahmed, F., Xiang, X., Jiang, C., Xiang, G., Yang, S.: Survey on traditional and AI based estimation techniques for hydrodynamic coefficients of autonomous underwater vehicle. Ocean Eng. **268**, 113300 (2023)
31. Lamb, H.: Hydrodynamics, pp. 134–139. Cambridge University Press (1932)
32. Imlay, F.H.: The complete expressions for added mass of a rigid body moving in an ideal fluid. Technical report, David Taylor Model Basin Washington DC (1961)
33. Fossen, T.I.: Handbook of Marine Craft Hydrodynamics and Motion Control. Wiley (2011)
34. Humphreys, D., Watkinson, K.: Prediction of acceleration hydrodynamic coefficients for underwater vehicles from geometric parameters. Technical report, NAVAL COASTAL SYSTEMS LAB PANAMA CITY FL (1978)
35. Watt, G.D.: Estimates for the added mass of a multi-component, deeply submerged vehicle. part 1. theory and program description. Technical report, DEFENCE RESEARCH ESTABLISHMENT ATLANTICDARTMOUTH (NOVA SCOTIA) (1988)

36. Doherty, S.M.: Cross body thruster control and modeling of a body of revolution autonomous underwater vehicle. Technical report, NAVAL POSTGRADUATE SCHOOL MONTEREY CA (2011)
37. Lee, S.K., Joung, T.H., Cheo, S.J., Jang, T.S., Lee, J.H.: Evaluation of the added mass for a spheroid-type unmanned underwater vehicle by vertical planar motion mechanism test. Int. J. Naval Arch. Ocean Eng. **3**(3), 174–180 (2011)
38. Munk, M.M.: Fluid mechanics, part ii. In: Aerodynamic Theory, pp. 224–304. Springer (1934)
39. Perrault, D., Bose, N., OYoung, S., Williams, C.D.: Sensitivity of AUV added mass coefficients to variations in hull and control plane geometry. Ocean Eng. **30**(5), 645–671 (2003)
40. Ahmed, F., Xiang, X., Wang, H., Zhang, J., Xiang, G., Yang, S.: Investigating wing-body lift interference effects on the dynamics of a novel flight-style AUV with bow-wings: Maneuvering simulations and experimental validations. Ocean Eng. **326**, 120778 (2025)
41. Ahmed, F., Xiang, X., Wang, H., Zhang, J., Xiang, G., Yang, S.: Nonlinear dynamics of novel flight-style autonomous underwater vehicle with bow wings, part i: Ase and cfd based estimations of hydrodynamic coefficients, part ii: Nonlinear dynamic modeling and experimental validations. Appl. Ocean Res. **141**, 103739 (2023)
42. Fossen, T.I.: Guidance and control of ocean vehicles. University of Trondheim, Norway, Printed Wiley, Chichester, England, ISBN: 0 471 94113 1, Doctors Thesis (1999)
43. Malvestuto, F.S., Gale, L.J.: Formulas for additional mass corrections to the moments of inertia of airplanes. Technical report (1947)
44. Triantafyllou, M.S., Hover, F.S.: Maneuvering and control of marine vehicles. Massachusetts of Institute of Technologyq (2003)
45. Kepler, M.E., Pawar, S., Stilwell, D.J., Brizzolara, S., Neu, W.L.: Assessment of auv hydrodynamic coefficients from analytic and semi-empirical methods. In: OCEANS 2018 MTS/IEEE Charleston, pp. 1–9 (2018)
46. Wieselsberger, C.v.: Weitere feststellungen uber die gesetze des flussigkeits und luftwiderstandes (other observations on the laws of fluid and air resistance). Physik Zeitschrift **23**, 219–224 (1922)
47. Wieselsberger, C.v.: Neuere feststellungen uber die gesetze des flussigkeits und luftwiderstands. Phys. Z. **22**, 321 (1921)
48. Potts, D.A., Binns, J.R., Potts, A.E., Marcollo, H.: The effect of aspect ratio on the drag of bare cylinders. In: International Conference on Offshore Mechanics and Arctic Engineering, vol. 58769, p. V001T01A028. American Society of Mechanical Engineers (2019)
49. Durand, W.F., Wieselsberger, C.: Airplane body (non lifting system) drag and influence on lifting system. Aerodynamic Theory: A General Review of Progress Under a Grant of the Guggenheim Fund for the Promotion of Aeronautics pp. 130–168 (1935)
50. Nielsen, J.N., Katzen, E.D., Tang, K.K.: Lift and pitching-moment interference between a pointed cylindrical body and triangular wings of various aspect ratios at mach numbers of 1.50 and 2.02. Technical report (1956)
51. Spreiter, J.R.: The aerodynamic forces on slender plane-and cruciform-wing and body combinations. Technical report (1950)
52. Bohlmann, H.J.: Berechnung hydrodynamischer koeffizienten von ubooten zur vorhersage des bewegungsverhaltens. Technical report (1990)
53. Morikawa, G.: Supersonic wing-body lift. J. Aeronaut. Sci. **18**(4), 217–228 (1951)
54. Pitts, W.C., Nielsen, J.N., Kaattari, G.E.: Lift and center of pressure of wing-body-tail combinations at subsonic, transonic, and supersonic speeds. Technical report (1957)
55. Barros, E.A., Dantas, J.L., Pascoal, A.M., Sá, E.: Investigation of normal force and moment coefficients for an AUV at nonlinear angle of attack and sideslip range. IEEE J. Oceanic Eng. **33**(4), 538–549 (2008)
56. Lyons, D., et al.: An analysis of the lift slope of aerofoils of small aspect ratio, including fins, with design charts for aerofoils and control surfaces (1945)
57. Qu, Y., Wu, Q., Zhao, X., Huang, B., Fu, X., Wang, G.: Numerical investigation of flow structures around the darpa suboff model. Ocean Eng. **239**, 109866 (2021)

# Chapter 5
# Computational Fluid Dynamics Based Estimation of Hydrodynamic Coefficients of AUVs

## 5.1 Introduction

CFD methods are widely used to design hydrodynamically stable and efficient underwater vehicles. Maneuvering analysis involves identifying fluid-generated forces and moments, represented as hydrodynamic derivatives, which characterize translational and rotational movements across all six degrees of freedom. These derivatives are crucial for predicting maneuvering performance and developing control strategies. Commercial CFD tools like ANSYS CFX, ANSYS Fluent, OpenFOAM, and STAR-CCM+ are commonly employed for this analysis [1]. Simulation approaches for AUV flows include DNS, LES, and RANSE, with RANSE being particularly effective for simulating complex fluid flows, capturing turbulence and boundary layer behavior. By averaging the Navier-Stokes equations over time, RANSE balances computational efficiency with the ability to predict turbulent flows, making it suitable for both steady and unsteady conditions. Its robustness in estimating hydrodynamic derivatives has been validated in numerous studies [2–11]. The choice of turbulence model in RANSE simulations is critical for accurately modeling turbulent flows around AUVs [12, 13]. Two-equation models, such as standard $k$-$\epsilon$, Realizable $k$-$\epsilon$, RNG $k$-$\epsilon$, and SST $k$-$\omega$, are commonly used for their balance of accuracy and efficiency [14, 15]. The standard $k$-$\epsilon$ model is efficient for preliminary analyses but struggles with complex boundary layer phenomena [16–19]. The Realizable and RNG $k$-$\epsilon$ models enhance accuracy by adjusting turbulence viscosity and incorporating smaller turbulence scales, respectively [11, 19–23]. The SST $k$-$\omega$ model combines advantages of both $k$-$\epsilon$ and $k$-$\omega$ models, excelling in boundary layer treatments and adverse pressure gradients [1, 15, 19, 24]. For unsteady flows involving AUVs, the SST $k$-$\omega$ model is preferred, especially for control surfaces and flow separation issues [12, 25, 26]. Potential flow theory and panel methods are also used for preliminary estimates, while Computational Fluid-Structure Interaction (FSI) combines fluid and structural analysis for dynamic coefficients.



X. Xiang et al., *Dynamics Modeling and Maneuvering of Autonomous Underwater Vehicles*, https://doi.org/10.1007/978-981-95-1521-9_5

Verification and validation of CFD simulations for AUV hydrodynamic performance involve several methods to ensure accuracy and reliability. Experimental tests compare CFD results with data from captive model tests of AUV prototypes, which help to verify accuracy [27, 28]. Benchmarking against standard models, such as the DARPA SUBOFF model [29], provides a cost-effective means to validate CFD methods by replicating well-documented experimental conditions [29–32]. Furthermore, uncertainty quantification involves varying input parameters within their uncertainty bounds to assess the impact on simulation outcomes, offering insights into the reliability and accuracy of the CFD results [1, 33–36].

In addition to shape optimizations, CFD methods are extensively used to predict the inertial and damping coefficients essential for AUV dynamic modeling [8, 37–41]. Foundational theoretical work by Watt [42] and Blevins [43] provides methods for predicting these coefficients, which can be calculated using the panel method, boundary element method [44–46], and CFD tools [26, 47–50]. For example, Raza et al. [49] validated their numerical estimations of added mass for an ellipsoid, while Mishra [47] focused on a torpedo-shaped AUV.

Recently, Javanmard et al. [26] introduced a CFD method for added mass coefficients of torpedo-shaped vehicles, validated against analytical results which are effective for both simple and complex geometries. Hydrodynamic damping coefficients have also been derived using CFD for various maneuvers and AUV types. Notably, Tyagi and Sen [2] calculated sway-velocity derivatives, while Phillips et al. [51] investigated dynamic stability using ANSYS CFX, successfully replicating experimental yawing and rotating tests. Additional notable studies, such as those by De Barros et al. [52] and Zhang et al. [53], highlighted CFD's accuracy in predicting coefficients for various AUV models, including the SUBOFF submarine. Recent advancements in CFD applications for AUV design include Huang et al. [54], who analyzed a streamlined I-AUV, and Liu et al. [41], who combined CFD with machine learning for efficient AUV shape design. These developments underline the increasing significance of CFD in accurately estimating hydrodynamic coefficients for AUV dynamic modeling and design.

### *5.1.1 Governing Equations*

The governing equations for CFD simulations of AUVs are derived from the fundamental principles of fluid mechanics. These equations are used to solve for the flow field around the AUV, enabling the estimation of hydrodynamic coefficients such as added mass, drag and lift coefficients. The primary equations used in CFD simulations are the Navier-Stokes equations, which describe the conservation of mass and momentum, respectively. The Navier-Stokes equations, after applying the Reynolds averaging rules, yield the Reynolds-Averaged Navier-Stokes (RANS) governing equations, which are used to solve the incompressible, Newtonian fluid flow field around underwater vehicles. The continuity equation, which ensures mass conservation, is given by:

$$\frac{\partial \overline{u}_i}{\partial x_i} = 0 \tag{5.1}$$

where $\overline{u}_i$ represents the mean flow velocity components. The momentum equation, which describes the conservation of momentum for the mean flow, is expressed as:

$$\frac{\partial \overline{u}_i}{\partial t} + \frac{\partial \overline{u_i u_j}}{\partial x_j} = -\frac{1}{\rho}\frac{\partial \overline{p}}{\partial x_i} + \nu \frac{\partial^2 \overline{u}_i}{\partial x_j \partial x_j} - \frac{\partial}{\partial x_j}\overline{u_i^{'} u_j^{'}} \tag{5.2}$$

In this equation, $\rho$ is the fluid density, $p$ is the pressure term, $\nu$ is the dynamic viscosity, and $\overline{u_i^{'} u_j^{'}}$ is the Reynolds stress tensor. The Reynolds stress tensor characterizes the turbulent behavior of the fluid flow and captures the correlations between the fluctuating velocities $\overline{u_i}$ and $\overline{u_j}$ within the flow field. The continuity equation ensures that the flow is divergence-free, while the momentum equation balances temporal acceleration, convective acceleration, pressure gradients, viscous diffusion, and Reynolds stresses.

To close the system of equations, turbulence models such as the $k$-$\epsilon$ or $k$-$\omega$ models are used to approximate the Reynolds stress tensor. These models provide additional equations to solve for turbulent kinetic energy ($k$) and its dissipation rate ($\epsilon$) or specific dissipation rate ($\omega$). The RANS equations, along with appropriate boundary conditions (e.g., no-slip at the AUV surface, inlet/outlet conditions, and free-surface conditions for air-water interfaces), form the basis for Computational Fluid Dynamics (CFD) simulations. These simulations solve the governing equations numerically using methods like the Finite Volume Method (FVM) or Finite Element Method (FEM), providing detailed insights into the flow field around the AUV. Typically, to compute the hydrodynamic drag and lift coefficients of underwater vehicle, URANSE with two equations turbulence models (standard $k - \epsilon$ or $k - \omega$ and SST$k - \omega$) are widely used [7, 25, 26, 28]. $k - \epsilon$ is appropriate when the flow needs to be simulated only around the circular hull of the AUV. However, SST $k - \omega$ turbulence model [24] is considered more suitable when flow separation problem occurs which in case of AUV, likely caused due to the control surfaces. Moreover, the turbulence model exhibits the ability to smoothly transit between low and high Reynolds number flows and demonstrates excellent adaptability in addressing boundary layer issues across various Reynolds number flow regimes [55].

The solution to these equations enables the estimation of hydrodynamic coefficients such as added mass, damping, and drag. For example, the added mass is derived from the pressure distribution on the AUV surface, while damping coefficients are obtained from the viscous forces acting on the vehicle.

By solving governing equations and turbulence models, CFD simulations provide relatively accurate predictions of hydrodynamic forces and moments, enabling the design and optimization of efficient and stable underwater vehicles. Taking Flight-Style AUV as reference AUV, CFD method is applied to calculate the drag and lift coefficients.

## 5.2 Drag Coefficients

CFD simulations have been performed to compute the drag coefficients, particularly cross flow drag past over the FSAUV and circular cylinders using 'STAR-CCM+'. Accordingly, SST $k - \omega$ turbulence model has been applied to model the Reynolds stress terms $\rho\overline{u_i^{'}u_j^{'}}$ given in the equation (3.9) to solve the flow field around the FSAUV.

### 5.2.1 *Computational Fluid Domain and Boundary Conditions*

A three-dimensional cuboidal computational fluid domain has been established around the full-scale 3D models of $\text{FSAUV}_{1,2}$ to simulate the flow behavior around the vehicle. The dimensions of the domain–length, width, and height–used for both axial and cross-flow simulations are illustrated in Fig. 5.1. This domain size is carefully chosen to adequately capture the fluid flow characteristics around the vehicle, as evidenced in Fig. 5.5, where the flow field is fully resolved from upstream to downstream. The boundary conditions applied to the computational domain include a prescribed inlet velocity, a pressure outlet, free-slip walls, and a no-slip wall condition on the submerged surfaces of the AUV, as depicted in Fig. 5.1.

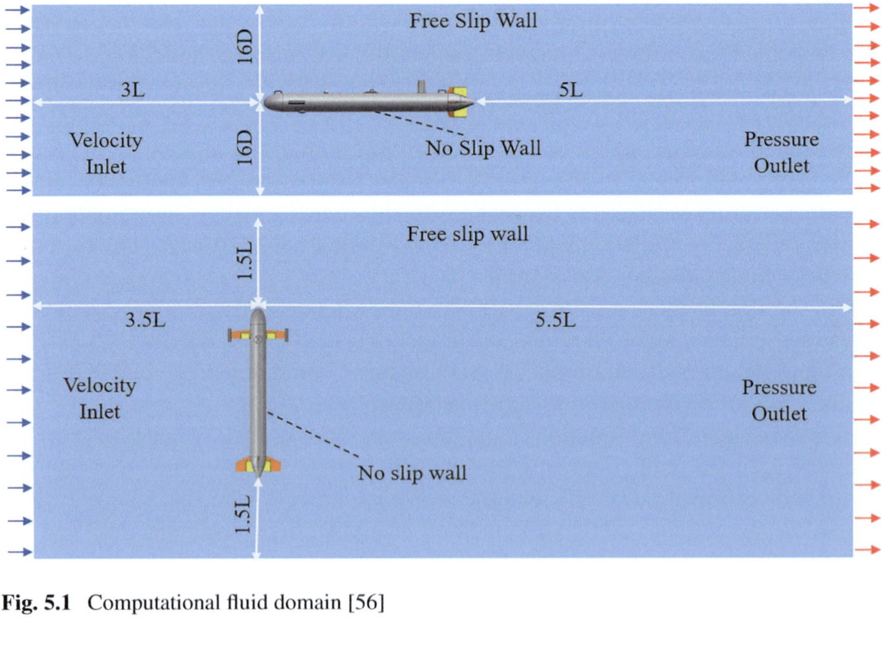


**Fig. 5.1** Computational fluid domain [56]

### 5.2.2 Mesh Generation and Grid Convergence

In CFD, mesh convergence and grid independence study are critical steps to ensure the accuracy and reliability of simulation results. These processes involve systematically refining the computational mesh (or grid) and analyzing how the results change with increasing mesh resolution. The goal is to determine the optimal mesh size that provides accurate results without excessive computational cost. Mesh convergence refers to the process of refining the computational mesh until the solution becomes independent of further refinement. This ensures that numerical errors due to discretization (e.g., truncation errors) are minimized, and the solution is reliable. A coarse mesh may introduce numerical errors, while an excessively fine mesh increases computational cost without significant improvement in accuracy. Mesh convergence is achieved by starting with a coarse mesh and progressively refining it while monitoring key output parameters (e.g., drag coefficient, lift coefficient, pressure distribution). Convergence is confirmed when the change in these parameters between successive refinements falls below a predefined tolerance (e.g., $< 1\%$).

A grid independence study is a systematic investigation to determine the mesh resolution at which the solution becomes independent of the grid size. This study ensures that the simulation results are accurate and reliable without unnecessary computational expense. The process involves defining key output parameters (e.g., drag force, lift force, pressure coefficient), creating multiple meshes with increasing resolution (e.g., coarse, medium, fine, and very fine), running simulations for each mesh, and analyzing the results to determine the point at which further refinement does not significantly change the results. For example, in a study of an underwater vehicle, the drag coefficient $(C_D)$ is often used as the key parameter. As the mesh is refined, the $C_D$ value should stabilize, indicating grid independence.

Underwater vehicle simulations present unique challenges for mesh convergence and grid independence. The complex geometries of underwater vehicles (e.g., hulls, fins, propellers) require careful mesh generation to accurately capture flow features. Additionally, resolving the boundary layer is critical for predicting drag and pressure distribution, often necessitating fine meshes near the vehicle surface and in regions of high gradients. However, fine meshes increase computational time and resource requirements, making it essential to balance accuracy and cost.

Best practices for achieving mesh convergence and grid independence include using Adaptive Mesh Refinement (AMR), which automatically refines the mesh in regions of high gradients (e.g., near the vehicle surface or in wake regions) while keeping the mesh coarse in less critical areas. It is also important to monitor key parameters relevant to the simulation objectives, such as drag, lift, or pressure distribution, and to set convergence criteria (e.g., $< 1\%$ change in $C_D$ between mesh refinements). Validating results by comparing CFD predictions with experimental data or analytical solutions further ensures accuracy.

For instance, an overset grid has been used to simulate the fluid flow underwater vehicle maneuvering, particularly when the relative motion of the underwater vehicle parts is also important [57, 58]. To simulate the fluid flow past over both the

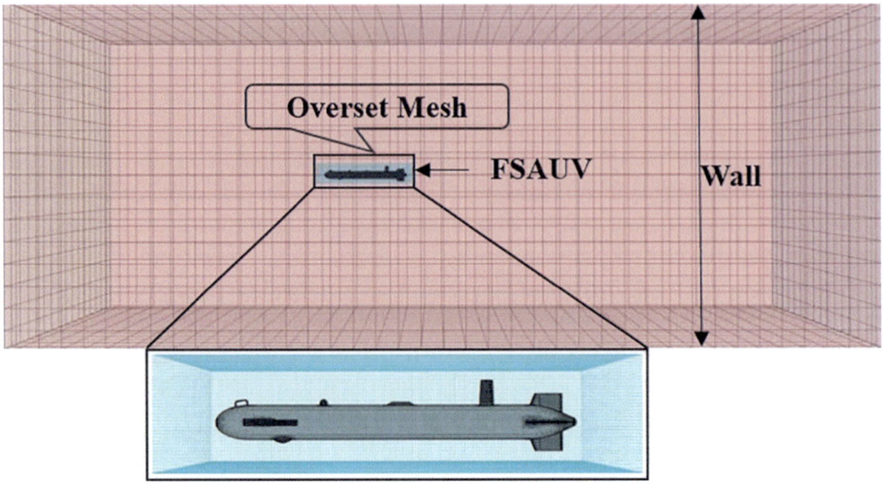


**Fig. 5.2** Meshed CFD domain [60]

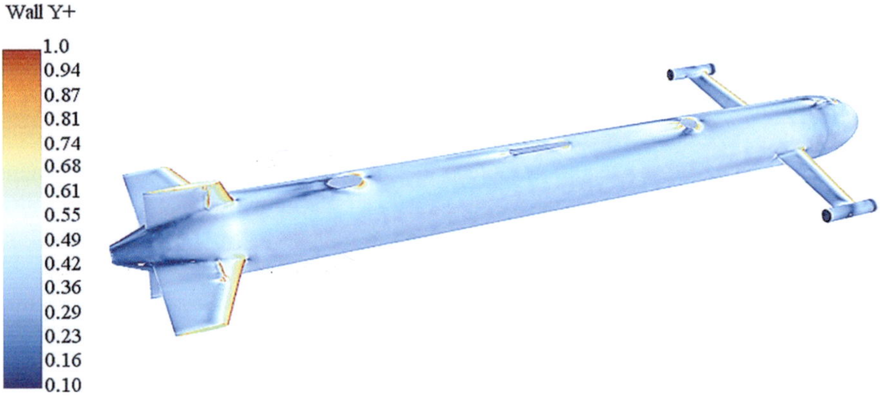


**Fig. 5.3** $y^+$ value distribution in CFD simulation of $FSAUV_1$ [60]

configurations of FSAUV for surge, sway and heave maneuvers, the overset grid has been generated around the FSAUV as shown in Fig. 5.2. The overset meshing technique provides great flexibility to modify the grid and provides better control over the local mesh [59]. Since, SST $k - \omega$ turbulence model is appropriate for near-wall treatment and therefore, $y^+$ is kept around 1 (i.e. $y^+ \approx 0.7$-$0.9$)[15, 57]. The $y^+$ value distribution over FSAUV model is shown in Fig. 5.3.

A grid convergence study was performed using three mesh configurations: coarse, medium, and fine. The grid refinement followed an orderly ratio of $r_G = \sqrt{2}$, progressively increasing the mesh resolution. For the axial drag coefficient evaluation, simulations were conducted with fluid flowing over an ellipsoid at a velocity of $U = 1$ m/s. In contrast, the cross-flow drag coefficients were obtained by simulating

**Table 5.1** Grid convergence study for velocity ($U = 1$ m/s)

| Flow direction | Grid level | Mesh refinement | Elements (Millions) | Drag (N) | $C_D$ | RD (%) |
|---|---|---|---|---|---|---|
| Axial flow | 1 | Coarse | 1.16 | 2.45 | 0.1085 | 4.7% |
| | 2 | Medium | 3.13 | 2.56 | 0.1134 | 0.4% |
| | 3 | Fine | 4.34 | 2.57 | 0.1138 | – |
| Cross-Flow | 1 | Coarse | 1.03 | 164 | 0.5039 | 2.5% |
| | 2 | Medium | 2.09 | 161 | 0.4947 | 0.625% |
| | 3 | Fine | 3.17 | 160 | 0.4916 | – |

flow past a circular cylinder at subcritical Reynolds numbers. The length-to-diameter ratios of both the ellipsoid and the cylinder were matched to that of the FSAUV model. Table 5.1 summarizes the number of elements in each mesh, the computed drag forces, and their relative differences compared to the fine mesh results. Based on this study, the refined mesh was selected for subsequent simulations of flow around the FSAUV.

To ensure monotonic convergence of the grid, the grid convergence ratio $R_G$ should lie between 0 and 1. The ratio $R_G$ is defined as

$$R_G = \frac{\epsilon_{23}}{\epsilon_{12}}, \tag{5.3}$$

where $\epsilon_{23} = C_{D2} - C_{D3}$ and $\epsilon_{12} = C_{D1} - C_{D2}$. Here, $C_{D1}$, $C_{D2}$, and $C_{D3}$ represent the drag coefficients obtained from the coarse, medium, and fine mesh configurations, respectively.

The computed values of $R_G$ for the axial and cross-flow cases were found to be 0.1 and 0.3, respectively. Since both values satisfy the condition $0 < R_G < 1$, the grid is considered to be monotonically convergent. Accordingly, the fine mesh was selected for calculating the axial and cross-flow drag coefficients for flow past the FSAUV.

### 5.2.3 *ASE and CFD Results of Drag Coefficients: A Quantitative Analysis*

**(1) Axial Flow Drag Coefficients**

The axial flow drag coefficient ($C_{d_a}$) is a pivotal parameter in the design of underwater vehicles, directly influencing the thrust required to propel the vehicle efficiently. To thoroughly investigate this parameter, both ASE and CFD techniques were employed. These methods were used to estimate the drag coefficient and the total drag force for three distinct bare-hull geometries: the FSAUV, an ellipse, and $\text{FSAUV}_1$.

**Table 5.2** $C_{d_a}$ and corresponding nonlinear axial drag coefficient $X_{u|u|}$ (Kg/m)

| Body | Coefficients | $ASE_1$ (A) [62, 63] Eq. (4.14) | $ASE_2$ (B) [61] Eqs. (4.15 and 4.16) | CFD (C) | $RD_A(\%)$ $\frac{\|C-A\|}{\|A\|}$ | $RD_B(\%)$ $\frac{\|C-B\|}{\|B\|}$ | $\Delta$RD (%) $RD_A - RD_B$ |
|---|---|---|---|---|---|---|---|
| Hull | $C_{da}$ | 0.141 | 0.141 | 0.148 | 5.0% | 5.0% | 0.0% |
| Hull | $X_{u\|u\|}$ | −3.2 | −3.2 | −3.34 | 4.4% | 4.4% | 0.0% |
| Ellipse | $C_{da}$ | 0.13 | 0.11 | 0.114 | 12.3% | 3.6% | 8.7% |
| Ellipse | $X_{u\|u\|}$ | −2.9 | −2.50 | −2.60 | 10.3% | 4.0% | 6.3% |
| $FSAUV_1$ | $C_{da}$ | 0.19 | 0.21 | 0.22 | 15.6% | 4.7% | 10.9% |
| $FSAUV_1$ | $X_{u\|u\|}$ | −6.6 | −7.33 | −7.70 | 16.7% | 5.0% | 11.7% |

The calculated values for $C_{d_a}$ and their corresponding **nonlinear drag coefficient** ($X_{u|u|}$) are summarized in Table 5.2. For comparative analysis, reference was also made to experimental results presented by Hoerner [61] (Fig. 21 on Page 3–12). For a cylinder with rounded or streamlined head forms, possessing an $l/d$ (length-to-diameter ratio) equivalent to the FSAUV, Hoerner's data indicates an approximate $C_{d_a}$ value of 0.21. This comparison helps validate the estimations derived from the ASE and CFD approaches, providing confidence in the predicted drag characteristics for these vehicle designs.

**Remarks on Table** 5.2: The key observations from Table 5.2 reveal that for the hull, both $C_{d_a}$ and $X_{u|u|}$ exhibit identical relative differences ($RD_A$ and $RD_B$) with $\Delta RD = 0.0\%$, indicating close agreement between $ASE_1$, $ASE_2$, and CFD results. However, for the ellipse and $FSAUV_1$, $ASE_2$ consistently shows smaller relative deviations ($RD_B$) compared to ($RD_A$) for $ASE_1$, with $\Delta$RD ranging from 6.3% to 11.7%. Notably, $ASE_2$ provides higher accuracy for complex geometries like $FSAUV_1$, where $ASE_1$ shows significantly larger deviations. Overall, $ASE_2$ demonstrates superior agreement with CFD predictions, particularly for intricate underwater vehicle shapes, highlighting its reliability for axial drag coefficient estimation.

The axial drag forces for both FSAUV configurations ($FSAUV_1$ and $FSAUV_2$) were calculated using CFD simulations for surge speeds of 1 to 3 m/s. The drag-velocity curves, shown in Fig. 5.4, reveal that $FSAUV_1$ experiences higher drag due to the bow-wings with electromagnetic arrays. The drag difference increases with speed as flow transitions from laminar to turbulent, raising resistance. The linear relationship between speed and drag indicates a proportional increase in drag with surge speed.

**(2) Cross Flow Drag Coefficients**

The cross-flow drag force coefficients, $Y_{v|v|}$ and $Z_{w|w|}$, estimated through both ASE and CFD methods, are summarized in Table 5.4. According to Eqs. (4.17) to (4.24), aside from water density and geometric parameters, the drag coefficient $C_{dc}$ significantly influences the nonlinear drag force and moment coefficients $Y_{v|v|}$ and $Z_{w|w|}$. Based on experimental data for three-dimensional flow past a circular cylinder–with a length-to-diameter ratio matching that of the FSAUV and free boundary conditions

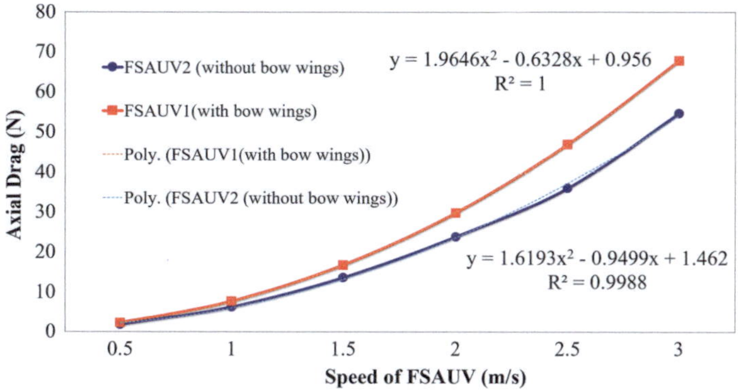


**Fig. 5.4** Correlation Between Axial Drag and Velocity of FSAUV

**Table 5.3** Experimental results–cross flow past circular cylinder l/d = 11.3 [60]

| Cross-flow drag coefficient | Experiment (2D) | Experiment (3D) |
|---|---|---|
| $C_{dc}$ | 1.2 | 0.84 |

**Table 5.4** Cross flow drag force coefficients $Y_{v|v|}$ and $Z_{w|w|}$ in Kg/m

| Body | Coefficient | $ASE_1$(A) (2D) [61, 62, 64] | $ASE_2$(B) (3D) [65] | CFD(C) (3D) | $RD_A(\%)$ $\frac{(C-A)}{\lvert A\rvert}$ | $RD_B(\%)$ $\frac{(C-B)}{\lvert B\rvert}$ | $\Delta RD(\%)$ $RD_A - RD_B$ |
|---|---|---|---|---|---|---|---|
| Cylinder | $C_{d_c}$ | 1.20 | 0.84 | 0.69 | 42.5% | 18.0% | 24.5% |
| $FSAUV_1$ | $Y_{v\lvert v\rvert}$ | −403 | −292 | −224 | 44.4% | 23.3% | 21.1% |
| $FSAUV_2$ | $Y_{v\lvert v\rvert}$ | −403 | −292 | −224 | 44.4% | 23.3% | 21.1% |
| $FSAUV_1$ | $Z_{w\lvert w\rvert}$ | −475 | −364 | −283 | 41.0% | 22.0% | 19.0% |
| $FSAUV_2$ | $Z_{w\lvert w\rvert}$ | −429 | −318 | −218 | 49.0% | 31.0% | 18.0% |

at both ends (refer to Table 5.3)–a value of $C_{dc} = 0.84$ is adopted for the present analysis.

The results obtained from the ASE and CFD methods are compared by calculating the relative difference, which quantifies the percentage variation between the two approaches. These comparative results are presented in Table 5.4. The analysis demonstrates that the current ASE method achieves improved accuracy over the previously used ASE approach with $C_{dc} = 1.2$. Specifically, a notable enhancement of approximately 20% is observed in the sway and heave force coefficients compared to the earlier method. This indicates that the refined ASE approach produces results that align more closely with experimental data. Additionally, the heave force coefficient ($Z_{w|w|}$) is higher for the FSAUV equipped with bow-wings, as these appendages introduce extra resistance during vertical plane maneuvers. Conversely, the sway force coefficient ($Y_{v|v|}$) remains nearly identical for both AUV configurations, since the bow-wings contribute negligibly to the resistance experienced in the horizontal plane.

**Remarks on Table** 5.4: The key observations from Table 5.4 highlight significant deviations between CFD predictions and analytical estimations ($ASE_1$ and $ASE_2$) for cross-flow drag force coefficients. For the cylinder, $ASE_2$ provides a more accurate estimation compared to $ASE_1$, with a $\Delta$RD of 24.5%. Similarly, for $FSAUV_1$ and $FSAUV_2$, $ASE_2$ consistently exhibits lower relative difference ($RD_B$) compared to $ASE_1$ ($RD_A$), with $\Delta$RD ranging from 18.0% to 21.1%. The coefficients $Y_{v|v|}$ and $Z_{w|w|}$ for FSAUV geometries indicate that $ASE_2$ captures 3D flow effects better, yielding closer agreement with CFD results. These findings emphasize the enhanced accuracy of $ASE_2$ in modeling complex 3D cross-flow dynamics, highlighting its suitability for predicting drag force coefficients for streamlined AUVs. Furthermore, the observed discrepancy between the proposed ASE and CFD results (i.e. 20% approx.) has been further investigated in Sect. 5.2.3.

Figure 5.5 presents CFD simulation visualizations for the flow past both FSAUV configurations, illustrating the resistance caused by the vehicle hull and the wings in surge, sway, and heave directions. The figure also shows velocity contours, providing visual representations of the flow distribution around the FSAUV hull and bow-wings, highlighting areas of higher and lower velocities.

The cross flow drag force and moment coefficients of FSAUV with bow-wings using equations (4.17) to (4.24) have been estimated. In these equations, the value of $C_{dc}$ has been taken as 1.2 ($ASE_1$), 0.84 ($ASE_2$) and 0.69 (CFD). The results are presented in Table 5.5.

**(3) Cross flow Drag Coefficients: Experimental Validation of CFD Results**

To investigate the 20% difference between ASE and CFD results for cross-flow drag coefficients, three additional CFD simulations were conducted for a circular cylinder with length-to-diameter ratios of 5, 10, and 11.3, in the sub-critical Reynolds number region ($Re = 88000$). Figure 5.6a shows the simulated and experimental results, with a relative variation of approximately 20%. This discrepancy is likely due to the limitations of the SST $k - \omega$ turbulence model in simulating flow over a circular cylinder in the sub-critical to supercritical Reynolds number regimes. A similar study using the $k - \epsilon$ model [66] reported similar findings. The investigation also explored the effect of the length-to-diameter ratio on drag reduction for flow past a circular cylinder at $Re = 88000$, referencing work by Knudsen & Katz [67, 68]. The drag reduction factor ($k_d$) [69, 70] correlates 2D and 3D drag coefficients, with $C_{D_\infty} = 1.2$ for sub-critical flow [61, 65]. Figure 5.6b compares CFD results with Wieselsberger's experimental drag coefficients, showing better agreement with the drag reduction factor.

**Remarks on Table** 5.6: Table 5.6 compares drag coefficient predictions from CFD simulations, experimental data, and the drag reduction factor ($k_d$) for a circular cylinder at $Re = 88000$ across various length-to-diameter ratios ($l/d$). The relative difference between CFD results and experimental/drag reduction factor values, along with the differential deviation ($\Delta$RD), shows that CFD results are consistently closer to the drag reduction factor, with a 15% better agreement than experimental data.

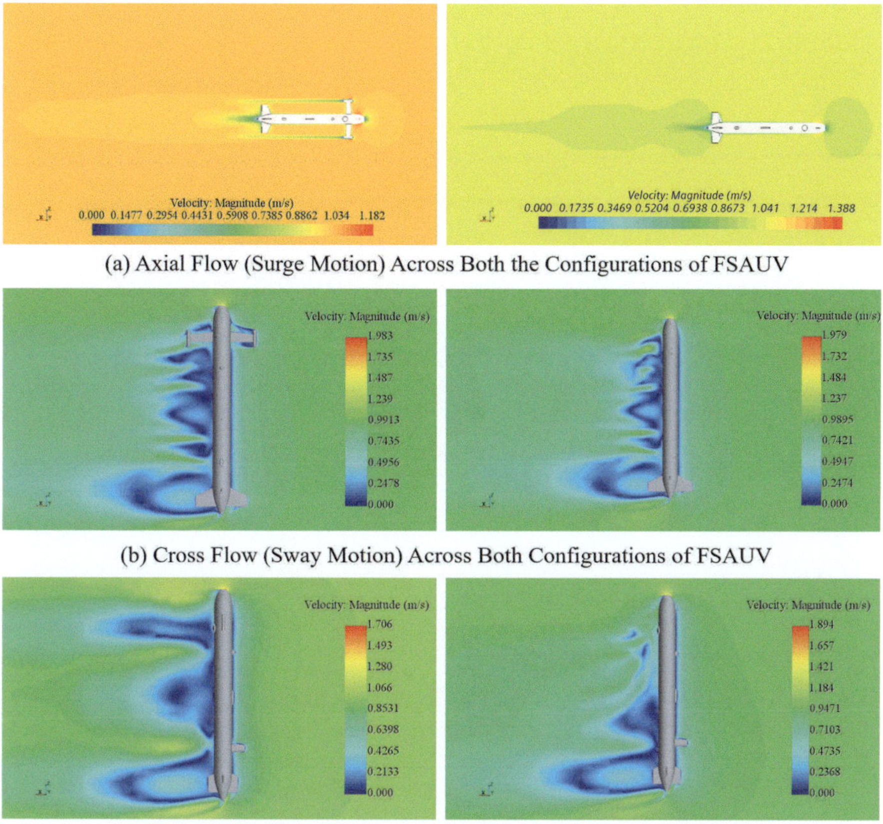


(a) Axial Flow (Surge Motion) Across Both the Configurations of FSAUV

(b) Cross Flow (Sway Motion) Across Both Configurations of FSAUV

(c) Cross Flow (Heave Motion) Across Both Configurations of FSAUV

**Fig. 5.5** Flow past over $FSAUV_1$ (Left) and $FSAUV_2$ (Right) in $x$, $y$ and $z$ directions [60]

**Table 5.5** Cross flow drag force and moment coefficients [60]

| Coefficients | $ASE_1$ (A) $C_{dc}^{2D} = 1.2$ | $ASE_2$ (B) $C_{dc}^{3D} = 0.84$ | CFD + ASE (C) $C_{dc}^{3D} = 0.69$ | Units |
|---|---|---|---|---|
| $Y_{v\|v\|}$ | −403.14 | −292.10 | −245.83 | kg/m |
| $Z_{w\|w\|}$ | −475.40 | −364.4 | −318.13 | kg/m |
| $M_{w\|w\|}$ | +11.87 | +3.05 | −0.63 | kg |
| $N_{v\|v\|}$ | +2.36 | +11.2 | +14.86 | kg |
| $Y_{r\|r\|}$ | −5.30 | +5.94 | +10.60 | $kg \cdot m/rad^2$ |
| $Z_{q\|q\|}$ | +13.42 | +2.20 | −2.47 | $kg \cdot m/rad^2$ |
| $M_{q\|q\|}$ | −330 | −268.33 | −242.70 | $kg \cdot m^2/rad^2$ |
| $N_{r\|r\|}$ | −239 | −177.20 | −151.50 | $kg \cdot m^2/rad^2$ |

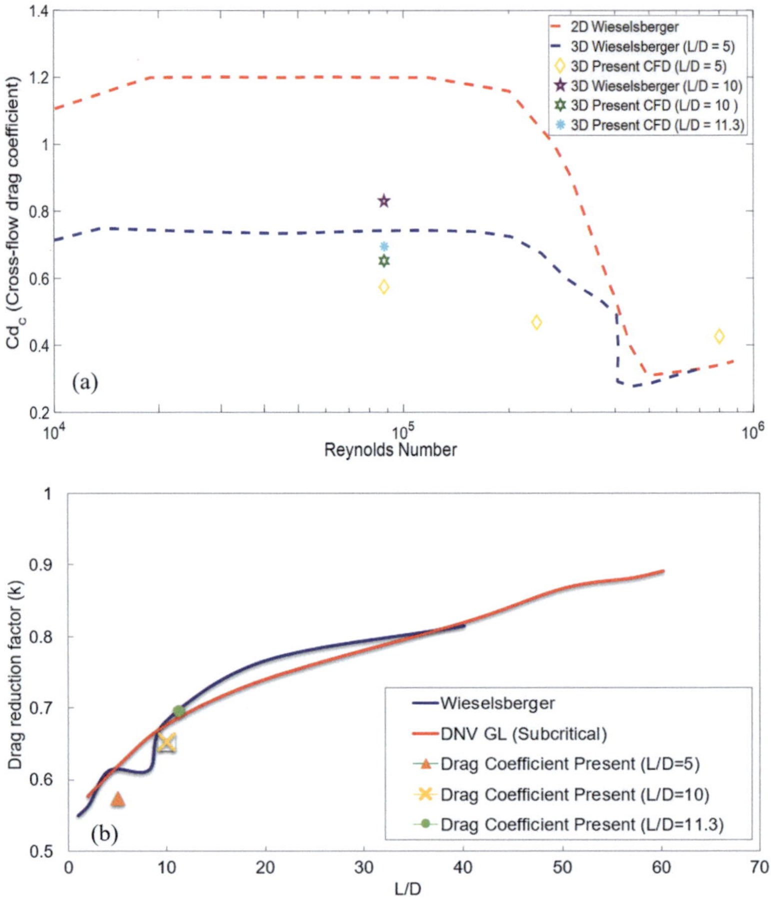


**Fig. 5.6** **a** Cross Flow Drag Coefficient ($C_{d_c}$) versus Reynolds Number ($R_e$) **b** Drag Reduction Factor ($k$) versus Length-to-Diameter Ratio ($l/d$) [60]

**Table 5.6** CFD versus experiment—drag coefficient for circular cylinder at $Re = 88{,}000$ [60]

| $l/d$ | Exp. (E) [65, 69, 71] | $k_d$ [65, 68, 69] | CFD (C) (%) | $\mathrm{RD}_E$ $\frac{\lvert C-E\rvert}{\lvert E\rvert}$ | $\mathrm{RD}_k$ $\frac{\lvert C-k\rvert}{\lvert k\rvert}$ | $\Delta$RD $\mathrm{RD}_E$–$\mathrm{RD}_k$ |
|---|---|---|---|---|---|---|
| 5 | 0.74 | 0.62 | 0.57 | 23% | 8% | 15% |
| 10 | 0.82 | 0.68 | 0.65 | 20% | 4% | 16% |
| 11.3 | 0.84 | 0.7 | 0.69 | 18% | 1.4% | 16.6% |

An approximate 20% difference observed between the ASE method and CFD results is considered acceptable and can be attributed to inherent approximations in the ASE formulation as well as limitations in the CFD simulations. Based on the comprehensive comparative analysis and the data summarized in Table 5.6, the drag coefficient $C_{dc}$ is adopted as 0.84 for three-dimensional flow conditions. This value is used to estimate the drag force and moment coefficients via the ASE formulations outlined in Eqs. (4.17) to (4.24) for the FSAUV, which has a length-to-diameter ratio of 11.3 and operates within the subcritical Reynolds number regime.

## 5.3 Lift Coefficients and Wing-Body Lift Interference Effects

CFD simulations were conducted to replicate experimental towing tank tests for steady drift analysis, calculating the force and moment coefficients $Y$, $Z$, $N$, and $M$ across various side-slip/drift angles ($\beta$) and angles of attack ($\alpha$) in both horizontal and vertical planes. The FSAUV drift angles in both planes have been selected between 0° and 25° to obtain a detailed CFD-informed dataset [72]. Subsequently, the sway-induced and heave-induced forces and moment coefficients were determined through regression methods using the CFD results. The CFD simulation settings, including initial and boundary conditions, discretization schemes, solver configurations, and mesh elements, are summarized in Table 5.7.

To simulate the flow around the FSAUV, a cylindrical domain with a structured mesh is constructed, as shown in Fig. 5.7a. The cylindrical domain is selected for its rotational symmetry and efficient mesh control, which is suitable for symmetric FSAUV. A mesh comprising three million structured cells is generated, with an overset mesh settings to ensure higher density near the FSAUV surface to resolve flow dynamics and boundary layer effects accurately. Figures 5.8, 5.9, 5.10, 5.11, and 5.12 illustrate the vortex shedding, $y^+$ distribution, pressure contours, and velocity contours from the CFD simulations.

The vortex magnitude is higher with pronounced pressure contour formation at the wing-body juncture, as depicted in Figs. 5.8 and 5.11 respectively. These observations highlight the critical role of the wing-body interference in influencing lift coefficients. The amplified vortex activity indicates strong flow interactions, enhancing lift generation by increasing the pressure differential between the upper and lower wing surfaces. The localized high-pressure zones, evident in the pressure contours, further contribute to the overall lift force. This interplay between vortex dynamics and pressure distribution highlights the importance of the wing-body interference effects for improved hydrodynamic performance.

The nondimensional lift coefficients derived from CFD analyses, denoted as $Y'_{uv}$, $N'_{uv}$, $Z'_{uw}$, and $M'_{uw}$, are summarized in Table 5.8. The lateral force ($Y$), heave force ($Z$), along with the corresponding yawing moment ($N$) and pitching moment ($M$) obtained through CFD simulations, are detailed in Tables 5.9 and 5.10, respectively.

**Table 5.7** CFD simulation settings: wing-body interference (WBI) effects

| Parameter | Details |
|---|---|
| Solver type | Unsteady reynolds-averaged navier-stokes (URANS) Solver |
| Turbulence model | Shear stress transport (SST) $k - \omega$ Model |
| Discretization scheme | Second-order upwind scheme for momentum and turbulence equations |
| Mesh type | Structured mesh with refinement near the AUV surface |
| Mesh resolution | Approximately 3 million elements |
| Near-Wall treatment | Wall functions; $y^+$ values maintained around 1 $(0.7 \leq y^+ \leq 0.9)$ (Fig. 5.9) |
| Domain type | Cylindrical domain (Fig. 5.7a) |
| Domain dimensions | Length: $17L$, height and width: $32D$ (Fig. 5.7b) |
| AUV placement | Positioned $5L$ from the front boundary and $10L$ from the rear boundary |
| Boundary conditions (Fig. 5.7b) | – Inlet: velocity inlet<br>– Outlet: pressure outlet<br>– Outer boundary: free-slip wall<br>– AUV surface: no-slip wall |
| Residual error criterion | $10^{-5}$ for solution convergence |
| Simulation type | Transient (unsteady flow simulation) |
| Reynolds number range | Based on AUV geometry and operational speed |
| Software used | STAR-CCM+ |

These hydrodynamic forces and moments have been nondimensionalized using the single prime notation system (System I), consistent with the SNAME nomenclature [74]. The nondimensional forms of the forces and moments are represented as $Y'$, $Z'$, $N'$, and $M'$.

For the FSAUV, the nondimensional lift coefficients were extracted by fitting linear and polynomial regression models to the CFD-generated lateral and heave force and moment data. The resulting approximations are illustrated in Fig. 5.13 for lateral force and yawing moment, and Fig. 5.14 for heave force and pitching moment, providing an analytical representation of the hydrodynamic behavior captured by the simulations.

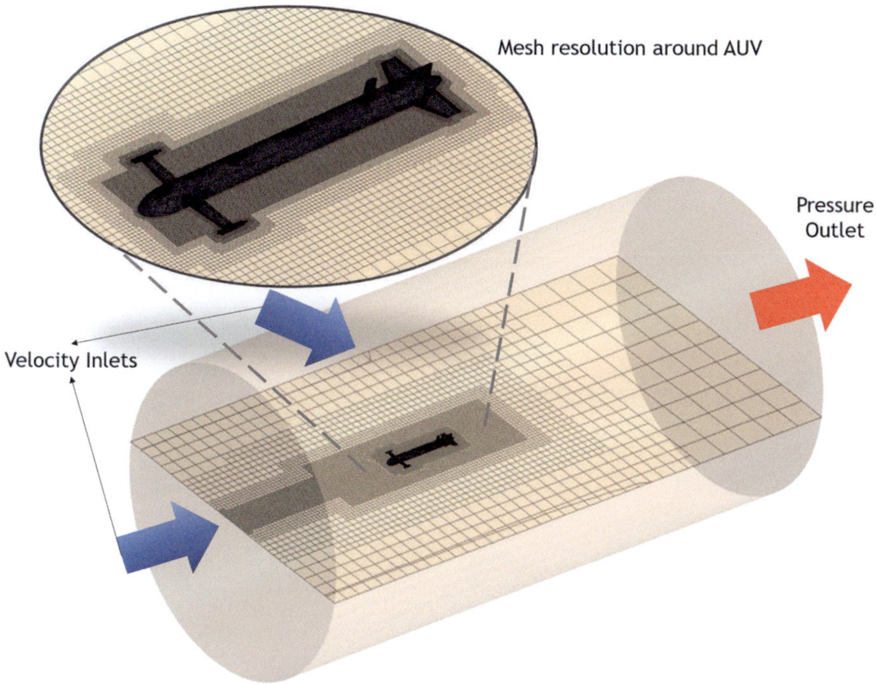


a. Meshed computational domain with 3.0 million (approx.) cells distributed around the AUV

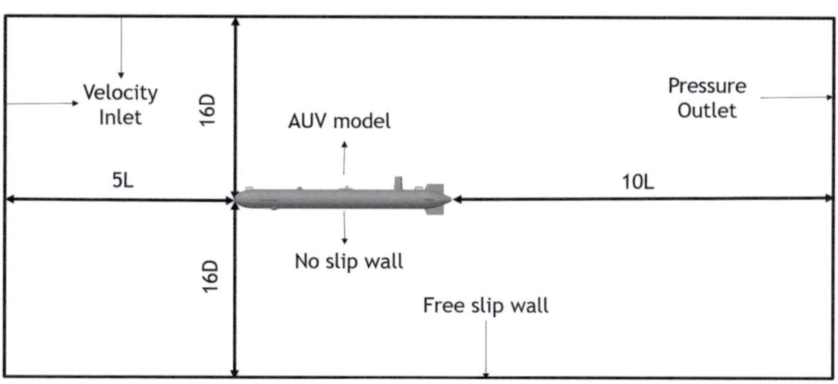


b. Computational domain size relative to AUV with boundary conditions.

**Fig. 5.7** Computational domain [73]

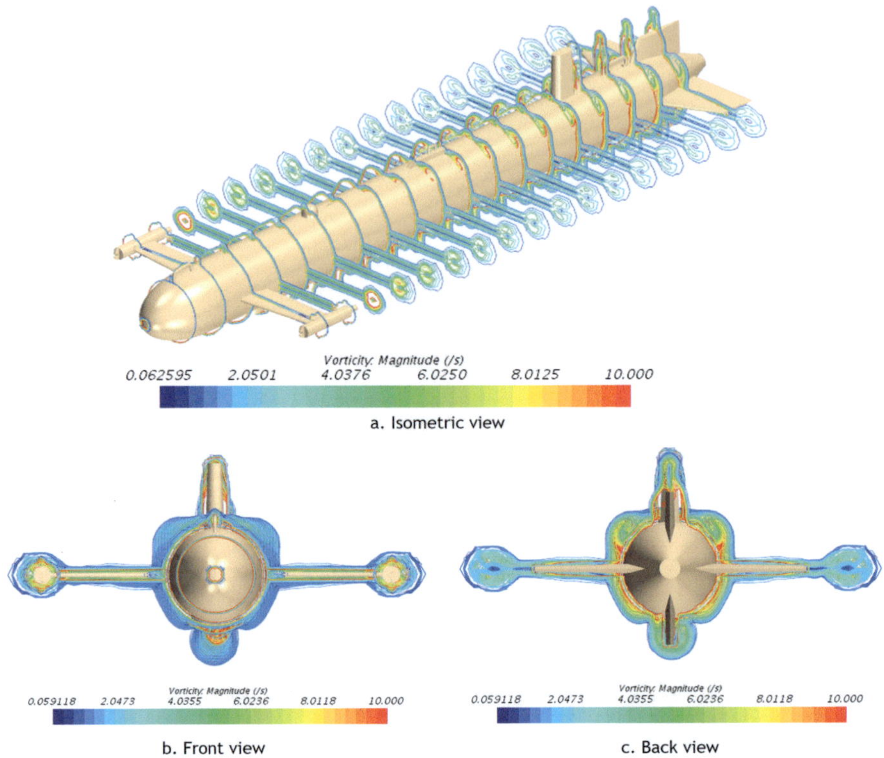


**Fig. 5.8** Vortex Shedding—FSAUV [73]

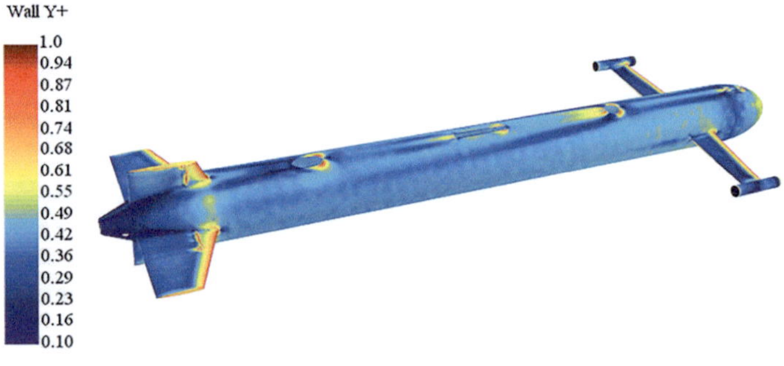


**Fig. 5.9** $y^+$ Distribution over FSAUV [73]

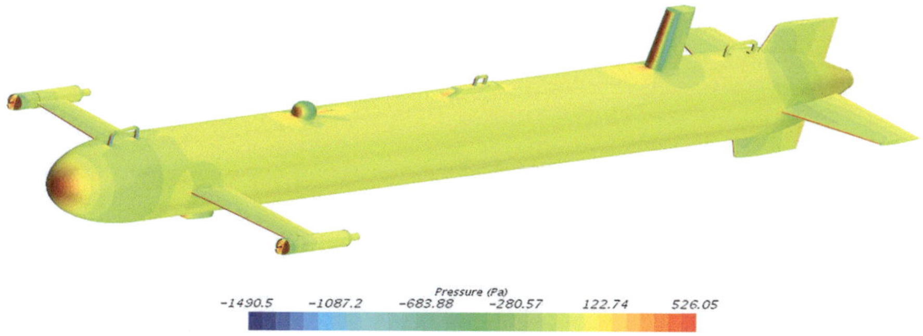


**Fig. 5.10** Pressure distribution on FSAUV surface [73]

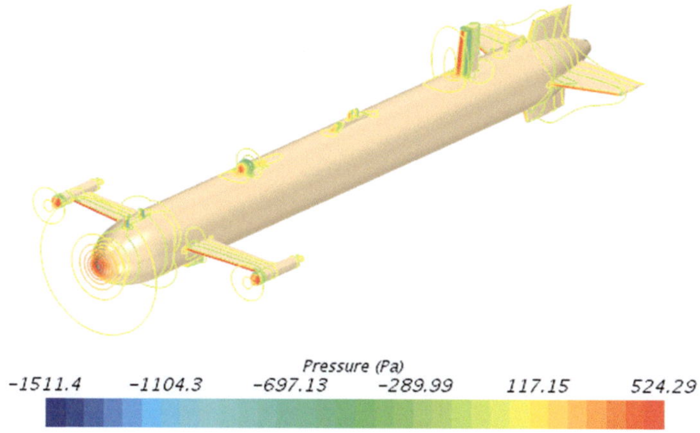


**Fig. 5.11** Pressure contours—visualization of WBI effects [73]

### *5.3.1 Quantitative Analysis of Wing-Body Interference Effects Using ASE and CFD Results*

The lift coefficients listed in Table 4.3 reveal notable differences between values computed with and without accounting for WBI effects. This disparity stems from interference factors, which range approximately from 1.5 to 3.1 (see Table 4.2), exerting a multiplicative influence on the lift coefficients of fins, wings, and other appendages. Due to sign conventions, the overall impact on vehicle behavior is best assessed through maneuvering simulations of the FSAUV.

The lift coefficients estimated via CFD inherently include WBI effects and serve as a benchmark to evaluate the performance of the ASE method, with results presented both excluding ($ASE_A$) and including ($ASE_B$) WBI effects. Table 4.4 summarizes this comparison.

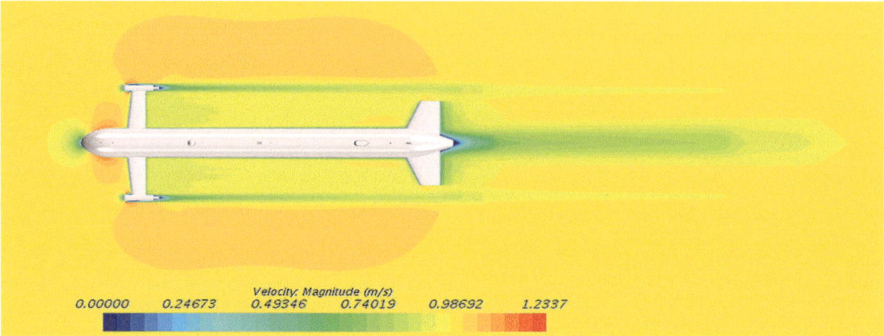


**Fig. 5.12** Velocity contours[73]

**Table 5.8** CFD-Estimated nondimensionalized lift coefficients ($Y'_{uv}$, $N'_{uv}$, $Z'_{uw}$&$M'_{uw}$)[73]

| $Y'_{uv}$ (Fig. 5.13b) | $N'_{uv}$ (Fig. 5.13d) | $Z'_{uw}$ Fig. (5.14b) | $M'_{uw}$ (Fig. 5.14d) |
|---|---|---|---|
| $5.48 \times 10^{-2}$ | $-5.20 \times 10^{-3}$ | $-1.45 \times 10^{-1}$ | $-5.30 \times 10^{-2}$ |

**Table 5.9** Computed lateral hydrodynamic forces and yaw moments from CFD simulations [73]

| Sideslip angle $\beta(°)$ | Radians $\beta$ (rad) | Lateral force $Y$ (N) | Yaw moment $N$ $(N \cdot m)$ | Nondimensional $Y'$ | Nondimensional $N'$ |
|---|---|---|---|---|---|
| 5 | 0.087 | 8.43 | −3.8 | $2.24 \times 10^{-3}$ | $-3.72 \times 10^{-4}$ |
| 10 | 0.175 | 25 | −1.65 | $6.63 \times 10^{-3}$ | $-1.61 \times 10^{-4}$ |
| 15 | 0.262 | 42 | 0.2 | $1.11 \times 10^{-2}$ | $1.96 \times 10^{-5}$ |
| 20 | 0.349 | 63.7 | 3.73 | $1.69 \times 10^{-2}$ | $3.64 \times 10^{-4}$ |
| 25 | 0.436 | 89.5 | 8.37 | $2.37 \times 10^{-2}$ | $8.19 \times 10^{-4}$ |

**Table 5.10** Hydrodynamic heave forces and pitching moments from CFD simulations [73]

| Angle of attack $\alpha(°)$ | Radians $\alpha$ (rad) | Heave force $Z$ (N) | Pitching moment $M(N \cdot m)$ | Nondimensional $Z'$ | Nondimensional $M'$ |
|---|---|---|---|---|---|
| 0 | 0.000 | 1138 | 87.9 | $3.02 \times 10^{-1}$ | $8.60 \times 10^{-3}$ |
| 5 | 0.087 | 1102 | 68.6 | $2.92 \times 10^{-1}$ | $6.71 \times 10^{-3}$ |
| 10 | 0.175 | 1067 | 60.4 | $2.83 \times 10^{-1}$ | $5.91 \times 10^{-3}$ |
| 15 | 0.262 | 1042 | 54.3 | $2.76 \times 10^{-1}$ | $7.27 \times 10^{-3}$ |
| 20 | 0.349 | 1032 | 57.4 | $2.74 \times 10^{-1}$ | $5.61 \times 10^{-3}$ |
| 25 | 0.436 | 1007 | 51.9 | $2.67 \times 10^{-1}$ | $5.08 \times 10^{-3}$ |

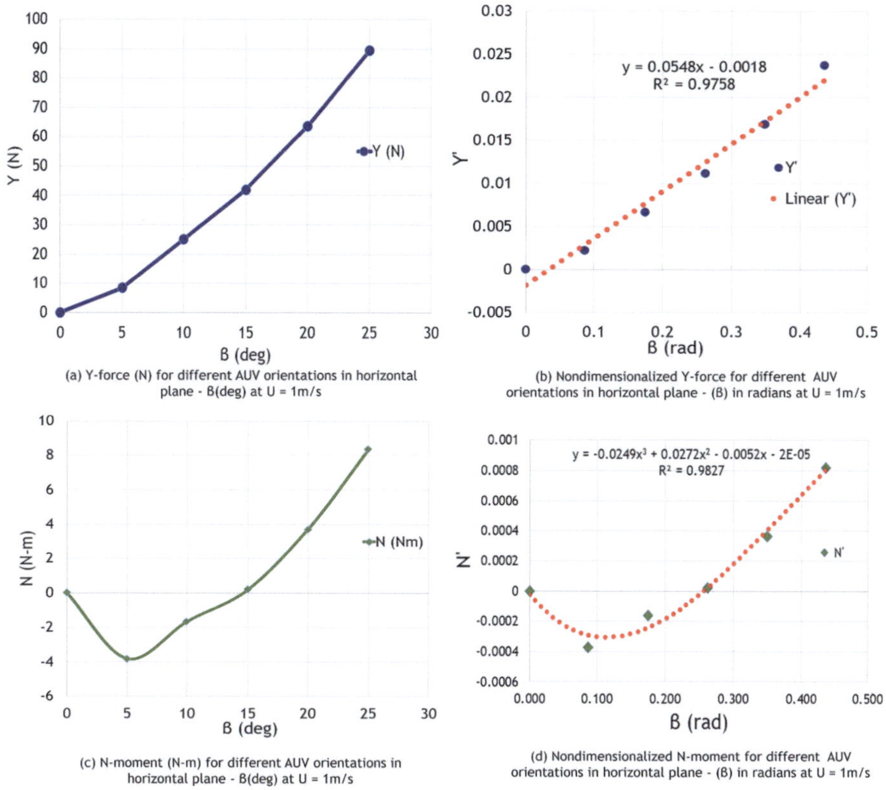


**Fig. 5.13** Y-Force & N-moment curves with linear and polynomial regression fits [73]

For a consistent quantitative analysis, absolute values of the nondimensionalized forces and moments were used to focus on magnitudes rather than directions. This approach ensures the nondimensional coefficients positively represent the force or moment magnitude relative to the chosen reference, independent of their orientation.

Table 5.11 provides a detailed comparison between ASE predictions and CFD reference data. It highlights the absolute differences and relative difference in percentage terms, enabling a clear assessment of the accuracy improvements achieved by including WBI effects within the ASE framework.

The comparison clearly demonstrates that ASE results incorporating wing-body interference effects ($ASE_B$) consistently yield closer agreement with CFD data than those neglecting WBI ($ASE_A$). Relative differences for $ASE_B$ range from 16% to 26%, which are substantially lower than those for $ASE_A$, ranging from 27% up to 62%. This indicates that the inclusion of WBI effects within the component-based ASE method significantly enhances the accuracy of lift coefficient estimation, thereby improving the fidelity of dynamic modeling for the FSAUV.

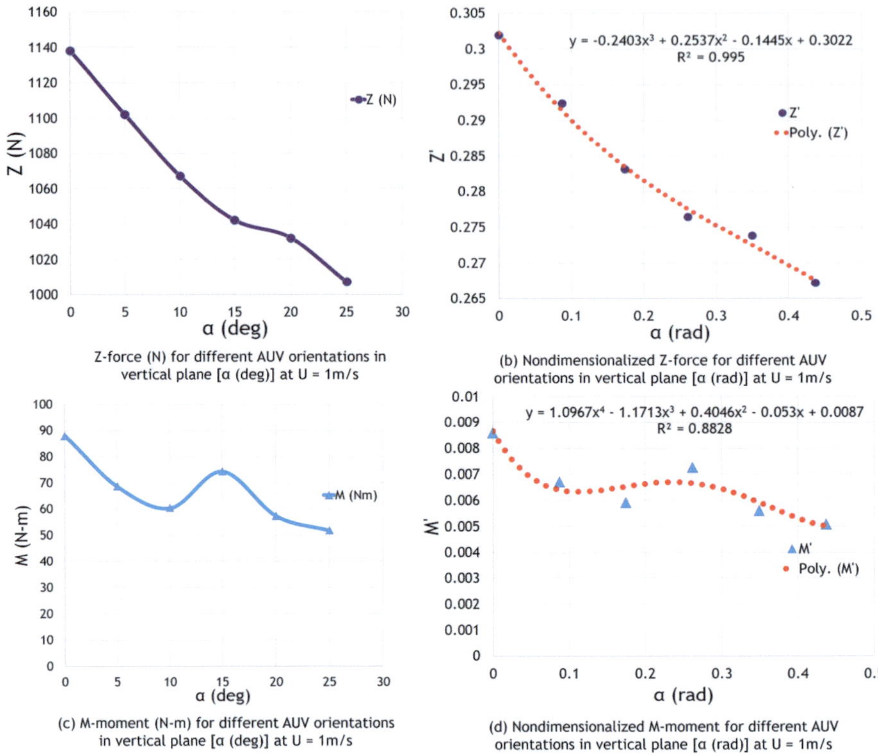


**Fig. 5.14** Z-Force and M-moment curves with polynomial regression fits [73]

**Table 5.11** Comparing ASE and CFD estimated nondimensionalized lift coefficients [73]

| Coefficient | $ASE_A$ $\|X_1\|$ | $ASE_B$ $\|X_2\|$ | CFD $\|X\|$ | Absolute diff. $\|\|X\|-\|X_1\|\|$ | Absolute diff. $\|\|X\|-\|X_2\|\|$ | RD(%) $\frac{\|\|X\|-\|X_1\|\|}{\|X\|}$ | RD (%) $\frac{\|\|X\|-\|X_2\|\|}{\|X\|}$ |
|---|---|---|---|---|---|---|---|
| $Y'_{uv}$ | $-3.33 \times 10^{-2}$ | $6.38 \times 10^{-2}$ | $5.48 \times 10^{-2}$ | $2.15 \times 10^{-2}$ | $9.03 \times 10^{-3}$ | 39% | 16% |
| $N'_{uv}$ | $-7.57 \times 10^{-3}$ | $3.83 \times 10^{-3}$ | $-5.20 \times 10^{-3}$ | $2.37 \times 10^{-3}$ | $1.37 \times 10^{-3}$ | 46% | 26% |
| $Z'_{uw}$ | $-1.05 \times 10^{-1}$ | $-1.68 \times 10^{-1}$ | $-1.45 \times 10^{-1}$ | $3.90 \times 10^{-2}$ | $2.30 \times 10^{-2}$ | 27% | 16% |
| $M'_{uw}$ | $-2.03 \times 10^{-2}$ | $-6.42 \times 10^{-2}$ | $-5.30 \times 10^{-2}$ | $3.2 \times 10^{-2}$ | $1.12 \times 10^{-2}$ | 62% | 21% |

## 5.4 Summary

A detailed CFD analysis aimed at estimating the hydrodynamic coefficients of a novel FSAUV, as a practical example, is provided in this chapter. The analysis focuses on the estimation of cross-flow drag coefficients of FSAUV, specifically $Y_{v|v|}$, $Y_{r|r|}$, $N_{v|v|}$, $N_{r|r|}$, $Z_{w|w|}$, $Z_{q|q|}$, $M_{w|w|}$, and $M_{q|q|}$, with the improved ASE approach validated through CFD simulations using the URANSE solver in Star-CCM+. The drag coefficient $C_{dc}$ was identified as a critical factor in determining the nonlinear drag force and moment coefficients in ASE formulations, significantly influencing the accuracy of the results. A comparative analysis between three different approaches–ASE, experimental, and a hybrid method combining ASE and CFD–highlighted a $C_{dc}$ value of 0.84, based on experimental data, which resulted in a notable 20% improvement in the estimation of sway and heave-induced drag forces and moments compared to previous ASE approaches. Experimental data from the study of 3D flow past a circular cylinder, with an equivalent length-to-diameter ratio and both ends free, further supported the recommended $C_{dc}$ value of 0.84. This value was validated by the comparative analysis between ASE and CFD methods, demonstrating that the improved ASE approach provides superior accuracy over the earlier ASE method, which utilized a $C_{dc}$ value of 1.2. The experimental data served as a benchmark for evaluating cross-flow over a circular cylinder, further highlighting the impact of configuration. Subsequently, CFD analysis has been extended to investigate the wing-body lift interference effects. Based on the CFD computations of flow past FSAUV, lift coefficients $Y_{uv}$, $Z_{uw}$, $N_{uv}$, and $M_{uw}$ are estimated, and fluid flow, vortex shedding, and pressure distribution around the FSAUV are visualized. The CFD simulations were designed to replicate experimental towing tests, calculating the force and moment coefficients $Y$, $N$, $Z$, and $M$ for various side-slip angles ($\beta$) and angles of attack ($\alpha$). The drift angles studied ranged from 0° to 25°, with nondimensionalized lift coefficients $Y'_{uv}$, $Z'_{uw}$, $N'_{uv}$, and $M'_{uw}$ extracted using regression equations. These CFD results were then compared with ASE estimations. The lift coefficients, which accounted for wing-body interference effects in ASE formulations, demonstrated better agreement with the CFD-simulated results. CFD simulated vortex shedding and pressure distribution visualizations provided deeper insights to better comprehend the wing body interactions. The effectiveness of incorporating WBI effect in the ASE formulations have been validated by the consistency between the CFD results and ASE predictions.

## References


1. Hong, L., Wang, X., Zhang, D.S.: Cfd-based hydrodynamic performance investigation of autonomous underwater vehicles: a survey. Ocean Eng. **305**, 117911 (2024)
2. Tyagi, A., Sen, D.: Calculation of transverse hydrodynamic coefficients using computational fluid dynamic approach. Ocean Eng. **33**(5–6), 798–809 (2006)

3. Phillips, A.B., Turnock, S.R., Furlong, M.: Comparisons of cfd simulations and in-service data for the self propelled performance of an autonomous underwater vehicle (2008)
4. Kim, H., Leong, Z.Q., Ranmuthugala, D., Forrest, A.: Cfd modelling and validation of an AUV undergoing variable accelerations. In: The Twenty-fourth International Ocean and Polar Engineering Conference. OnePetro (2014)
5. Huang, H., Zhou, Z., Li, H., Zhou, H., Xu, Y.: The effects of the circulating water tunnel wall and support struts on hydrodynamic coefficients estimation for autonomous underwater vehicles. Int. J. Naval Arch. Ocean Eng. **12**, 1–10 (2020)
6. Min, F., Pan, G., Xu, X.: Modeling of autonomous underwater vehicles with multi-propellers based on maximum likelihood method. J. Marine Sci. Eng. **8**(6), 407 (2020)
7. Javanmard, E., Mansoorzadeh, S., Pishevar, A., Mehr, J.: Determination of drag and lift related coefficients of an AUV using computational and experimental fluid dynamics methods. Int. J. Maritime Eng. **162**(A2) (2020)
8. Le, T.L., Hong, D.T.: Computational fluid dynamics study of the hydrodynamic characteristics of a torpedo-shaped underwater glider. Fluids **6**(7), 252 (2021)
9. Li, G., Zhang, S.: The hydrodynamic coefficient analysis and motion control of the lingyun moveable lander. Geofluids **2021** (2021)
10. Rasekh, M., Mahdi, M.: Combining cfd, ase, and hekf approaches to derive all of the hydrodynamic coefficients of an axisymmetric AUV. Proc. Inst. Mech. Eng. Part M: J. Eng. Maritime Environ. **236**(2), 474–492 (2022)
11. Safari, F., Rafeeyan, M., Danesh, M.: Estimation of hydrodynamic coefficients and simplification of the depth model of an AUV using cfd and sensitivity analysis. Ocean Eng. **263**, 112369 (2022)
12. Panda, J.P., Mitra, A., Warrior, H.V.: A review on the hydrodynamic characteristics of autonomous underwater vehicles. Proc. Inst. Mech. Eng. Part M: J. Eng. Maritime Environ. **235**(1), 15–29 (2021)
13. Lu, D., Lin, W., Duan, J., Sun, T.: Hydrodynamic performance of a water-air trans-media flying submersible vehicle. Ocean Eng. **307**, 118102 (2024)
14. Du, X., Zheng, Z., Guan, S.: Numerical calculation of hydrodynamic interactions of submarine flow on AUV. In: 2018 OCEANS-MTS/IEEE Kobe Techno-Oceans (OTO), pp. 1–5 (2018)
15. Lin, Y.H., Chiu, Y.C.: The estimation of hydrodynamic coefficients of an autonomous underwater vehicle by comparing a dynamic mesh model with a horizontal planar motion mechanism experiment. Ocean Eng. **249**, 110847 (2022)
16. Xu, H., Hong, L., Wang, X., Zhao, M.: Numerical investigation on turbulence models and the hydrodynamics of a UVMs. In: International Conference on Intelligent Robotics and Applications, pp. 299–310. Springer (2022)
17. Bao, H., Zhu, H., Liu, D.: Research on hydrodynamic modeling and simulation of streamlined autonomous underwater vehicle based on cfd method. In: 2023 35th Chinese Control and Decision Conference (CCDC), pp. 4795–4800. IEEE (2023)
18. Perron, A.J.: Maneuvering of slender x-fin AUVs with hydrodynamic derivatives informed through cfd. Ph.D. thesis, Virginia Tech (2023)
19. Zheng, M., Liu, Y., Wang, Y., He, Y.: Simulation and experimental research on hydrodynamic performance of fully attached submarine in the surface and near the surface modes. Ocean Eng. **281**, 114785 (2023)
20. Cooper-Baldock, Z.L., Santos, P.E., Brinkworth, R.S., Sammut, K.: Hydrodynamic analysis of payload bay berthing for underwater vehicles. IEEE J. Oceanic Eng. (2024)
21. Ao, Y., Xu, J., Zhang, D., Li, S.: Artificial intelligence aided design (aiad) of hull form of unmanned underwater vehicles (UUVs) for minimization of energy consumption. J. Comput. Inf. Sci. Eng. **24**(1) (2024)
22. Chen, S., Liu, F.: Multi-objective shape optimization of underwater vehicles based on an adaptive sampling algorithm. Appl. Ocean Res. **146**, 103950 (2024)
23. Huang, X., Dai, Y., Liu, C., Su, Q., Zhu, X.: Water-exit impact of deep-sea mining vehicles: experimental and numerical investigations. Ocean Eng. **302**, 117444 (2024)

24. Menter, F.R.: Two-equation eddy-viscosity turbulence models for engineering applications. AIAA J. **32**(8), 1598–1605 (1994)
25. Javanmard, E., Mansoorzadeh, S.: A computational fluid dynamics investigation on the drag coefficient measurement of an AUV in a towing tank. J. Appl. Fluid Mech. **12**(3), 947–959 (2019)
26. Javanmard, E., Mansoorzadeh, S., Mehr, J.A.: A new cfd method for determination of translational added mass coefficients of an underwater vehicle. Ocean Eng. **215**, 107857 (2020)
27. Zhang, X.G., Zou, Z.J.: Estimation of the hydrodynamic coefficients from captive model test results by using support vector machines. Ocean Eng. **73**, 25–31 (2013)
28. Go, G., Ahn, H.T.: Hydrodynamic derivative determination based on cfd and motion simulation for a tow-fish. Appl. Ocean Res. **82**, 191–209 (2019)
29. Roddy, R.F.: Investigation of the stability and control characteristics of several configurations of the darpa suboff model (dtrc model 5470) from captive-model experiments. Technical report, David Taylor Research Center Bethesda MD Ship Hydromechanics Dept (1990)
30. Qu, Y., Wu, Q., Zhao, X., Huang, B., Fu, X., Wang, G.: Numerical investigation of flow structures around the darpa suboff model. Ocean Eng. **239**, 109866 (2021)
31. Efremov, D., Milanov, E.: Hydrodynamics of darpa suboff submarine at shallowly immersion conditions. TransNav: Int. J. Marine Navig. Safety of Sea Trans. **13**(2) (2019)
32. Shadlaghani, A., Mansoorzadeh, S.: Calculation of linear damping coefficients by numerical simulation of steady state experiments. J. Appl. Fluid Mech. **9**(2), 653–660 (2016)
33. Barth, T.J., Mishra, S., Schwab, C.: Uncertainty quantification in computational fluid dynamics (2013)
34. Dantas, J.L.D., Barros, E.: Numerical analysis of control surface effects on AUV manoeuvrability. Appl. Ocean Res. **42**, 168–181 (2013)
35. Mathelin, L., Hussaini, M.Y., Zang, T.A.: Stochastic approaches to uncertainty quantification in cfd simulations. Numer. Alg. **38**, 209–236 (2005)
36. Hammond, B.M.: Real-time autonomy and maneuvering simulation of an unmanned underwater vehicle near a moving submarine using actively sampled gaussian process surrogate models. Ph.D. thesis, Massachusetts Institute of Technology (2023)
37. Vasudev, K., Sharma, R., Bhattacharyya, S.: A multi-objective optimization design framework integrated with cfd for the design of AUVs. Methods Oceanograp. **10**, 138–165 (2014)
38. Gao, T., Wang, Y., Pang, Y., Cao, J.: Hull shape optimization for autonomous underwater vehicles using cfd. Eng. Appl. Comput. Fluid Mech. **10**(1), 599–607 (2016)
39. Phillips, A., Turnock, S., Furlong, M.: The use of computational fluid dynamics to aid cost-effective hydrodynamic design of autonomous underwater vehicles. Proc. Inst. Mech. Eng. Part M: J. Eng. Maritime Environ. **224**(4), 239–254 (2010)
40. Du, H., Yan, T., Sun, T., Liu, S., He, B., Wei, X.: Study of cfd prediction and surface roughness effect on AUV hull resistance performance. J. Marine Sci. Technol. 1–19 (2024)
41. Liu, M., Song, Y., Yang, S., Yang, M.: Rapid data-driven individualised shape design of AUVs based on cfd and machine learning. Ships Offshore Struct. 1–15 (2024)
42. Watt, G.D.: Estimates for the added mass of a multi-component, deeply submerged vehicle. part 1. theory and program description. Technical report, DEFENCE RESEARCH ESTABLISHMENT ATLANTICDARTMOUTH (NOVA SCOTIA) (1988)
43. Blevins, R.D., Plunkett, R.: Formulas for natural frequency and mode shape. J. Appl. Mech. **47**(2), 461 (1980)
44. Nishimura, N., Yoshida, K., Kobayashi, S.: A fast multipole boundary integral equation method for crack problems in 3d. Eng. Anal. Bound. Elem. **23**(1), 97–105 (1999)
45. Gomez, J., Powert, H.: A multipole direct and indirect bem for 2d cavity flow at low reynolds number. Eng. Anal. Bound. Elem. **19**(1), 17–31 (1997)
46. Lin, Z., Liao, S.: Calculation of added mass coefficients of 3d complicated underwater bodies by fmbem. Commun. Nonlinear Sci. Numer. Simul. **16**(1), 187–194 (2011)
47. Mishra, V., Vengadesan, S.: Translational added mass of axisymmetric underwater vehicles with forward speed using computational fluid dynamics. J. Ship Res. **55**(03), 185–195 (2011)

48. Malik, S.A., Guang, P.: Transient numerical simulations for hydrodynamic derivatives predictions of an axisymmetric submersible vehicle. Res. J. Appl. Sci. Eng. Technol. **5**(21), 5003–5011 (2013)
49. Raza, N., Mehmood, I., Rafiuddin, H., Rafique, M.: Numerical simulation of added mass determination of standard ellipsoids. In: Proceedings of 2012 9th International Bhurban Conference on Applied Sciences and Technology (IBCAST), pp. 270–273. IEEE (2012)
50. Lihua, S.: Calculation of added mass for underwater vehicles based on fvm (2016)
51. Phillips, A., Furlong, M., Turnock, S.R.: The use of computational fluid dynamics to determine the dynamic stability of an autonomous underwater vehicle (2007)
52. Barros, E., Pascoal, A., Sa, E.: Investigation of a method for predicting AUV derivatives. Ocean Eng. **35**(16), 1627–1636 (2008)
53. Zhang, H., Xu, Y.R., Cai, H.P.: Using cfd software to calculate hydrodynamic coefficients. J. Marine Sci. Appl. **9**(2), 149–155 (2010)
54. Huang, H., Bian, X., Jiang, T., Tang, Q., Qin, H., Wang, Z.: Hydrodynamic analysis and manipulation control on a streamlined i-AUV. ISA Trans. (2024)
55. Du, X.X., Wang, H., Hao, C.Z., Li, X.l.: Analysis of hydrodynamic characteristics of unmanned underwater vehicle moving close to the sea bottom. Def. Technol. **10**(1), 76–81 (2014)
56. Ahmed, F., Xiang, X., Zhou, G., Xiang, G., Yang, S.: Dynamic modeling and maneuvering of remus 100 AUV: The impact of added mass coefficients. In: 2023 42nd Chinese Control Conference (CCC), pp. 1424–1429. IEEE (2023)
57. Han, K., Cheng, X., Liu, Z., Huang, C., Chang, H., Yao, J., Tan, K.: Six-dof cfd simulations of underwater vehicle operating underwater turning maneuvers. J. Marine Sci. Eng. **9**(12), 1451 (2021)
58. He, G., Zhang, C., Xie, H., Liu, S.: The numerical simulation of a submarine based on a dynamic mesh method. J. Marine Sci. Eng. **10**(10), 1417 (2022)
59. Fan, S.S., Ci, X.H., Bose, N., Cheng, X.: Structural and operational optimization of a flapping fin used as a self-propulsor for AUV propulsion. China Ocean Eng. **36**(1), 86–99 (2022)
60. Ahmed, F., Xiang, X., Wang, H., Zhang, J., Xiang, G., Yang, S.: Nonlinear dynamics of novel flight-style autonomous underwater vehicle with bow wings, part i: Ase and cfd based estimations of hydrodynamic coefficients, part ii: nonlinear dynamic modeling and experimental validations. Appl. Ocean Res. **141**, 103739 (2023)
61. Hoerner, S.F.: Fluid Dynamic Drag, pp. 16–35. Published by the Author, Midland Park, NJ (1965)
62. Prestero, T.T.J.: Verification of a six-degree of freedom simulation model for the remus autonomous underwater vehicle (2001)
63. Triantafyllou, M.S., Hover, F.S.: Maneuvering and control of marine vehicles. Massachusetts of Institute of Technologyq (2003)
64. Kepler Jr, M.E.: Dynamics of a small autonomous underwater vehicle that tows a large payload. Ph.D. thesis, Virginia Tech (2018)
65. Wieselsberger, C.V.: Neuere feststellungen uber die gesetze des flussigkeits und luftwiderstands. Phys. Z. **22**, 321 (1921)
66. Zhang1a, X.T., Li, Z.Y., Fu, S.X.: Study of the flow around a cylinder from the subcritical to supercritical regimes (2014)
67. Knudsen, J.G., Katz, D.L., Street, R.E.: Fluid dynamics and heat transfer. Phys. Today **12**(3), 40–44 (1959)
68. Heddleson, C., Brown, D., Cliffe, R.: Summary of drag coefficients of various shaped cylinders. Technical report, GENERAL ELECTRIC CO CINCINNATI OH (1957)
69. Potts, D.A., Binns, J.R., Potts, A.E., Marcollo, H.: The effect of aspect ratio on the drag of bare cylinders. In: International Conference on Offshore Mechanics and Arctic Engineering, vol. 58769, p. V001T01A028. American Society of Mechanical Engineers (2019)
70. Veritas, N.: Environmental Conditions and Environmental Loads. Det Norske Veritas Oslo, Norway (2000)

71. Xiang, G., Soares, C.G.: Improved dynamical modelling of freely falling underwater cylinder based on cfd. Ocean Eng. **211**, 107538 (2020)
72. Njaka, T., Miller, L.M., Brizzolara, S., Stilwell, D.J.: Method for improving existing maneuvering models to accommodate large drift angles. In: Global Oceans 2020: Singapore–US Gulf Coast, pp. 1–4. IEEE (2020)
73. Ahmed, F., Xiang, X., Wang, H., Zhang, J., Xiang, G., Yang, S.: Investigating wing-body lift interference effects on the dynamics of a novel flight-style AUV with bow-wings: maneuvering simulations and experimental validations. Ocean Eng. **326**, 120778 (2025)
74. Sname, T.: Nomenclature for treating the motion of a submerged body through a fluid. In: The Society of Naval Architects and Marine Engineers, Technical and Research Bulletin, pp. 1–5 (1950)

# Chapter 6
# Experimental and Data-Driven Approaches for Hydrodynamic Coefficient Estimation

## 6.1 Introduction

The hydrodynamic characterization of AUVs is essential for accurate dynamic modeling and control system design. This chapter explores experimental and data-driven approaches for determining hydrodynamic coefficients, which govern an AUV's maneuvering behavior. Experimental methods, such as captive model tests (CMT) in towing tanks and free-running tests in open water, provide foundational data through standardized procedures like the Planar Motion Mechanism (PMM) and Rotating Arm (RA) setups. Recent advancements, including the Intelligent Towing Tank (ITT) at MIT, integrate artificial intelligence to enhance testing efficiency. Additionally, system identification techniques–both parametric (e.g., Kalman Filters, Support Vector Machines) and non-parametric (e.g., neural networks, Gaussian Processes)–offer data-driven alternatives that capture real-world dynamics more effectively. By reviewing these methodologies, this chapter highlights the evolution of hydrodynamic coefficient estimation, from traditional experimental techniques to modern machine learning-based approaches.

### *6.1.1 Experimental Methods*

To predict the hydrodynamic coefficients of an AUV through experimental methods, researchers typically conduct two types of maneuvering tests: captive model tests (CMT) performed in controlled towing tank environments (Fig. 6.2) [1–4], and free-running model tests carried out in open-water conditions such as lakes or the sea (Fig. 6.1) [5–8]. Historically, hydrodynamic coefficients have been obtained through wind tunnel experiments, towing tank tests, and full-scale captive vehicle testing [9–13].



X. Xiang et al., *Dynamics Modeling and Maneuvering of Autonomous Underwater Vehicles*, https://doi.org/10.1007/978-981-95-1521-9_6

(a) SPARUS-II AUV (b) Flight-Style AUV

**Fig. 6.1** Free running underwater testing of Torpedo-Shaped AUVs [18]

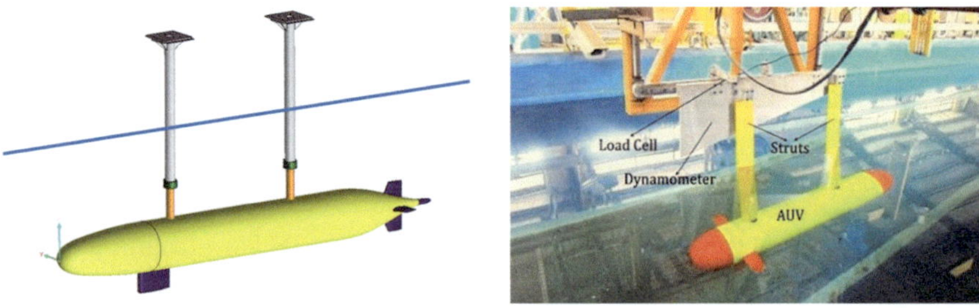


(a) SUBOFF Model with Two Strut Supports (b) AUV in Towing Tank with Strut Supports

**Fig. 6.2** Typical setup for captive model testing of Torpedo-Shaped AUVs [18]

In CMT, measurements are taken for three forces (surge, sway, and heave) and three moments (roll, pitch, and yaw) following the standardized procedures outlined in the "ITTC Recommended Procedures and Guidelines for Captive Model Tests for Underwater Vehicles, 2021" [3], with all measurements referenced to a body-fixed coordinate system as originally defined by Abkowitz [14].

The most common experimental setup for maneuvering tests in towing tanks is the Planar Motion Mechanism (PMM), developed by Gertler [15] to determine hydrodynamic coefficients for submerged bodies. The PMM consists of two oscillators mounted on a towing tank carriage at the bow and stern of the vehicle, generating controlled transverse motions while the AUV moves at a constant speed. By adjusting the phase difference between the oscillators, different motion profiles—such as pure sway, pure yaw, or combined motions—can be produced [16]. These tests are essential for deriving hydrodynamic coefficients related to horizontal plane dynamics (yaw, sway, and rudder deflections) and vertical plane dynamics (heave, pitch, and control surface deflections).

Additionally, the Rotating Arm (RA) setup is employed to evaluate steady-state turning behavior and estimate nonlinear hydrodynamic coefficients in towing tank experiments. Examples of such tests include studies on the DARPA SUBOFF submarine model and torpedo-shaped AUVs, both supported by struts inside the towing tank (Fig. 6.2a, b).

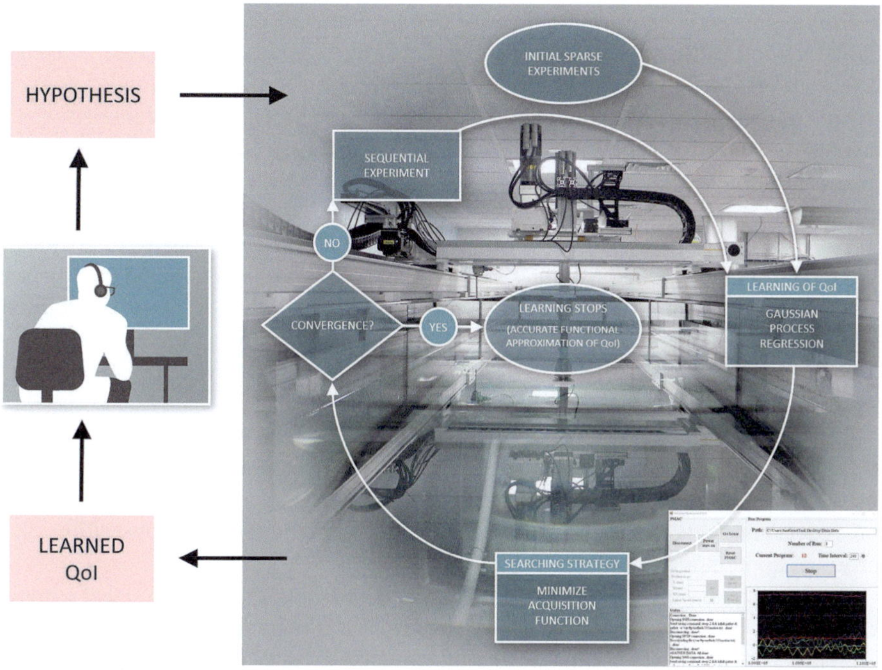


**Fig. 6.3** A novel intelligent towing tank facility at MIT [18]

Recent advancements in experimental hydrodynamics include the development of the Intelligent Towing Tank (ITT) by MIT researchers [17] (Fig. 6.3), an automated facility that leverages active learning and human-computer-robot collaboration to optimize experimental sequences, such as vortex-induced vibration studies. By incorporating artificial intelligence, the ITT accelerates the experimental process and enhances the efficiency of hydrodynamic testing, paving the way for faster scientific discoveries in marine vehicle research. This innovative approach represents a significant step forward in fluid dynamics experimentation, enabling more precise and rapid determination of hydrodynamic coefficients for AUVs.

The experimental characterization of hydrodynamic coefficients for torpedo-shaped AUVs through captive model testing has evolved significantly over several decades, building upon foundational studies while incorporating modern technological advancements. This progression began with the seminal work at the David Taylor Research Center (DTRC), where Roddy's 1990 investigation [19] established comprehensive baseline data through systematic PMM tests on DARPA SUBOFF configurations in their model basin. These pioneering experiments not only revealed the Reynolds number dependence of non-dimensional hydrodynamic coefficients but also created a benchmark dataset that continues to serve as a reference point for subsequent studies [20].

Building directly upon DTRC's methodology, Lin et al. [21] expanded the experimental scope at National Cheng Kung University by examining a half-scale SUBOFF model with and without control surfaces. Their rigorous test program, encompassing oblique towing, pure sway/yaw motions, surge acceleration, and constant drift angle maneuvers, confirmed the robustness of earlier findings while extending validation to more complex motion scenarios. This continuity between studies demonstrates the reproducible nature of well-conducted towing tank experiments.

The experimental paradigm further evolved to address environmental factors, as evidenced by Efremov and Milanov's 2019 work [22] which investigated free surface effects and Froude number dependencies. By focusing on shallow water conditions, their research bridged the gap between ideal towing tank environments and operational scenarios, particularly regarding control surface effectiveness in constrained depths.

This trajectory of experimental research builds upon earlier foundational studies including Sayer's 1996 ROV hydrodynamic characterization [23], Prestero's full-scale REMUS AUV tests at WHOI [12], and Jagadeesh et al.'s 2009 vertical plane force measurements [24]. Each of these contributed methodological innovations that informed contemporary approaches.

Recent years have witnessed a synergistic integration of experimental and computational methods, exemplified by Javanmard and Mansoorzadeh's 2019–2020 studies [1, 2] that systematically compared towing tank results with CFD predictions for drag and lift coefficients. This dual approach has been enhanced by technological advances such as Pozzoli's 2021 dynamic measurement apparatus [25], which improved testing accuracy, and Byun & Lee's 2024 bio-inspired UUV study [26] that applied oblique towing tests to validate numerical models of unconventional hull forms.

The cumulative impact of these interconnected studies demonstrates how captive model testing has progressed from establishing fundamental hydrodynamic principles to supporting cutting-edge AUV development. Each generation of researchers has built upon previous methodologies while introducing innovations that address emerging challenges, maintaining towing tank experiments as an indispensable tool for underwater vehicle development and validation.

### *6.1.2 Procedure for Determining Hydrodynamic Coefficients Following ITTC Guidelines*

The International Towing Tank Conference (ITTC) provides standardized procedures for captive model testing of underwater vehicles [3]. The following methodology outlines the key steps for determining hydrodynamic coefficients:

**Step 1. Test Preparation**

1. **Model Design and Scaling**:
    - Design the scaled model maintaining geometric similarity with the full-scale vehicle
    - Ensure surface roughness satisfies $k_s/L \leq 10^{-5}$ (ITTC 7.5-02-03-01.4)

- Install necessary instrumentation (force transducers, accelerometers, etc.)

2. **Towing Tank Setup**:
   - Calibrate the Planar Motion Mechanism (PMM) system according to ITTC 7.5-02-07-02.1
   - Verify water quality and temperature (maintain within $\pm 1\,^\circ$C during tests)
   - Establish the body-fixed coordinate system per Abkowitz (1964) convention [14]

**Step 2. Test Execution**

1. **Static Tests**:
   - Conduct straight-line towing tests at multiple speeds to determine:

$$X = X_0 + X_{uu}u^2 + X_{vv}v^2 + X_{ww}w^2 \tag{6.1}$$

   - Perform oblique towing tests at various drift angles (typically $-20°$ to $+20°$)

2. **Dynamic Tests Using PMM**:
   - Pure sway tests: Sinusoidal motion with amplitude $y_0$ and frequency $\omega$

$$Y = Y_v v + Y_{\dot{v}}\dot{v} + Y_{|v|v}|v|v \tag{6.2}$$

   - Pure yaw tests: Sinusoidal rotation about z-axis

$$N = N_r r + N_{\dot{r}}\dot{r} + N_{|r|r}|r|r \tag{6.3}$$

   - Combined sway-yaw tests with phase shifts (typically 90°)

3. **Rotating Arm Tests (if applicable)**:
   - Conduct steady circular motions at various radii
   - Measure forces and moments during turns

**Step 3. Data Analysis**

1. **Force/Moment Decomposition**:
   - Separate measured forces into components using Fourier analysis
   - Apply linear regression to determine coefficients

2. **Dimensional Analysis**:

   - Convert to non-dimensional coefficients using:

$$C_Y = \frac{Y}{\frac{1}{2}\rho L^2 U^2}, \quad C_N = \frac{N}{\frac{1}{2}\rho L^3 U^2} \tag{6.4}$$

   where $\rho$ is water density, $L$ is vehicle length, and $U$ is velocity

3. **Uncertainty Analysis**:

   - Calculate uncertainties following ITTC 7.5-02-07-02.5
   - Typical acceptable uncertainty: $\leq 5\%$ for linear coefficients

**Step 4. Validation and Reporting**

1. Compare results with available benchmark data (e.g., DARPA SUBOFF [19])
2. Document all test conditions and parameters per ITTC reporting standards
3. Perform repeatability tests on critical measurements.

This procedure ensures consistent determination of hydrodynamic coefficients across different facilities while maintaining compliance with ITTC recommended practices [3].

## 6.2 Data-Driven and System Identification Techniques

### *6.2.1 Parametric and Non-Parametric Dynamics Modeling*

Traditional dynamic modeling approaches using ASE, CFD, or Captive Model Tests (CMT) often observe limitations to capture real-time environmental variations and the full complexity of marine vehicle dynamics. Alternately, System Identification (SI) techniques have emerged as a powerful alternative, enabling data-driven modeling through free-running tests that inherently account for vehicle appendages and environmental interactions [11, 27]. These methods achieve superior accuracy by directly correlating model outputs with experimental measurements, offering an efficient and scalable solution applicable to both scaled and full-size vehicles. The implementation requires instrumented vehicles capable of executing standard maneuvering patterns, effectively eliminating the need for costly captive test setups while providing more operationally relevant data. SI-based approaches broadly fall into two categories: parametric and non-parametric modeling.

Parametric modeling employs predefined mathematical structures where hydrodynamic coefficients or datasets serve as state variables. The general form of the system's dynamics can be expressed as:

$$\dot{\mathbf{x}} = f(\mathbf{x}, \mathbf{u}, \boldsymbol{\theta}) + \mathbf{w} \tag{6.5}$$

where $\mathbf{x}$ represents the state vector of the AUV, which includes variables such as position, velocity, and orientation; $\mathbf{u}$ denotes the control input, such as thrust or rudder angles; $\boldsymbol{\theta}$ represents the hydrodynamic parameters (e.g., drag, added mass, and lift coefficients) that may vary with environmental conditions; and $\mathbf{w}$ is the process noise, accounting for uncertainties or unmodeled dynamics in the system.

In parametric modeling, traditional implementations utilize Kalman Filters, with the Extended Kalman Filter (EKF) suffering from linearization limitations that the Unscented Kalman Filter (UKF) overcomes through sigma-point sampling [28]. Further refinement comes through the Optimized UKF (OUKF), which demonstrated enhanced precision in identifying dynamics for the NPS AUV-II [29].

Machine learning has significantly advanced parametric approaches, particularly through Support Vector Machines (SVMs) including $\nu$-SVM, $\varepsilon$-SVM, and Support Vector Regression (SVR). These methods robustly estimate coefficients while $\nu$-SVM specifically addresses parameter drift and overfitting [30]. SVR techniques have proven particularly effective when trained on either captive test or free-running maneuver data [31, 32]. Gaussian Processes (GPs) complement these methods by providing probabilistic coefficient estimates that naturally handle measurement uncertainty. While parametric models offer interpretability advantages for control system design, their accuracy remains constrained by the chosen model structure.

Non-parametric or "black-box" modeling circumvents structural limitations by directly mapping input-output relationships without explicit hydrodynamic parameters [33]. Traditional implementations use transfer functions or state-space representations, while modern approaches employ neural networks (NNs)—including Long Short-Term Memory (LSTM) networks and Neural Ordinary Differential Equations (Neural ODEs)—to capture unmodeled nonlinearities and memory effects. Reinforcement Learning (RL) methods enable adaptive control in varying sea states through continuous environmental interaction, while kernel methods like Radial Basis Function (RBF) networks provide effective trajectory prediction [34]. Though non-parametric models excel at handling complex, poorly-understood dynamics, they demand substantial training data and computational resources while offering limited physical interpretability.

The evolving frontier of dynamics modeling combines both paradigms through hybrid approaches that leverage their complementary strengths. Representative examples include using UKF/OUKF for state estimation while employing NNs to learn residual dynamics, or initializing models with SVR-derived coefficients that subsequently adapt via RL. These integrated methods maintain physical interpretability where needed while accommodating unmodeled effects, representing a promising direction for next-generation marine vehicle modeling that balances accuracy, adaptability, and computational efficiency.

## 6.3 Summary

This chapter examines the methodologies for determining hydrodynamic coefficients of AUVs, focusing on experimental and data-driven techniques. Experimental approaches, including CMT using PMM and RA setups, follow ITTC guidelines to measure forces and moments in controlled environments. Recent innovations like the Intelligent Towing Tank demonstrate how AI can optimize hydrodynamic testing. Beyond experiments, system identification techniques such as parametric modeling (EKF, UKF, SVM) and non-parametric modeling (LSTMs, Neural ODEs, GPs)–provide adaptive, data-driven alternatives that account for real-time environmental variations. Hybrid approaches that combine physical models with machine learning are emerging as a robust solution for accurate and efficient hydrodynamic prediction. Together, these methods advance the field by improving the precision and applicability of AUV dynamic modeling for diverse operational scenarios.

## References

1. Javanmard, E., Mansoorzadeh, S., Pishevar, A., Mehr, J.: Determination of drag and lift related coefficients of an AUV using computational and experimental fluid dynamics methods. Int. J. Maritime Eng. **162**(A2) (2020)
2. Javanmard, E., Mansoorzadeh, S.: A computational fluid dynamics investigation on the drag coefficient measurement of an AUV in a towing tank. J. Appl. Fluid Mech. **12**(3), 947–959 (2019)
3. ITTC: Procedures and guidelines-captive model test for underwater vehicles (2021)
4. Mansoorzadeh, S., Javanmard, E.: An investigation of free surface effects on drag and lift coefficients of an autonomous underwater vehicle (AUV) using computational and experimental fluid dynamics methods. J. Fluids Struct. **51**, 161–171 (2014)
5. Cardenas, P., Barros, E.A.: Estimation of AUV hydrodynamic coefficients using analytical and system identification approaches. IEEE J. Oceanic Eng. **45**(4), 1157–1176 (2019)
6. Dantas, J.L., Caetano, W.S., Vale, R.T., Barros, E.A.: Analysis of identification methods applied to free model tests of the Pirajuba AUV. IFAC Proc. Vol. **46**(33), 185–190 (2013)
7. Zhang, J., Xiang, X., Li, W.: Advances in marine intelligent electromagnetic detection system, technology and applications: a review. IEEE Sens. J. 1–15 (2021)
8. Zhang, J., Xiang, X., Zhang, Q., Li, W.: Neural network-based adaptive trajectory tracking control of underactuated AUVs with unknown asymmetrical actuator saturation and unknown dynamics. Ocean Eng. **218**, 108193 (2020)
9. Goheen, K.R.: Modeling methods for underwater robotic vehicle dynamics. J. Robot. Syst. **8**(3), 295–317 (1991)
10. Hopkin, D., Davies, M., Gartshore, I.: The aerodynamics and control of a remotely-piloted underwater towed vehicle. Canadian Aeronaut. Space J. **36**(3), 122–129 (1990)
11. Nahon, M.: A simplified dynamics model for autonomous underwater vehicles. In: IEEE Proceedings of Symposium on Autonomous Underwater Vehicle Technology, pp. 373–379 (1996)
12. Allen, B., Vorus, W.S., Prestero, T.: Propulsion system performance enhancements on Remus AUVs. In: OCEANS 2000 MTS/IEEE Conference and Exhibition. Conference Proceedings (Cat. No. 00CH37158), vol. 3, pp. 1869–1873. IEEE (2000)
13. Hopkin, D., Den Hertog, V.: The hydrodynamic testing and simulation of an autonomous underwater vehicle. In: Proceedings of the Second Canadian Marine Dynamics Conference, pp. 274–281 (1993)

14. Abkowitz, M.: Ship hydrodynamics-steering and manoeuvrability. Hydro-and Aerodynamics Laboratory, Hydrodynamics Section, Lyngby, Denmark, Report No. Hy-5, Lectures (1964)
15. Gertler, M.: The dtmb planar-motion-mechanism system. Technical report, David W Taylor Naval Ship Research and Development Center Bethesda MD DEPT (1967)
16. Phillips, A., Furlong, M., Turnock, S.: Virtual planar motion mechanism tests of the autonomous underwater vehicle autosub (2007)
17. Fan, D., Jodin, G., Consi, T., Bonfiglio, L., Ma, Y., Keyes, L., Karniadakis, G.E., Triantafyllou, M.S.: A robotic intelligent towing tank for learning complex fluid-structure dynamics. Sci. Robot. **4**(36), eaay5063 (2019)
18. Ahmed, F., Xiang, X., Jiang, C., Xiang, G., Yang, S.: Survey on traditional and AI based estimation techniques for hydrodynamic coefficients of autonomous underwater vehicle. Ocean Eng. **268**, 113300 (2023)
19. Roddy, R.F.: Investigation of the stability and control characteristics of several configurations of the darpa suboff model (dtrc model 5470) from captive-model experiments. Technical report, David Taylor Research Center Bethesda MD Ship Hydromechanics Dept (1990)
20. Lin, Y.H., Chiu, Y.C.: The estimation of hydrodynamic coefficients of an autonomous underwater vehicle by comparing a dynamic mesh model with a horizontal planar motion mechanism experiment. Ocean Eng. **249**, 110847 (2022)
21. Lin, Y.H., Tseng, S.H., Chen, Y.H.: The experimental study on maneuvering derivatives of a submerged body suboff by implementing the planar motion mechanism tests. Ocean Eng. **170**, 120–135 (2018)
22. Efremov, D., Milanov, E.: Hydrodynamics of darpa suboff submarine at shallowly immersion conditions. TransNav: Int. J. Marine Navig. Safety of Sea Trans. **13**(2) (2019)
23. Sayer, P.: Hydrodynamic forces on ROVS near the air-sea interface. Ocean. Lit. Rev. **12**(44), 1572 (1997)
24. Jagadeesh, P., Murali, K., Idichandy, V.: Experimental investigation of hydrodynamic force coefficients over AUV hull form. Ocean Eng. **36**(1), 113–118 (2009)
25. Pozzoli, M.: Development of a dynamic measuring apparatus for AUV in towing tank experiments (2021)
26. Byun, S.W., Lee, S.E.: Numerical assessment of the hydrodynamic loads for a manta type unmanned underwater vehicle: oblique towing test. J. Coastal Res. **116**(SI), 598–602 (2024)
27. Ouyang, Z.L., Zou, Z.J.: Nonparametric modeling of ship maneuvering motion based on gaussian process regression optimized by genetic algorithm. Ocean Eng. **238**, 109699 (2021)
28. Julier, S.J., Uhlmann, J.K.: New extension of the kalman filter to nonlinear systems. In: Signal Processing, Sensor Fusion, and Target Recognition VI, vol. 3068, pp. 182–193. Spie (1997)
29. Deng, F., Levi, C., Yin, H., Duan, M.: Identification of an autonomous underwater vehicle hydrodynamic model using three Kalman filters. Ocean Eng. **229**, 108962 (2021)
30. Wang, Z., Zou, Z., Soares, C.G.: Identification of ship manoeuvring motion based on nu-support vector machine. Ocean Eng. **183**, 270–281 (2019)
31. Xu, F., Zou, Z.J., Yin, J.C., Cao, J.: Identification modeling of underwater vehicles' nonlinear dynamics based on support vector machines. Ocean Eng. **67**, 68–76 (2013)
32. Vijay, A., Somayajula, A.: Identification of hydrodynamic coefficients using support vector regression. In: OCEANS 2022-Chennai, pp. 1–7. IEEE (2022)
33. Zhang, X.G., Zou, Z.J.: Black-box modeling of ship manoeuvring motion based on feed-forward neural network with chebyshev orthogonal basis function. J. Marine Sci. Technol. **18**(1), 42–49 (2013)
34. Wang, Z., Xu, H., Xia, L., Zou, Z., Soares, C.G.: Kernel-based support vector regression for nonparametric modeling of ship maneuvering motion. Ocean Eng. **216**, 107994 (2020)

# Chapter 7
# Maneuvering Performance Analysis and Evaluation

## 7.1 Introduction

The hydrodynamic coefficients of an AUV, computed using ASE, CFD, and/or experimental methods, are employed to simulate 3-DOF and 6-DOF AUV maneuvers. To demonstrate the practical application of the developed methodology for hydrodynamic coefficient estimation and nonlinear dynamics modeling of AUVs, maneuvering results for the REMUS 100 and a Flight-Style AUV (FSAUV) are presented.

The added mass estimation methods are validated by analyzing the circular and spiral motion responses of the REMUS 100 AUV, confirming their efficacy for AUV applications. Furthermore, improved ASE methods, for estimating drag coefficients and accounting for wing-body lift interference (WBI) effects, are incorporated into the FSAUV dynamics model. A series of maneuvering simulations, including zigzag pitching, zigzag yawing, circular, and spiral maneuvers, are performed. Additionally, the influence of cross-flow drag coefficients and WBI effects on FSAUV dynamics is investigated to provide detailed practical insights.

The simulated maneuvering results are compared with experimental data, validating the accuracy and robustness of the ASE-based FSAUV dynamics model across its full operational range, including circular, zigzag, and spiral motions. Discrepancies between simulated and experimental results are quantified using error metrics such as absolute error (AE), relative error (RE), mean absolute error (MAE), and root-mean-square error (RMSE), offering a comprehensive validation of the ASE-based SNDM (Simulated Nonlinear Dynamics Model) motion predictive capabilities.



X. Xiang et al., *Dynamics Modeling and Maneuvering of Autonomous Underwater Vehicles*, https://doi.org/10.1007/978-981-95-1521-9_7

## 7.2 Maneuvering Simulations and Experimental Validations

### 7.2.1 Interpreting Maneuvering Results and Error Metrics

#### (1) Zigzag Maneuvering Results: ITTC Protocol and Key Parameters

To accurately interpret the zigzag maneuvering parameters of the marine vehicle, the standardized procedures outlined in the International Towing Tank Conference (ITTC) protocol have been meticulously followed. The zigzag maneuver is a critical test in assessing the dynamic stability and maneuverability of marine vehicles, both in vertical and horizontal planes. These maneuvers involve alternately reversing the control planes by deflecting them to the port and starboard sides, which induces pitching or yawing from the vehicle's initial course. The measured parameters provide important insights into the vessel's response characteristics. Key parameters, as depicted in Fig. 7.1, include the initial turning or pitching time, which indicates how quickly the vessel responds to the control input, and the complete cycle time, representing the duration of one full zigzag maneuver cycle. Additionally, the overshoot pitch and yawing angles are measured to evaluate the extent of the vessel's deviation from its intended course during each maneuver, reflecting the precision and control of the vessel.

As another critical parameter, overshoot time, is recorded to understand the time taken by the vessel to reach the maximum overshoot angle before stabilizing. These measurements are carried out in strict accordance with the ITTC guidelines, ensuring that the results are consistent, reliable, and comparable with international standards. The adherence to the ITTC protocol, as referenced in [1], ensures that the zigzag maneuvering results are not only accurate but also standardized, facilitating a thorough evaluation of the vessel's maneuvering performance.

**(2) Quantitative Error Metrics for Simulated Results: AE, RE, MAE, and RMSE** In order to provide a comprehensive assessment of the accuracy and reliability of the simulated results compared to the experimental data, it is essential to quantify the deviation between these two sets of values. Accordingly, the evaluation is performed using a set of error evaluation metrics: Absolute Error (AE), Relative Error (RE), Mean Absolute Error (MAE), and Root Mean Square Error (RMSE). The

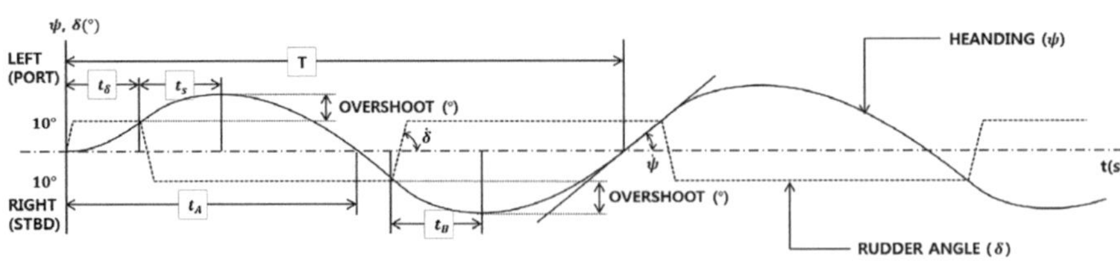


**Fig. 7.1** Zigzag maneuvering parameters (ITTC, 2021)

absolute error metrics represents the direct difference between a simulated value and the corresponding experimental value, offering a straightforward measure of error for individual data points. The relative error metrics further refines the observed variations by expressing the error as a proportion of the actual value, thus providing insight into the error relative to the magnitude of the experimental data.

To evaluate the overall accuracy across the entire dataset, the MAE is calculated, which aggregates the absolute errors across all data points, providing an average error that highlights the general level of discrepancy. Finally, the RMSE offers a more sensitive measure of error by giving greater weight to larger errors, due to its quadratic nature. This metric is particularly useful for identifying situations where larger errors may disproportionately affect the overall performance of the model.

Mathematically, the error metrics are defined in the following Eqs. (7.1), (7.2), (7.3), and (7.4):

$$\mathrm{AE} = |\hat{y}_i - y_i| \tag{7.1}$$

$$\mathrm{RE} = \frac{|\hat{y}_i - y_i|}{|y_i|} \tag{7.2}$$

$$\mathrm{MAE} = \frac{1}{n}\sum_{i=1}^{n} |\hat{y}_i - y_i| \tag{7.3}$$

$$\mathrm{RMSE} = \sqrt{\frac{1}{n}\sum_{i=1}^{n} (\hat{y}_i - y_i)^2} \tag{7.4}$$

where, $n$ is the number of data points in the dataset, $\hat{y}_i$ is the estimated value, and $y_i$ is the actual value which is experimental data in the present study.

### 7.2.2 *Open Water Lake Trials of FSAUV: Free Running Experiments*

The maneuvering performance of an AUV can be evaluated through a series of free-running underwater experiments conducted in an open water in lakes or sea. Accordingly, as a practical example free running experiments of FSAUV conducted in an inland lake (Fig. 7.2) are presented. Series of standard maneuvers were executed, including pure zigzag yawing, pure zigzag pitching, circling, and spiral maneuvers. These maneuvers were performed using predefined data sets to ensure consistency and accuracy. As an illustrative example, the spiral motion maneuver is used to explain the parameters recorded during these experiments, as shown in Fig. 7.3. The total velocity $U$ of the FSAUV recorded during the spiral motion is shown in Fig. 7.3b. The velocity curve provides a comprehensive view of its speed throughout

**Fig. 7.2** Open-loop/Free-running underwater experiments of FSAUV [2]

the maneuver. Further, Fig. 7.3l through q demonstrate the velocity component curves in the $x$, $y$, and $z$ directions, as well as within the inertial reference frame.

The roll, pitch, and heading of the FSAUV were recorded and are shown in Fig. 7.3i–k, respectively. These figures offer insights into the vehicle's orientation changes during the spiral maneuver. The FSAUV's trajectory in the longitude-latitude, $x$-$y$, and $z$ planes is illustrated in Fig. 7.3c–e, respectively. Moreover, the deflections of the stern plane, bow plane, and rudder are shown in Fig. 7.3f through h.

### 7.2.3 REMUS 100 AUV Motion Simulations: Verification of ASE Methodology for Added Mass Coefficients

The AUV's maneuvering performance is significantly influenced due to added mass and variation in these coefficients can affect critical parameters such as vehicle speed, turning radius, turning speed, stability, and energy consumption. To investigate these effects on the REMUS 100 AUV, circle and spiral maneuvers were simulated using the added mass coefficients listed in Table 7.1 and their corresponding cross terms. ASE-1 follows the method outlined by Prestero [3], while ASE-2 is the method treating the hulls, fins and wings separately given in the chapter 4. The comparative analyses of the results in Table 7.1 shows that except the coupled added mass coefficients ($Y_{\dot{r}}=N_{\dot{v}}$ & $M_{\dot{w}}=Z_{\dot{q}}$) and related cross-terms coefficients, both ASE approaches for all the other translational and rotational added mass coefficients are in good agreement. The proposed technique was further validated through AUV maneuvers performing circle maneuvers, descent rates, and 6-DOF spiral motion simulations, as shown in Figs. 7.6, 7.5, and 7.4.

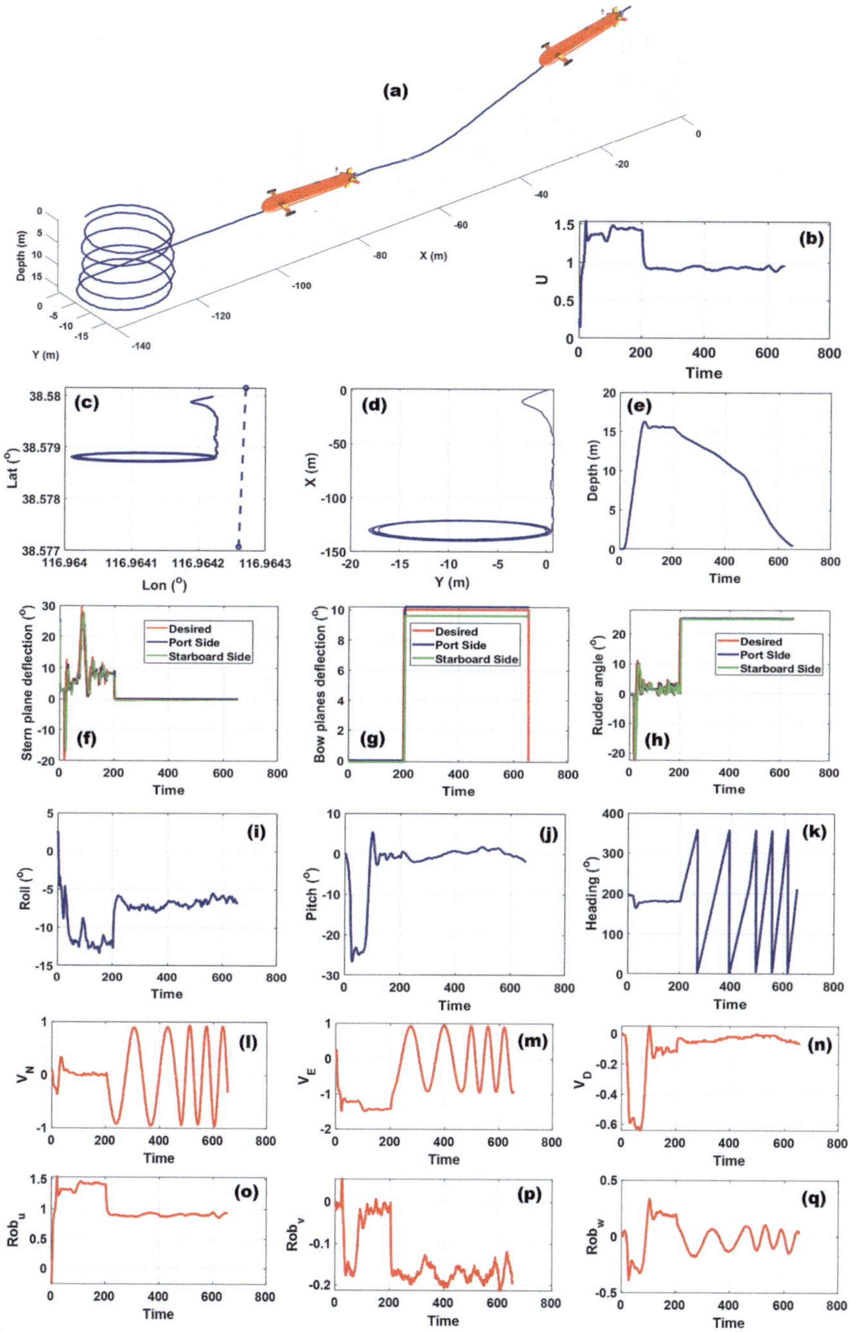


**Fig. 7.3** Spiral motion data—free-running underwater experiments of FSAUV

**Table 7.1** Comparison between two approached: added mass coefficients of REMUS 100 AUV [4]

| Coefficient | Prestero, MIT [3](A) | Present (B) | RE (%) | Unit |
|---|---|---|---|---|
| $X_{\dot{u}}$ $(m_{11})$ | −0.93 | −0.95 | 2.15 | Kg |
| $Y_{\dot{v}}$ $(m_{22})$ | −35.5 | −33.2 | 6.47 | Kg |
| $Z_{\dot{w}}$ $(m_{33})$ | −35.5 | −33.2 | 6.47 | Kg |
| $K_{\dot{p}}$ $(m_{44})$ | −0.0092 | −0.0093 | 1.08 | $\text{Kg} \cdot \text{m}^2/\text{rad}$ |
| $M_{\dot{q}}$ $(m_{55})$ | −4.88 | −3.8 | 22.13% | $\text{Kg} \cdot \text{m}^2/\text{rad}$ |
| $N_{\dot{r}}$ $(m_{66})$ | −4.88 | −3.8 | 22.13% | $\text{Kg} \cdot \text{m}^2/\text{rad}$ |

**Table 7.2** Simulation results for REMUS 100 AUV Maneuvers [4]

| Maneuver type | Fin angle $(\delta_r/\delta_s)$ | Speed (m/s) | $D_1$ (m) | $D_2$ (m) | Δ (m) | Percentage variations (%) |
|---|---|---|---|---|---|---|
| Turning-1 (Fig. 7.6) | −10° | 1.54 | 8.72 | 9.22 | 0.51 | 5.4 |
| Turning-2 (Fig. 7.6) | −5° | 1.03 | 9.73 | 10.4 | 0.67 | 6.4 |
| Turning-3 (Fig. 7.6) | −15° | 1.03 | 8.01 | 8.42 | 0.41 | 4.9 |
| Spiral (Fig. 7.4) | −10°/5° | 0.514 | 8.71 | 9.21 | 0.51 | 5.4 |

For conducting the circular and spiral maneuvering simulations, the input parameters including forward speed and rudder/stern deflection angles are provided in Table 7.2. The subscripts 1 and 2 denote the turning diameters ($D$) corresponding to the previously adopted and the present approach, respectively. The resulting maneuvering performance data are also summarized in Table 7.2.

The quantitative analysis from the simulated data presented in Table 7.2 reveals that the AUV effectively executed the circle and spiral maneuvers with approximately a 5% variation in results between the two approaches. However, the observed minor discrepancy is primarily due to differences in the yaw and sway-related added mass coefficients. As illustrated in Fig. 7.6, the results from both approaches align consistently across all parameters, including $u(t)$, $x(t)$, $y(t)$, and $\psi(t)$. To further validate the influence of added mass coefficients in the vertical plane, simulation results were compared with field experiment data from the REMUS 100 AUV, as shown in Fig. 7.5. The maneuvering results were consistent across linear and angular velocities, accelerations, yaw, and heading rates. Thus, the proposed ASE technique proved to be suitable for estimating the added mass coefficients of AUVs, especially when considering the distinct geometries of the hull and control fins as in the case of novel FSAUV.

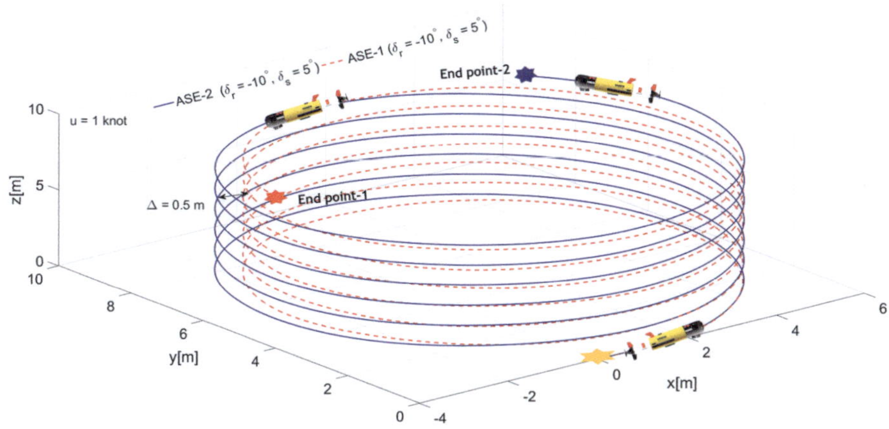


**Fig. 7.4** Simulated spiral motion of REMUS 100 AUV [4]

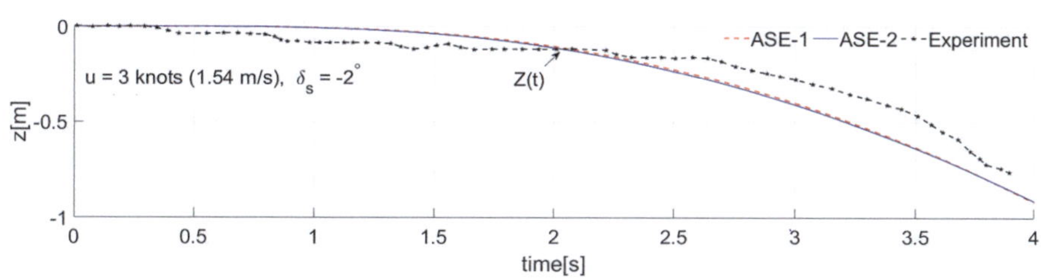


**Fig. 7.5** Depth rate change of REMUS 100 AUV maneuver: simulation and experiment comparison [4]

## *7.2.4 ASE Based FSAUV Dynamics and Experimental Validations*

To comprehensively evaluate the performance of the ASE-based simplified nonlinear dynamic model, a series of simulated maneuvers were conducted for the FSAUV. These simulations encompassed dynamic responses in both the horizontal and vertical planes, including zigzag yaw, zigzag pitch, circular, and spiral trajectories. Each maneuver was configured by setting specific input parameters such as control fin deflections, desired heading or pitch angles, and forward speed. By systematically varying these parameters, a wide range of maneuvering scenarios were replicated to assess the model's fidelity. The simulation outcomes, along with the corresponding maneuvering inputs, are summarized in Table 7.3.

**(1) Zigzag Pitching Maneuvers–1: (3-DOF Motion)**

Figure 7.7 illustrates the comparison between simulated and experimental results for zigzag pitch maneuvers, performed with an input stern angle of $\pm 10°$ at a forward speed of 3.0 knots (1.54 m/s). A quantitative comparison of key output parameters–

**Fig. 7.6** Simulated circle maneuvers of REMUS 100 AUV [4]

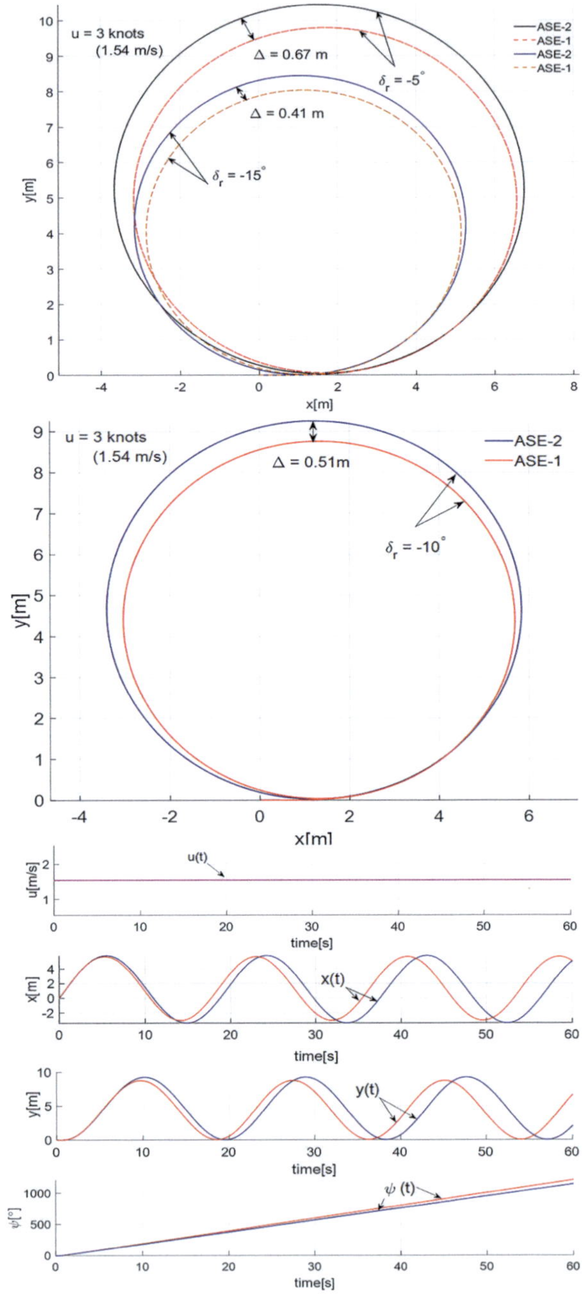

**Table 7.3** ASE Based FSAUV dynamics: simulations versus experimental results [5]

| Maneuver type | Parameters | SIM (S) | EXP (E) | AE $\|S-E\|$ | RE $\frac{\|S-E\|}{\|E\|} \times 100$ |
|---|---|---|---|---|---|
| | Zigzag yawing (Inputs: $\boldsymbol{\delta_r = \pm 20°, u \approx 2.6}$ knots)—(Fig. 7.8) | | | | |
| | Time of a complete cycle (T) | 24.3 s | 23.98 s | 0.32 s | 1.33 % |
| | Initial turning time ($t_i$) | 5.2 s | 5.1 s | 0.1 s | 2.0 % |
| | First overshoot angle ($\psi_{ov_1}$) | −7.5° | −12.7° | 5.2° | 41 % |
| | Time of first overshoot ($t_{ov_1}$) | 2.4 s | 2.3 s | 0.1 s | 4.35 % |
| | Second overshoot angle ($\psi_{ov_2}$) | 9.3° | 20.7° | 11.4° | 55 % |
| | Time of second overshoot ($t_{ov_2}$) | 3.1 s | 3.0 s | 0.1 s | 3.33 % |
| | Third overshoot angle ($\psi_{ov_3}$) | −9.5° | −13° | 3.5° | 27 % |
| | Fourth overshoot angle ($\psi_{ov_4}$) | 9.3° | 13° | 3.7° | 28.5 % |
| | Fifth overshoot angle ($\psi_{ov_5}$) | −9.5° | −10.8° | 1.3° | 12 % |
| | Sixth overshoot angle ($\psi_{ov_6}$) | 9.3° | 10.4° | 1.1° | 10.6 % |
| | Seventh overshoot angle ($\psi_{ov_7}$) | −9.5° | −13.5° | 4° | 29 % |
| | Eighth overshoot angle ($\psi_{ov_8}$) | 9.3° | 12.3° | 3° | 24.4 % |
| | RMSE ($\psi_{ov}$) = 5.13° | | | | |
| | RMSE ($\psi_{ov}$) excluding ($\psi_{ov_1}$ & $\psi_{ov_2}$) = 3.0° | | | | |
| | Zigzag pitching (Inputs: $\boldsymbol{\delta_s = \pm 10°}$, u ≈ 3 knots)—(Fig. 7.7) | | | | |
| | Time of a complete cycle (T) | 28.3 s | 28 s | 0.3 s | 1.1% |
| | Initial pitching time ($t_i$) | 10.9 s | 11 s | 0.1 s | 0.9% |

(continued)

**Table 7.3** (continued)

| Maneuver type | Parameters | SIM (S) | EXP (E) | AE $\|S - E\|$ | RE $\frac{\|S-E\|}{\|E\|} \times 100$ |
|---|---|---|---|---|---|
| | First overshoot angle ($\theta_{ov_1}$) | 0.7° | 5.9° | 5.19° | 88% |
| | Time of first overshoot ($t_{ov_1}$) | 1.5 s | 2.5 s | 1.0 s | 40% |
| | Second overshoot angle ($\theta_{ov_2}$) | −3.53° | −6.1° | 2.57° | 42.13% |
| | Time of second overshoot ($t_{ov_2}$) | 3.0 s | 3.1 s | 0.1 s | 3.23% |
| | Third overshoot angle ($\theta_{ov_3}$) | 4.35° | 5.9° | 1.55° | 26.3% |
| | Fourth overshoot angle ($\theta_{ov_4}$) | −4.48° | −6.2° | 1.72° | 27.74% |
| | Fifth overshoot angle ($\theta_{ov_5}$) | 4.5° | 5.9° | 1.4° | 23.73% |
| | Sixth overshoot angle ($\theta_{ov_6}$) | −4.52° | −6.3° | 1.78° | 28.25% |
| | RMSE ($\theta_{ov}$) = 2.71° | | | | |
| | RMSE ($\theta_{ov}$) excluding ($\theta_{ov_1}$ & $\theta_{ov_2}$) = 1.62° | | | | |
| | Circle maneuver–1 (Inputs: $\boldsymbol{\delta_s = 25°, u \approx 2.4}$ knots (1.3 m/s))—(Fig. 7.9) | | | | |
| | Circle diameter | $D_s$ = 17.75 m | $D_{e(\text{avg.})}$ = 18.02 m | 0.27 m | 1.5% |
| | Spiral maneuver–1 (Inputs: $\boldsymbol{\delta_r = 25°, \delta_s = 0°, \delta_b = 10°}$ **&** $\boldsymbol{u \approx 2}$ knots)—(Fig. 7.11) | | | | |
| | Pitch | 3.0 m | 2.8 m (avg.) | 0.2 m | 7.14% |
| | Circle diameter | 17.7 m | 18.1 m (avg.) | 0.4 m | 2.21% |
| | Rate of ascent | 0.053 m/s | 0.037 m/s | 0.016 m/s | 43.24% |
| | Spiral maneuver–2 (Inputs: $\boldsymbol{\delta_r = 25°, \delta_s = 10°, \delta_b = 0°}$ **&** $\boldsymbol{u \approx 2}$ knots)—(Fig. 7.12) | | | | |
| | Pitch | 3.2 m | 3.5 m | 0.3 m | 8.57% |
| | Circle Diameter | 16.9 m | 17.93 m | 1.03 m | 5.74% |
| | Rate of Ascent | 0.05 m/s | 0.0375 m/s | 0.0125 m/s | 33.33% |
| | Spiral maneuver–3 (Inputs: $\boldsymbol{\delta_r = 25°, \delta_s = 5°, \delta_b = 5°}$ **&** $\boldsymbol{u \approx 2}$ knots)—(Fig. 7.13) | | | | |
| | Pitch | 3.3 m | 4.75 m (avg.) | 1.45 m | 30.53 % |
| | Circle diameter | 16.9 m | 19.5 m (avg.) | 2.6 m | 13.33% |
| | Rate of ascent | 0.06 m/s | 0.058 m/s | 0.002 m/s | 3.45% |

including initial turning time ($t_i$), pitching cycle time ($T$), overshoot angles ($\theta_{ov}$), and the corresponding overshoot times ($t_{ov}$)–is provided in Table 7.7.

Unlike the zigzag yaw maneuvers, which were performed in deeper water, the pitch maneuvers were conducted closer to the surface due to safety considerations. As observed in zigzag yawing tests, notable discrepancies are found between the simulated and experimental results, particularly for the first and second pitch overshoot

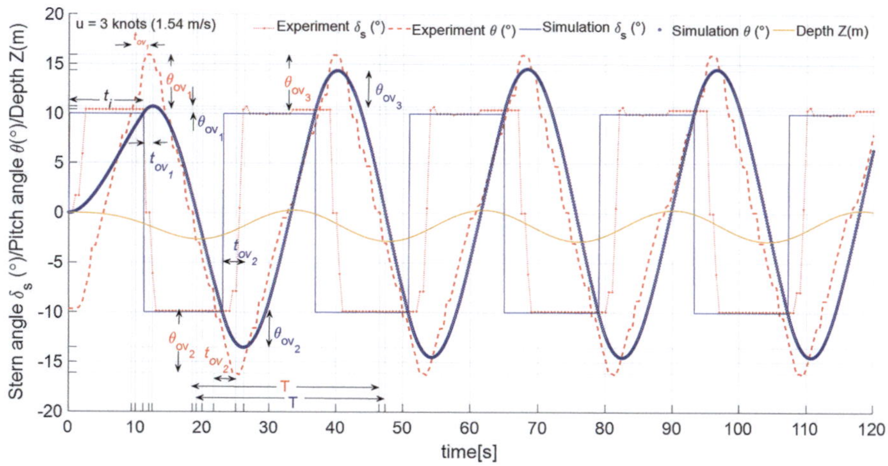


**Fig. 7.7** Zigzag pitching Maneuver–1 [5]

angles ($\theta_{ov_1}$ and $\theta_{ov_2}$). However, the variation is significantly reduced to approximately 26% from the third pitching cycle onward.

RMSE analysis was carried out for the first three pitching cycles, comprising six overshoot data points. The initial RMSE was computed as 2.7°, indicating a noticeable deviation between simulation and experiment. Upon excluding the first two overshoot values–identified as outliers–from the dataset, the RMSE reduced to 1.62°, suggesting a substantial improvement in the agreement between the two sets of results, as visually supported by Fig. 7.7.

Therefore, it can be inferred that the initial overshoot responses were largely responsible for the observed discrepancies. Furthermore, delays in switching the stern angle from positive to negative (and vice versa) during physical testing were observed. These delays, likely caused by actuator lag and/or environmental resistances such as hydrodynamic disturbances, contributed to higher overshoot angles in the experimental data.

Overall, the FSAUV exhibited consistent and stable behavior during zigzag pitch maneuvers in both simulation and underwater experiments, as illustrated in Fig. 7.7. The simulation results demonstrated reasonable accuracy, with a variation of 1.62° for an average pitch angle of approximately 15.2°, corresponding to a discrepancy of nearly 10% between the simulated and experimental outcomes.

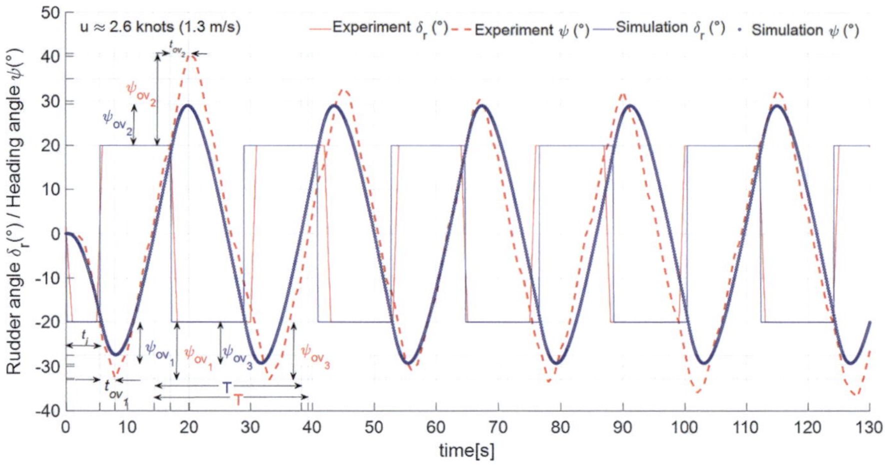


**Fig. 7.8** Zigzag yawing Maneuver–1 [5]

### (2) Zigzag Yawing Maneuvers–1: (3-DOF Motion)

Figure 7.8 illustrates the simulated and experimental zigzag yaw maneuvers conducted with an input rudder angle of $\pm 20°$ at a forward speed of 2.6 knots (1.3 m/s). To mitigate surface influence, these maneuvers were executed at an approximate depth of 5 meters. The comparative results, including the initial turning time ($t_i$), yawing cycle time ($T$), and overshoot angles ($\psi_{ov}$), are presented in Table 7.3.

The yaw response profiles in Fig. 7.8 demonstrate that the FSAUV maintains a stable and repeatable heading variation in both the simulated and underwater test environments. While notable deviations were observed between the simulated and experimental data for the first two overshoot angles, further analysis was carried out to assess the subsequent yaw cycles. An RMSE analysis was performed over the first four yaw cycles, encompassing eight overshoot data points, yielding an RMSE of 5.13°. Upon identifying the first two overshoot values as statistical outliers due to their relatively larger deviations, they were excluded from the analysis. This refinement led to a substantial reduction in the RMSE to approximately 3.0°. The improved agreement between the simulation and experimental results is also evident from Fig. 7.8.

Overall, the simulation results displayed a high degree of accuracy, with a deviation of 3° for an average heading change of approximately 33°, resulting in an estimated discrepancy of around 9% between the simulation and experimental outcomes. This level of variation is acceptable and can be attributed to underwater current effects, measurement sensor limitations, and model-based simplifications.

### (3) Circle Maneuver–1

The simulated results for the circular maneuver, conducted at an input rudder angle ($\delta_r$) of 25° and a speed of 2.4 knots (1.3 m/s), were compared with the experimental

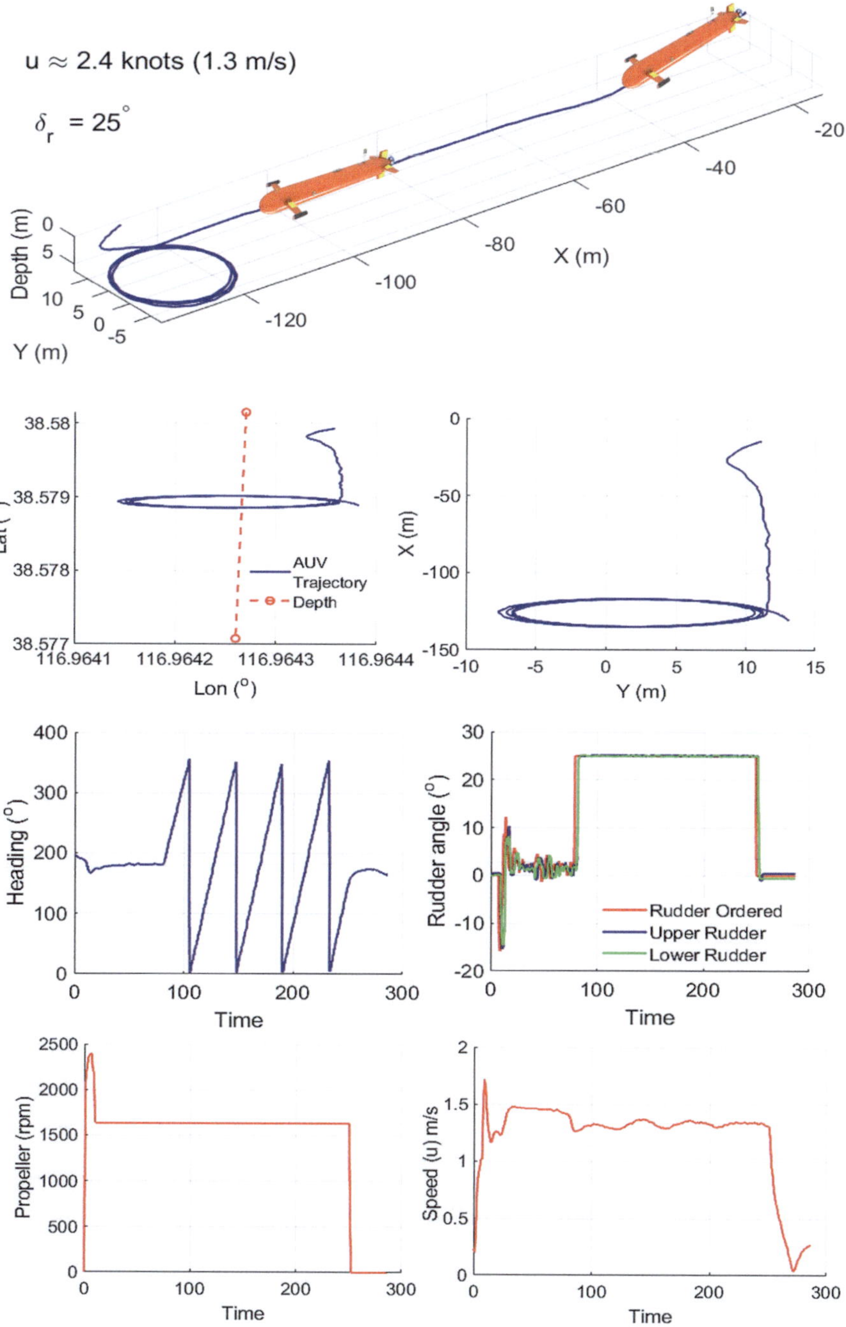


**Fig. 7.9** Experimental results of circle Maneuver–1 [5]

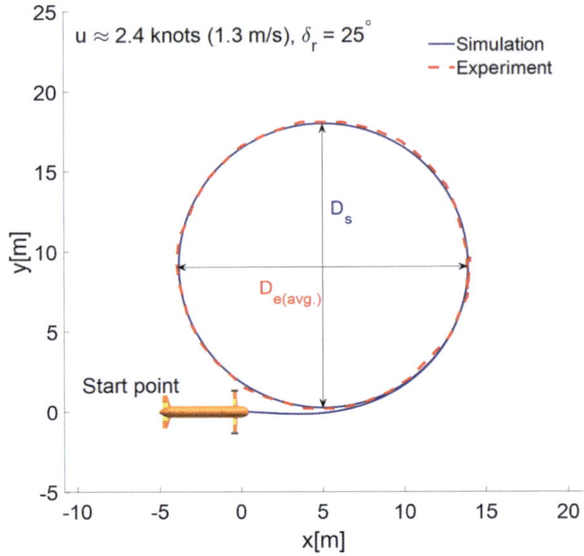


**Fig. 7.10** Comparison of simulated and experimental results of circle Maneuver–1 [5]

data obtained at an operational depth of approximately 5 meters to minimize surface-related disturbances, as illustrated in Fig. 7.9. The comparison of the FSAUV's circular trajectories from simulation and underwater trials is shown in Fig. 7.10, revealing a close match between the simulation and experimental results.

The circle diameters attained in both the simulation and the free-running underwater experiments are provided in Table 7.10. The relative difference between the results is estimated to be around 1.5%, which is considered negligible. This minor discrepancy can be attributed to environmental disturbances during underwater testing or potential inaccuracies in sensor measurements.

### (4) Spiral Maneuvers: (6-DOF Motion)

The spiral maneuver represents one of the most complex and challenging trajectories for AUVs, owing to the nonlinear and coupled dynamics exhibited across all six degrees of freedom (6-DOF). These dynamics involve intricate interactions between translational and rotational motions, as well as coupling effects between different motion axes, thereby necessitating advanced modeling strategies. Furthermore, the unpredictable nature of the underwater environment–characterized by currents, turbulence, and density gradients–adds to the difficulty of achieving accurate motion predictions and requires the deployment of sophisticated computational techniques.

To rigorously evaluate the capability of the ASE-based nonlinear dynamic model in capturing the full 6-DOF behavior of the FSAUV, a series of spiral maneuvers were simulated and subsequently validated against experimental results from underwater free-running tests. Each spiral maneuver was executed at a fixed rudder angle of $\delta_r = 25°$ and a constant speed of approximately 2 knots. The maneuvers were differentiated

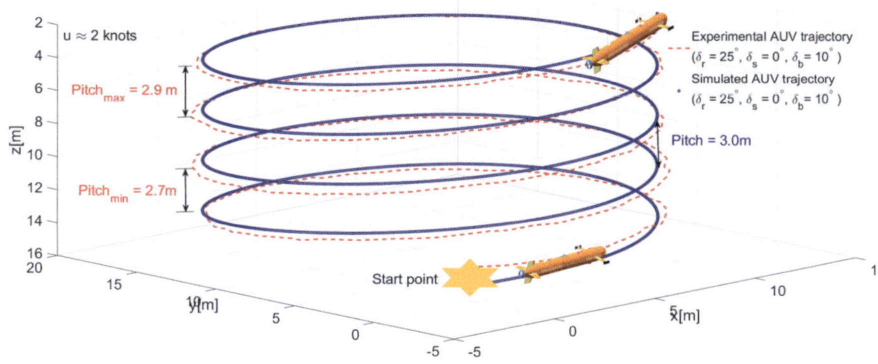


**Fig. 7.11** Spiral Maneuver–1 [5]

based on varying configurations of the stern and bow control surface angles, and the comparative results are detailed as follows:

- **Spiral Maneuver–1 (Fig.** 7.11): The bow fin angle ($\delta_b$) was set to 10° while the stern fin angle ($\delta_s$) remained at 0°. The pitch angle and circle diameter showed deviations of 6.7 and 2.2%, respectively, between simulation and experiment. However, the simulated ascending rate was observed to be approximately 30% higher than the experimental value.
- **Spiral Maneuver–2 (Fig.** 7.12): In this case, $\delta_s = 10°$ and $\delta_b = 0°$. The pitch angle and circle diameter exhibited discrepancies of 8.5 and 5.7%, respectively. Similar to Maneuver–1, the ascending rate showed a notable difference, with the simulated value being 25% higher than that observed experimentally.
- **Spiral Maneuver–3 (Fig.** 7.13): Both stern and bow fins were deflected at 5° each. The variations in pitch, circle diameter, and ascending rate were 30, 13.3, and 3.3%, respectively. Contrary to the previous two maneuvers, the experimental data showed higher pitch and ascending rates, possibly due to the cumulative lift generated by the simultaneous deflection of both control surfaces.

Overall, the comparative analysis between simulated and experimental trajectories indicates a strong correlation, affirming the suitability of the ASE-based 6-DOF nonlinear dynamic model for trajectory prediction and its potential application in model-based control strategies, particularly for missions such as underwater cable tracking. The observed discrepancies–particularly in ascending rate and pitch–may be attributed to external environmental disturbances (e.g., unmodeled hydrodynamic effects, underwater currents, or wave-induced motions), as well as potential simplifications or parameter uncertainties in the dynamic model.

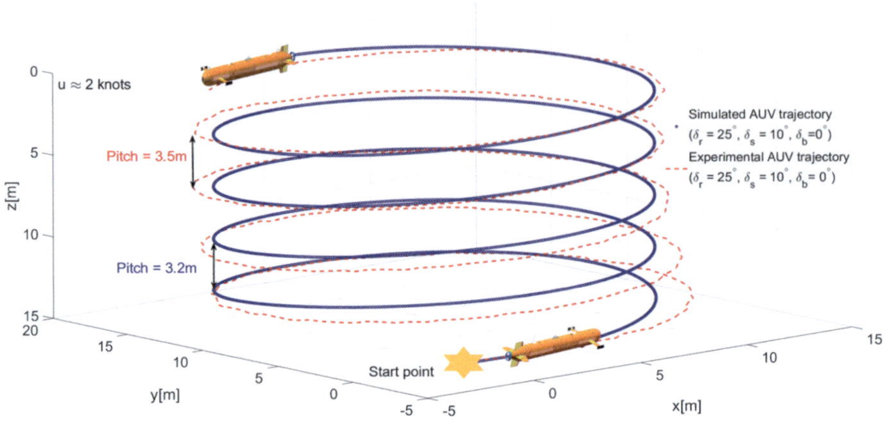


**Fig. 7.12** Spiral Maneuver–2 [5]

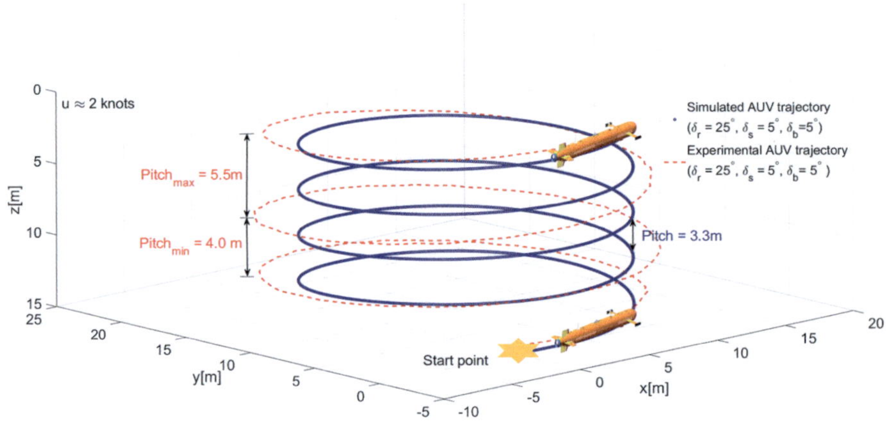


**Fig. 7.13** Spiral Maneuver–3 [5]

## 7.3 Improved ASE Method: Experimental Validation

To validate the effectiveness of the proposed improved ASE technique in modeling the 6-DOF dynamics of the FSAUV, a set of three maneuvering simulations–denoted as Cases A, B, and C–were conducted. These simulations differ solely in the set of nonlinear cross-flow drag coefficients used: $ASE_1$ (Case A), $ASE_2$ (Case B), and CFD-enhanced ASE (Case C). The specific values of the drag-related coefficients ($Y_{v|v|}$, $Z_{w|w|}$, $M_{w|w|}$, $N_{v|v|}$, $Y_{r|r|}$, $Z_{q|q|}$, $M_{q|q|}$, and $N_{r|r|}$) employed in each case were estimated in earlier chapters and are provided in Table 5.5.

All other hydrodynamic coefficients, including those related to added mass, lift forces, and moments (as listed in Table 4.5), were kept constant across the simulations to isolate the influence of the drag coefficients. By varying only the nonlinear

**Table 7.4** Improved ASE method: simulations versus experimental results [5]

| Maneuver Type | Parameters | EXP (E) | SIM (A) | SIM (B) | SIM (C) | $RE_A(\%)$ $\frac{\|A-E\|}{\|E\|}$ | $RE_B(\%)$ $\frac{\|B-E\|}{\|E\|}$ | $RE_C(\%)$ $\frac{\|C-E\|}{\|E\|}$ |
|---|---|---|---|---|---|---|---|---|
| | Zigzag pitching (Inputs: $\boldsymbol{\delta_s = \pm 10^\circ, u \approx 3}$ knots)—(Fig. 7.14) | | | | | | | |
| | Pitching angle ($\theta_{\text{avg.}}$) | 16° | 13.7° | 14.5° | 14.9° | 14.5% | 9.5% | 6.8% |
| | Zigzag yawing (Inputs: $\boldsymbol{\delta_r = \pm 20^\circ, u \approx 2.6}$ knots)—(Fig. 7.15) | | | | | | | |
| | Cycle time $T_{\text{avg.}}$ | 23.98 s | 24.5 s | 24.3 s | 24.26 s | 2.1% | 1.33% | 1.16% |
| | Heading angle ($\psi_{\text{avg.}}$) | 33.5° | 28.46° | 28.9° | 29.3° | 15% | 13.7% | 12.5% |
| | Circle maneuver (Inputs: $\boldsymbol{\delta_s = 25^\circ, u \approx 2.4}$ knots (1.3 m/s)—(Fig. 7.18) | | | | | | | |
| | Circle diameter | 18.02 m | 18.53 m | 17.75 m | 17.36 m | 2.83% | 1.5% | 3.7% |

damping terms, the simulation study enables an in-depth evaluation of the sensitivity of the FSAUV's dynamic behavior to cross-flow drag effects and the improvements achieved using the enhanced ASE methodology.

The motion responses of the FSAUV under zigzag yawing, zigzag pitching, circle, and spiral maneuvers were simulated for each coefficient set and benchmarked against corresponding free-running underwater experimental data. A quantitative comparison of the simulated results with the experimental trajectories is summarized in Table 7.4, highlighting the relative accuracy of each estimation approach in capturing the real-world dynamic behavior of the vehicle.

### *7.3.1 Zigzag Pitching Maneuver–2*

The analysis of zigzag pitching maneuvers confirms the reliability of the improved ASE methodology in accurately estimating nonlinear drag coefficients relevant to the vertical plane dynamics of the FSAUV. This evaluation highlights the critical role of cross-flow drag forces and associated moment coefficients in governing pitch motion characteristics. The maneuvering outcomes, presented in Table 7.4 and illustrated in Fig. 7.14, reveal that a reduction in the cross-flow drag coefficient ($C_{d_c}$) significantly enhances the correlation between simulated and experimental results.

Specifically, for a higher estimated value of $C_{d_c}^{2D} = 1.2$, the simulated average pitch angle ($\theta_{\text{avg.}}$) is computed as 13.7°, noticeably lower than the experimentally observed 16°, corresponding to a relative deviation of approximately 14.5%. However, for reduced coefficients of $C_{d_c}^{3D} = 0.84$ and 0.69, the simulated average pitch angles improve to 14.5° and 14.9°, respectively, indicating much closer alignment with the empirical data.

These observations highlights the substantial sensitivity of pitch dynamics to variations in $C_{d_c}$ and affirm the necessity of accurate drag coefficient estimation to improve the fidelity of vertical plane motion simulations for the FSAUV.

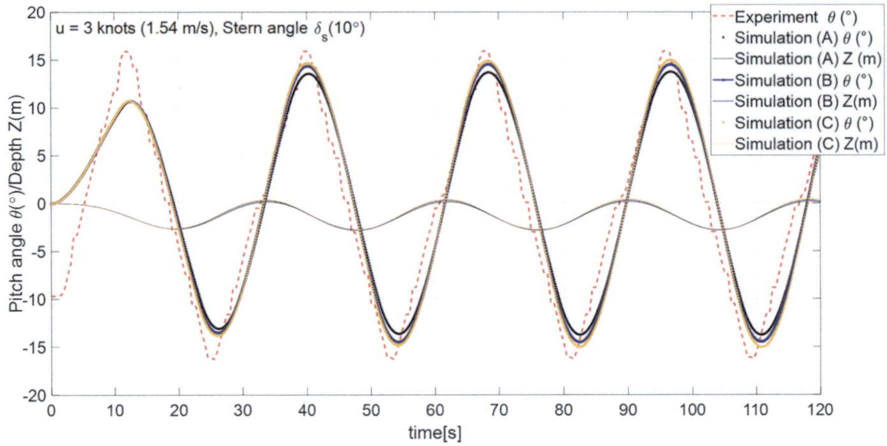


**Fig. 7.14** Zigzag pitching Maneuver–2 [5]

## 7.3.2 *Zigzag Yawing Maneuver–2*

The effectiveness of the improved ASE methodology for estimating drag coefficients has been experimentally validated for the horizontal plane dynamics of the FSAUV. A detailed investigation into the influence of the cross-flow drag coefficient ($C_{d_c}$) on the vehicle's yawing behavior during zigzag maneuvers has been conducted by comparing simulated outcomes with experimental observations. As presented in Table 7.4 and illustrated in Fig. 7.15, a progressive reduction in $C_{d_c}$ from 1.2 to 0.84 and subsequently to 0.69 results in enhanced agreement between simulation and experiment.

Notably, as $C_{d_c}$ decreases, the average cycle time $T_{\text{avg.}}$ for completing the maneuver is reduced from 24.5 s to 24.26 s, lowering the relative error from 2.1% to 1.16%. Furthermore, the average heading angle response ($\psi_{\text{avg.}}$) demonstrates improved correlation with the experimental data, indicating a more precise simulation of the yaw dynamics.

These findings emphasize the critical role of accurate estimation of $C_{d_c}$ in achieving higher fidelity simulations and improved prediction of the FSAUV's horizontal maneuvering performance during complex yawing motions.

## 7.3.3 *Circle and Spiral Maneuvers*

The performance of the proposed ASE-based estimation method for cross-flow drag coefficients has also been evaluated through dynamic simulations of circular and spiral maneuvers of the FSAUV. These free-running tests were conducted using a fixed rudder deflection of 25°, with forward speeds of 2.4 knots for circular motion

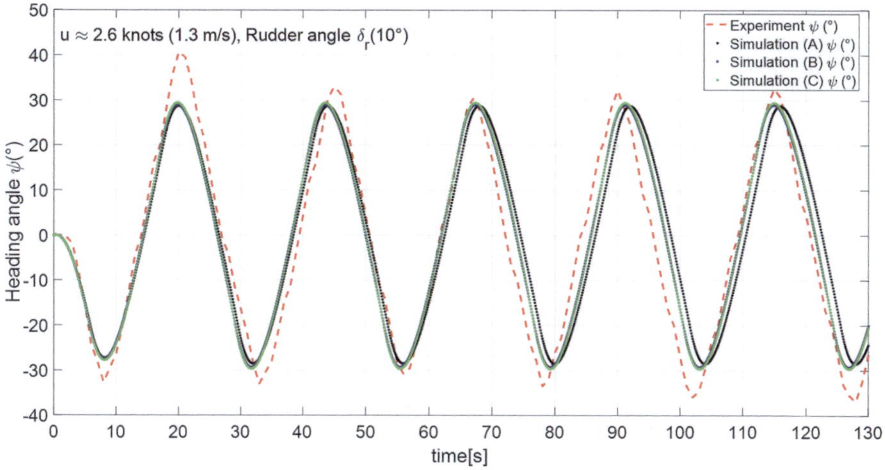


**Fig. 7.15** Zigzag yawing Maneuver–2 [5]

and 2.0 knots for spiral motion. For the spiral tests, two control fin configurations were applied: Spiral Maneuver–4 ($\delta_r = 25°$, $\delta_s = 0°$, $\delta_b = 10°$) and Spiral Maneuver–5 ($\delta_r = 25°$, $\delta_s = 10°$, $\delta_b = 0°$). Comparative simulation and experimental results are presented in Figs. 7.18, 7.16, and 7.17.

The experimental trials showed an average circling diameter of approximately 18.02 m. When simulating the circular and spiral motions with a cross-flow drag coefficient of $C_{d_c}^{2D} = 1.2$, the vehicle traced a larger turning diameter of 18.53 m. This overestimation is attributed to the increased drag impeding tighter turns, resulting in a relative deviation from the experiment. In contrast, simulations with reduced coefficients–specifically, $C_{d_c}^{3D} = 0.84$ and 0.69–yielded diameters of 17.75 m and 17.36 m, respectively. The value of 0.84 provided the closest match to the experimental diameter, indicating improved predictive fidelity of the FSAUV's maneuvering response.

Quantitative error analysis (see Table 7.4) further substantiates these findings. The simulated result with $C_{d_c}^{2D} = 1.2$ showed a positive deviation of approximately 2.83% from the experimental value. In comparison, the result with $C_{d_c}^{3D} = 0.84$ had a smaller negative deviation of about $-1.50\%$, reflecting a tighter agreement. However, further reduction to $C_{d_c}^{3D} = 0.69$ led to a larger negative deviation of $-3.7\%$, indicating overcompensation and suggesting that this value may underestimate the actual resistance.

These results clearly highlight the sensitivity of the FSAUV's maneuvering behavior to variations in $C_{d_c}$. Reduced cross-flow drag coefficients enhance turning performance due to diminished lateral resistance, allowing for smaller turning radii and improved agility in horizontal-plane maneuvers.

Among all examined trajectories, spiral motion stands out as the most complex, involving simultaneous variation in heading and pitch angles while maintaining a

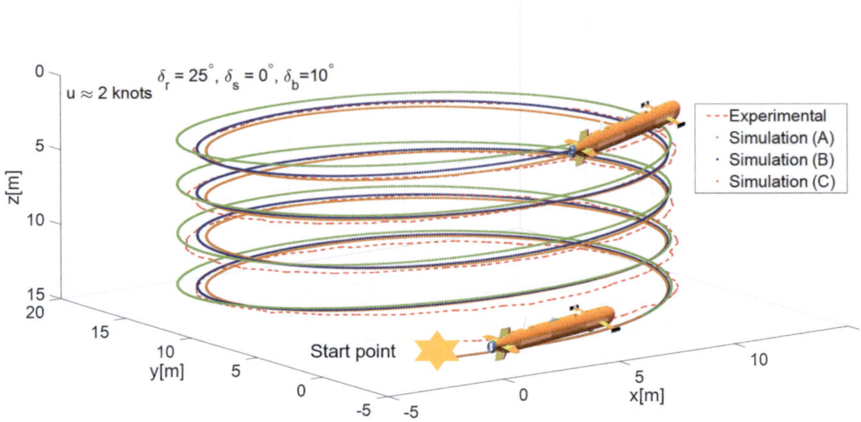


**Fig. 7.16** Spiral Maneuver–4 [5]

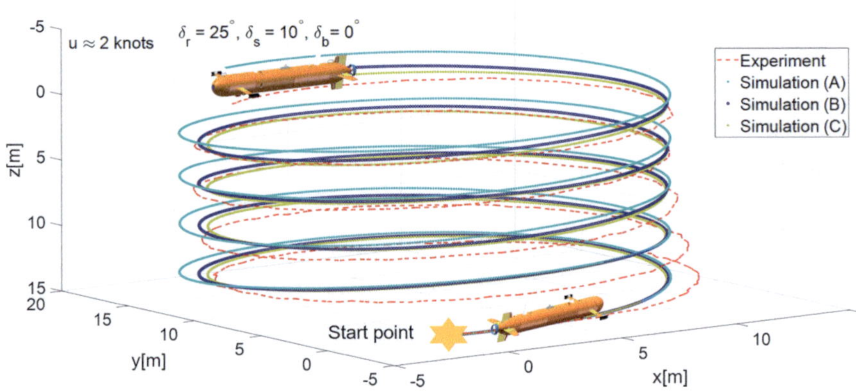


**Fig. 7.17** Spiral Maneuver–5 [5]

circular path–constituting a full six-degree-of-freedom (6-DOF) dynamic condition. The simulation conducted using $C_{d_c}^{3D} = 0.84$ (identified as $ASE_2$) exhibited the highest fidelity in replicating the experimental spiral trajectory. This indicates that the optimized coefficient value captures the essential dynamics of the FSAUV under compound motion modes, thereby affirming the robustness and accuracy of the improved ASE approach in modeling intricate 6-DOF underwater behavior.

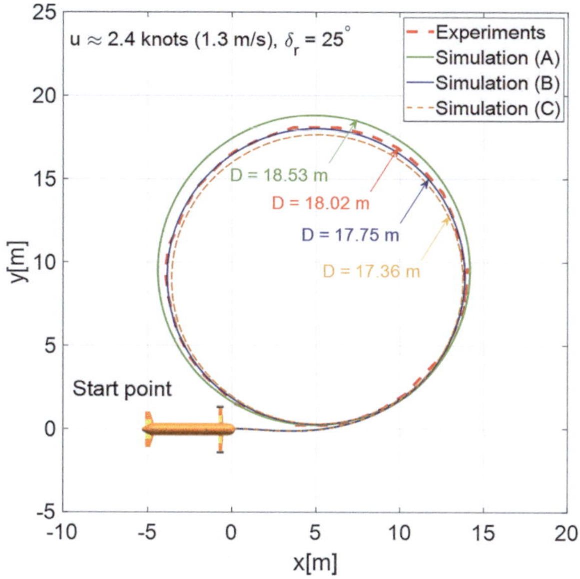


**Fig. 7.18** Circle Maneuver–2 [5]

## 7.4 Wing-Body Lift Interference Effects on FSAUV Dynamics

The influence of wing-body lift interference effects on the maneuvering performance of the FSAUV has been examined through the combined lift interference factor $K_c$, previously estimated using slender body theory and incorporated into the nonlinear dynamic modeling framework. To evaluate the impact of these interference effects in both the vertical and horizontal maneuvering planes, a series of simulations were carried out for zigzag pitching and yawing maneuvers using the ASE-based nonlinear dynamic model.

Two distinct simulation sets, denoted as (A) and (B), were performed using the lift coefficient configurations detailed in Table 4.3. Simulation (A) employed a set of lift coefficients derived without accounting for wing-body lift interference effects, while Simulation (B) incorporated coefficients modified to reflect these effects. All other hydrodynamic parameters, including added mass and drag coefficients, were held constant across both cases to isolate the impact of lift interference. The simulation outcomes from both configurations were subsequently compared against experimental results to assess the fidelity and influence of the lift interference modeling.

### 7.4.1 WBI Effects on FSAUV Vertical Plane Dynamics

**(1) Impact of WBI on Zigzag Pitching at $\delta_s = \pm 10°$ and $\delta_s = \pm 20°$**

The outcomes of the zigzag pitching simulations for the FSAUV are summarized in Table 7.5 and illustrated in Fig. 7.19a. Two sets of simulations were conducted, with stern fin deflections of $\delta_s = \pm 10°$ and $\delta_s = \pm 20°$, respectively, to generate complete zigzag pitching cycles. In all cases, the forward speed of the FSAUV was maintained at approximately 3.0 knots.

In the first simulation set, Simulation (B)–which includes the wing-body lift interference (WBI) effects–achieved a shorter initial pitch response time ($t_i = 7.3$ s) compared to Simulation (A) ($t_i = 10.9$ s), indicating a faster reaction to control input. However, the total cycle time ($T$) was slightly longer in Simulation (B) (28.9 s) than in Simulation (A) (28.3 s), suggesting prolonged maneuvering behavior. Moreover, Simulation (B) yielded greater pitch overshoot angles ($\theta_{ov}$), reflecting a more dynamic pitch response.

In the second set, conducted at the same speed ($u = 3.0$ knots) with larger fin deflections ($\delta_s = \pm 20°$), Simulation (B) again demonstrated a quicker initial pitch response and more significant overshoot angles, further confirming the enhanced maneuverability attributable to WBI effects. The incorporation of WBI in the lift coefficients led to increased lift forces, which in turn amplified the vehicle's pitch dynamics.

Despite differences in initial pitch response and complete cycle time, the overshoot angles exhibited a consistent pattern within each simulation set. For instance, in the first set with $\delta_s = \pm 10°$, Simulation (A) recorded overshoot angles ranging from 0.7° to 4.5°, while Simulation (B) exhibited a range from 3.9° to 5.85°, indicating an average increase of approximately 1.86° due to WBI. Similarly, in the second set with $\delta_s = \pm 20°$, Simulation (A) showed overshoot angles between 1.09° and 4.69°, whereas Simulation (B) produced overshoot angles from 7.44° to 9.22°, resulting in an average increase of 5.25° due to WBI.

Further evaluation of the WBI effects was carried out by analyzing the angular velocity, heave velocity, and vertical displacement, as shown in Fig. 7.19b–d. These parameters align well with the corresponding zigzag pitching trajectories illustrated in Fig. 7.19a, reinforcing the significant impact of wing-body lift interference on the vertical-plane maneuvering performance of the FSAUV.

### 7.4.2 Zigzag Pitching Maneuvers–3: Experimental Validations

A comparative evaluation between the simulated and experimental outcomes for the zigzag pitching maneuver of the FSAUV in the vertical plane, executed with a stern fin deflection of $\delta_s = \pm 10°$ and a forward speed of approximately $u \approx 3$ knots, is illustrated in Fig. 7.6. The experimental data served as a reference to assess the

**Table 7.5** Maneuvering simulation input parameters and simulated results [2]

| Maneuver type | Parameters | SIM (A) | SIM (B) | Absolute difference $\|A - B\|$ |
|---|---|---|---|---|
| | Zigzag pitching (Inputs: $\boldsymbol{\delta_s} = \mathbf{\pm 10°}, \boldsymbol{u} = \mathbf{3.0}$ knots)—(Fig. 7.19) | | | |
| | Initial pitching time ($t_i$) | 10.9 s | 7.3 s | 3.6 s |
| | Complete cycle time (T) | 28.3 s | 28.9 s | 0.6 s |
| | 1st overshoot ($\theta_{ov_1}$) | 0.7° | 3.9° | 3.2° |
| | 2nd overshoot ($\theta_{ov_2}$) | −3.53° | −5.83° | 2.3° |
| | 3rd pitch overshoot ($\theta_{ov_3}$) | 4.35° | 5.95° | 1.6° |
| | 4th pitch overshoot ($\theta_{ov_4}$) | −4.48° | −5.9° | 1.42° |
| | 5th pitch overshoot ($\theta_{ov_5}$) | 4.5° | 5.85° | 1.35° |
| | 6th pitch overshoot ($\theta_{ov_6}$) | −4.52° | −5.86° | 1.34° |
| | Zigzag pitching (Inputs: $\boldsymbol{\delta_s} = \mathbf{\pm 20°}, \boldsymbol{u} = \mathbf{3.0}$ knots)—(Fig. 7.19) | | | |
| | Initial pitching time ($t_i$) | 11.9 s | 6.6 s | 5.3 s |
| | Complete cycle time (T) | 28.6 s | 28.8 s | 0.2 s |
| | 1st pitch overshoot ($\theta_{ov_1}$) | 1.09° | 7.44° | 6.35° |
| | 2nd pitch overshoot ($\theta_{ov_2}$) | −4.26° | −11° | 6.74° |
| | 3rd pitch overshoot ($\theta_{ov_3}$) | 4.55° | 9.03° | 4.48° |
| | 4th pitch overshoot ($\theta_{ov_4}$) | −4.52° | −9.27° | 4.75° |
| | 5th pitch overshoot ($\theta_{ov_5}$) | 4.69° | 9.22° | 4.53° |
| | 6th pitch overshoot ($\theta_{ov_6}$) | −4.56° | −9.23° | 4.67° |
| | Zigzag yawing (Inputs: $\boldsymbol{\delta_r} = \mathbf{\pm 10°}, \boldsymbol{u} = \mathbf{2.6}$ knots)—(Fig. 7.21) | | | |
| | Initial turning time ($t_i$) | 5.5 s | 5.1 s | 0.4 s |
| | Complete Cycle time (T) | 24.3 s | 24.3 s | 0.6 s |
| | 1st yaw overshoot ($\psi_{ov_1}$) | −4.18° | −4.9° | 0.72° |
| | 2nd yaw overshoot ($\psi_{ov_2}$) | 5.17° | 6.79° | 1.62° |

(continued)

**Table 7.5** (continued)

| Maneuver type | Parameters | SIM (A) | SIM (B) | Absolute difference $\|A-B\|$ |
|---|---|---|---|---|
| | 3rd yaw overshoot ($\psi_{ov_3}$) | −5.08° | −6.82° | 1.74° |
| | 4th yaw overshoot ($\psi_{ov_4}$) | 5.15° | 7.16° | 2.01° |
| | 5th yaw overshoot ($\psi_{ov_5}$) | −5.08° | −6.8° | 1.72° |
| | 6th yaw overshoot ($\psi_{ov_6}$) | 5.15° | 7.16° | 2.01° |
| | 7th yaw overshoot ($\psi_{ov_7}$) | −5.08° | −6.8° | 1.72° |
| | 8th yaw overshoot ($\psi_{ov_8}$) | 5.15° | 7.16° | 2.01° |
| | Zigzag yawing (Inputs: $\boldsymbol{\delta_r = \pm 20^\circ, u = 2.6}$ knots)—(Fig. 7.21) | | | |
| | Initial turning time ($t_i$) | 5.2 s | 5.0 s | 0.2 s |
| | Complete cycle time (T) | 24.3 s | 23.7 s | 0 s |
| | 1st yaw overshoot ($\psi_{ov_1}$) | −7.5° | −9.1° | 1.6° |
| | 2nd yaw overshoot ($\psi_{ov_2}$) | 9.3° | 12.56° | 3.26° |
| | 3rd yaw overshoot ($\psi_{ov_3}$) | −9.5° | −12.91° | −3.4° |
| | 4th yaw overshoot ($\psi_{ov_4}$) | 9.3° | 13.28° | 3.98° |
| | 5th yaw overshoot ($\psi_{ov_5}$) | −9.5° | −12.86° | −3.36$° |
| | 6th yaw overshoot ($\psi_{ov_6}$) | 9.3° | 13.28° | 3.98° |
| | 7th yaw overshoot ($\psi_{ov_7}$) | −9.5° | −12.86° | −3.36° |
| | 8th yaw overshoot ($\psi_{ov_8}$) | 9.3° | 13.28° | 3.98° |

accuracy of the simulations, with absolute and relative error metrics computed to quantify deviations. The corresponding error values are listed in Table 7.6, while the mean absolute error (MAE) and root mean square error (RMSE) values are summarized in Table 7.7.

Simulation (B), which incorporates the influence of wing-body lift interference (WBI), demonstrated a reduced initial pitch response time ($t_i$) compared to Simulation (A), indicating a more prompt reaction to control inputs. However, the duration

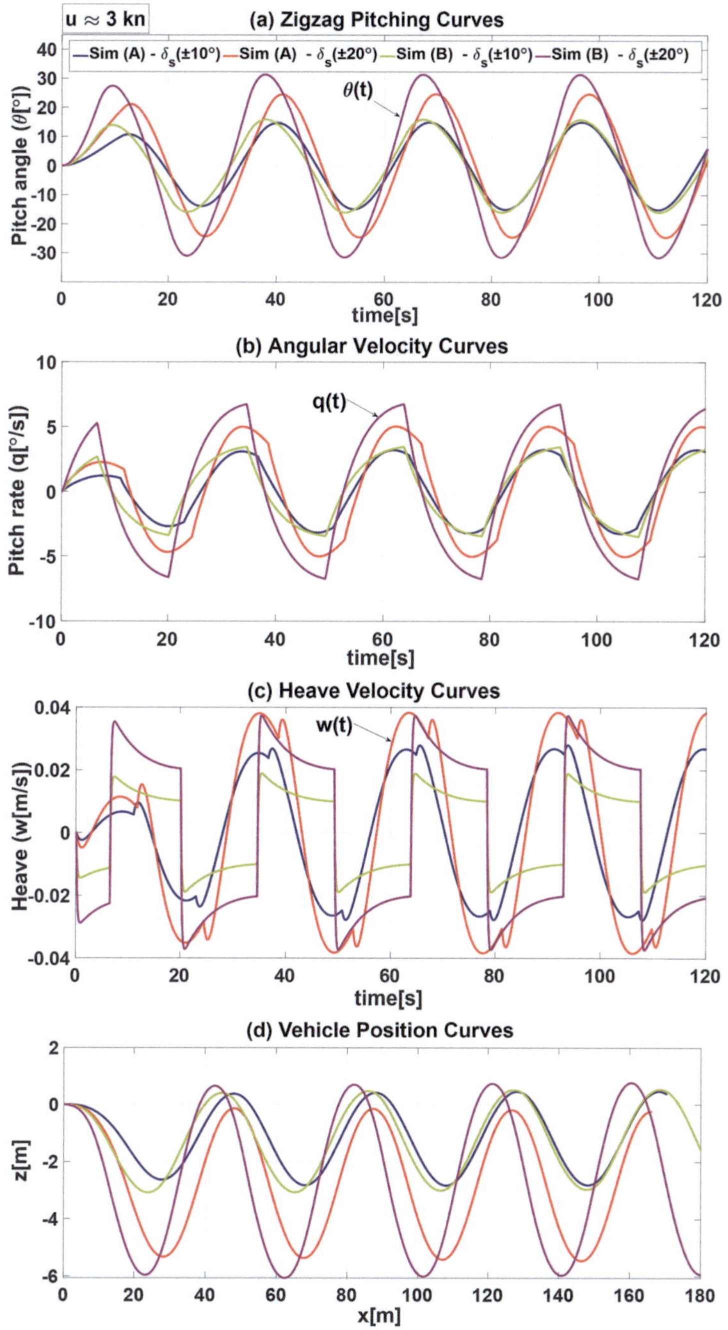


**Fig. 7.19** Time traces and position curves in zigzag pitching simulations: **a** Pitch angle $\theta(t)$, **b** Pitch rate $q(t)$, **c** Heave rate $w(t)$, and **d** Vertical position $z$ vs $x$—impact of WBI effects on vertical plane dynamics [2]

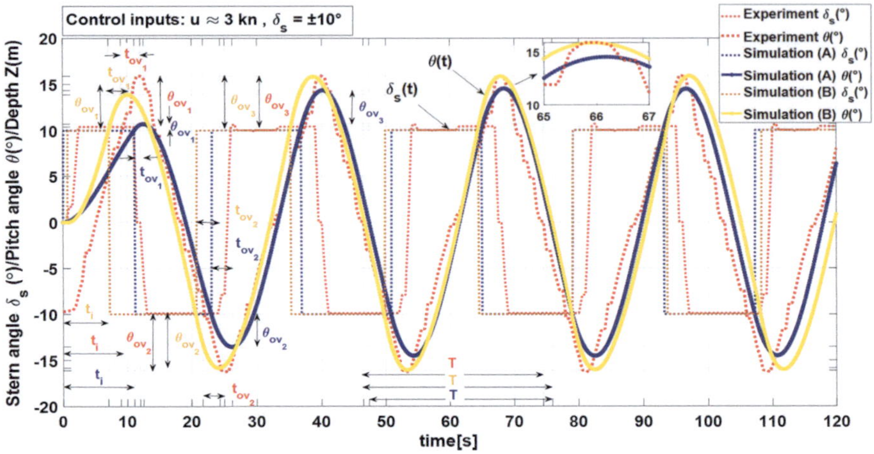


**Fig. 7.20** Zigzag pitch Maneuvers–3: simulated and experimental results of FSAUV [2]

of the complete pitching cycle ($T$) was marginally longer in Simulation (B), reflecting a more sustained oscillatory behavior due to the WBI effects. Additionally, Simulation (B) produced noticeably higher pitch overshoot angles ($\theta_{ov}$), indicating enhanced maneuvering intensity. The pitch overshoot times ($t_{ov}$) also varied, with Simulation (B) generally exhibiting shorter durations.

Further analysis through MAE and RMSE revealed that Simulation (B) yielded lower error magnitudes, particularly when the initial overshoot peaks ($\theta_{ov_1}$ and $\theta_{ov_2}$) were excluded from the evaluation. These findings underscore the critical role of WBI in refining the lift coefficient estimations, thereby improving the fidelity of the simulated zigzag pitching behavior and achieving closer alignment with experimental observations.

### 7.4.3 *WBI Effects on FSAUV Horizontal Plane Dynamics*

#### (1) Impact of WBI on Zigzag Yawing at $\delta_r = \pm 10°$ and $\delta_r = \pm 20°$

The simulated results of zigzag yawing maneuvers of FSAUV are illustrated in Fig. 7.21a, whereas, the recorded values of the maneuvering parameters are given in Table 7.5. Similar to the zigzag pitch maneuvers, two sets of simulations were conducted: In the first set, the rudder deflection angle was $\delta_r = \pm 10°$, while in the second set, $\delta_r$ was set at $\pm 20°$ to complete the zigzag yawing cycles. The AUV propulsion speed was approximately 2.6 knots in both sets of simulations. While comparing the simulated results of Simulation (A) and (B), it have been observed that the AUV in Simulation (B) took a slightly shorter initial turning time ($t_i$) compared to Simulation (A). Moreover, the AUV took same time to complete the yawing cycle

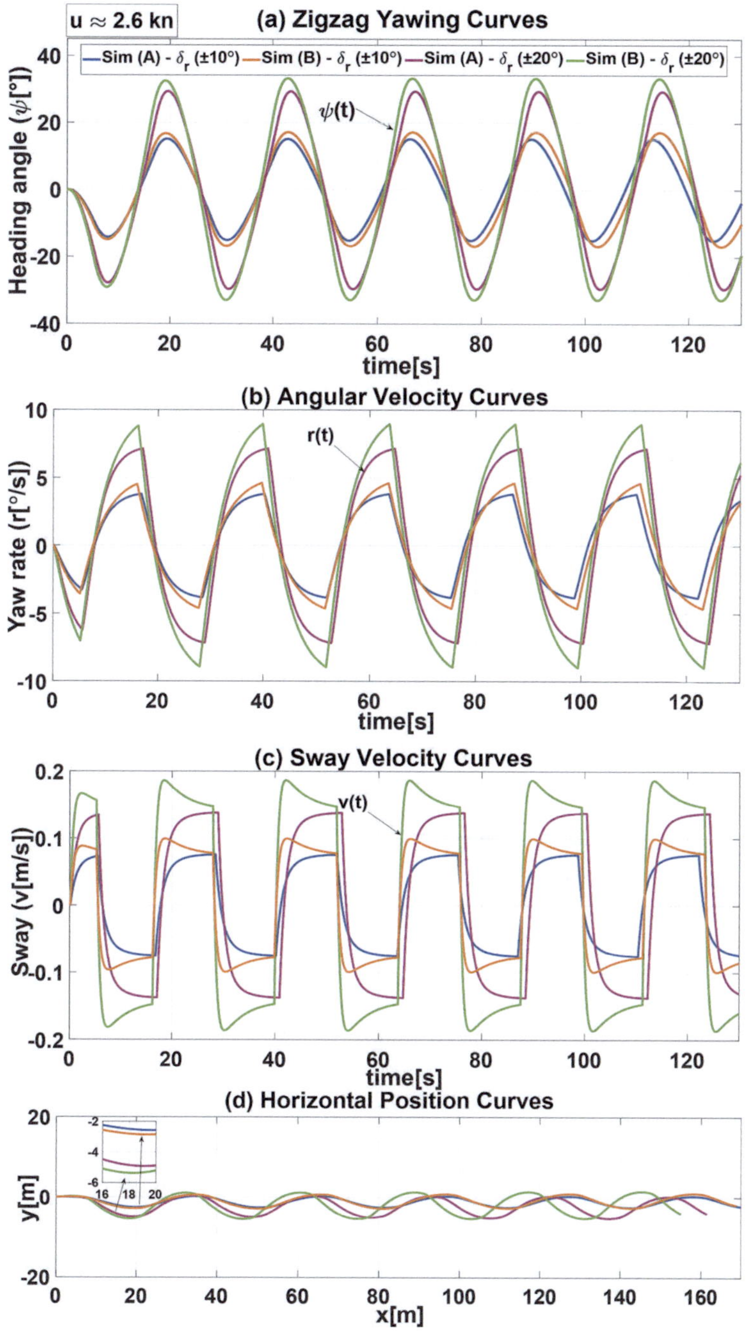


**Fig. 7.21** Time traces and position curves in zigzag yawing simulations: **a** Yaw angle $\psi(t)$, **b** Yaw rate $r(t)$, **c** Velocity $v(t)$, and **d** Position $y$ versus $x$—impact of WBI effects on horizontal plane dynamics [2]

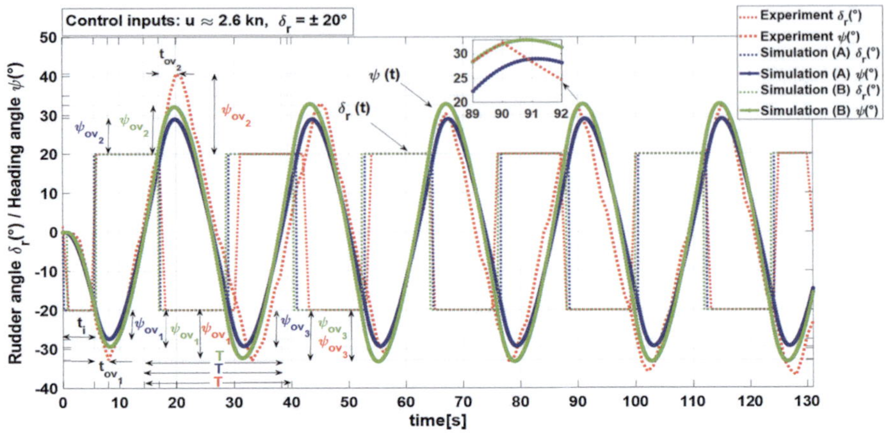


**Fig. 7.22** Zigzag Yawing Maneuvers–3: simulated and experimental results of FSAUV [2]

which suggests stable performance of AUV dynamics modeled either with or without considering wing-body lift interference effects.

Additionally, as observed in the zigzag pitch maneuvers, the yaw overshoot angles remain relatively consistent across all cycles for both sets of simulations. For instance, in the first set of simulations with $\delta_r = \pm 10°$, the yaw overshoot angles for the first eight cycles ranged from $-4.18°$ to $5.15°$ in Simulation (A) and from $-4.9°$ to $7.16°$ in Simulation (B). Due to wing-body lift interference effects, an average increase of $1.72°$ in yaw overshoot was observed across all eight cycles of the AUV's yaw maneuvers. Similarly, in the second set of simulations with $\delta_r = \pm 20°$, the yaw overshoot angles for the first eight cycles varied consistently between $-7.5°$ and $9.3°$ in Simulation (A) and between -9.1° and 13.28° in Simulation (B). Here, the wing-body lift interference led to an average increase of $3.98°$ in yaw overshoot across all eight cycles of the AUV's yaw maneuvers.

Similar to the zigzag pitch maneuvers, wing-body lift interference effects on maneuvering parameters such as angular velocity, sway velocity, and horizontal position of the FSAUV have been conducted. Corresponding curves are shown in Fig. 7.21b–d respectively. The simulated results for these parameters also demonstrated consistency with the zigzag yawing curves depicted in Fig. 7.21a.

### (2) Zigzag Yawing Maneuvers–3: Experimental Validations

The comparison between simulated and experimental results for zigzag yawing maneuvers of FSAUV in the horizontal plane conducted at rudder deflection angle $\delta_r = \pm 20°$ at speed of $u \approx 2.6$ knots, is depicted in Fig. 7.6 and the corresponding values are tabulated in Table 7.6.

Similar to the approach used for zigzag pitching maneuvers, the experimental results serve as the reference for evaluating the deviations in the simulated results for zigzag yawing maneuvers. By comparing the simulation outcomes with the experimental data, the variations in terms of error metrics have been observed. Specifically,

**Table 7.6** Comparison between maneuvering simulations and experimental results

| Maneuver type | Parameters | SIM (A) | SIM (B) | EXP (E) | $AE_A$ $\|A-E\|$ | $AE_B$ $\|B-E\|$ | $RE_A$ (%) $\frac{\|A-E\|}{\|E\|}$ | $RE_B$ (%) $\frac{\|B-E\|}{\|E\|}$ |
|---|---|---|---|---|---|---|---|---|
| | Zigzag pitching (Inputs: $\boldsymbol{\delta_s = \pm 10^\circ, u \approx 3}$ knots)—(Fig. 7.20) | | | | | | | |
| | Initial pitching time ($t_i$) | 10.9 s | 7.3 s | 11 s | 0.1 s | 3.67 s | 0.9% | 33.6% |
| | Time of a complete cycle (T) | 28.3 s | 28.9 s | 28 s | 0.3 s | 0.9 s | 1.1% | 3.2% |
| | 1st overshoot angle ($\theta_{ov_1}$) | 0.7° | 3.9° | 5.9° | 5.19° | 2° | 88% | 34% |
| | Time of 1st overshoot ($t_{ov_1}$) | 1.5 s | 2.9 s | 2.5 s | 1.0 s | 0.4 s | 40% | 16% |
| | 2nd overshoot angle ($\theta_{ov_2}$) | −3.53° | −5.83° | −6.1° | 2.57° | 0.47° | 42.13% | 4.4% |
| | Time of 2nd overshoot ($t_{ov_2}$) | 3.0 s | 3.4 s | 3.1 s | 0.1 s | 0.3 s | 3.23% | 9.7% |
| | 3rd overshoot angle ($\theta_{ov_3}$) | 4.35° | 5.95° | 5.9° | 1.55° | 0.05° | 26.3% | 0.85% |
| | 4th overshoot angle ($\theta_{ov_4}$) | −4.48° | −5.9° | −6.2° | 1.72° | 0.3° | 27.74% | 4.83% |
| | 5th overshoot angle ($\theta_{ov_5}$) | 4.5° | 5.85° | 5.9° | 1.4° | 0.05° | 23.73% | 0.85% |
| | 6th overshoot angle ($\theta_{ov_6}$) | −4.52° | -5.86° | −6.3° | 1.78° | 0.44° | 28.25% | 6.7% |
| | Zigzag yawing (Inputs: $\boldsymbol{\delta_r = \pm 20^\circ, u \approx 2.6}$ knots)—(Fig. 7.22) | | | | | | | |
| | Initial turning time ($t_i$) | 5.2 s | 5.0 s | 5.1 s | 0.1 s | 0.1 s | 2.0% | 2.0 % |
| | Time of a complete cycle (T) | 24.3 s | 23.7 s | 23.98 s | 0.32 s | 0.28 s | 1.33% | 1.16% |

(continued)

**Table 7.6** (continued)

| Maneuver type | Parameters | SIM (A) | SIM (B) | EXP (E) | $AE_A$ $\|A-E\|$ | $AE_B$ $\|B-E\|$ | $RE_A$ (%) $\frac{\|A-E\|}{\|E\|}$ | $RE_B$ (%) $\frac{\|B-E\|}{\|E\|}$ |
|---|---|---|---|---|---|---|---|---|
| | 1st overshoot angle ($\psi_{ov_1}$) | −7.5° | −9.1° | −12.7° | 5.2° | 3.6° | 41% | 28.34% |
| | Time of 1st overshoot ($t_{ov_1}$) | 2.4 s | 2.3 s | 2.3 s | 0.1 s | 0 s | 4.35% | 0% |
| | 2nd overshoot angle ($\psi_{ov_2}$) | 9.3° | 12.56° | 20.7° | 11.4° | 8.14° | 55% | 39.32% |
| | Time of 2nd overshoot ($t_{ov_2}$) | 3.1 s | 3.0 s | 3.0 s | 0.1 s | 0 s | 3.33% | 0 % |
| | 3rd overshoot angle ($\psi_{ov_3}$) | −9.5° | -12.91° | −13° | 3.5° | 0.1° | 27 % | 0.7% |
| | 4th overshoot angle ($\psi_{ov_4}$) | 9.3° | 13.28° | 13° | 3.7° | 0.28° | 28.5% | 2.15% |
| | 5th overshoot angle ($\psi_{ov_5}$) | −9.5° | −12.86° | −10.8° | 1.3° | 2.06° | 12% | 19% |
| | 6th overshoot angle ($\psi_{ov_6}$) | 9.3° | 13.28° | 10.4° | 1.1° | 2.88° | 10.6% | 27.7% |
| | 7th overshoot angle ($\psi_{ov_7}$) | −9.5° | −12.86° | −13.5° | 4° | 0.64° | 29% | 4.7% |
| | 8th overshoot angle ($\psi_{ov_8}$) | 9.3° | 13.28° | 12.3° | 3° | 0.98° | 24.4% | 7.9% |

the Absolute Error and Relative Error are quantified to assess the magnitude of deviations in the simulated results, as presented in Table 7.6. Similarly, the Mean Absolute Error and Root Mean Square Error, which provide a more comprehensive evaluation of the accuracy of the simulations, are detailed in Table 7.7. To visually represent the

**Table 7.7** Maneuvering simulations and experimental results—MAE and RMSE metrics [2]

| Zigzag pitching ($\delta_s = \pm 10°, u \approx 3$ knots) (Fig. 7.20) | Zigzag yawing ($\delta_r = \pm 20°, u \approx 2.6$ knots) (Fig. 7.22) |
|---|---|
| $MAE_1$ ($\theta_{ov}$) = 2.2° | $MAE_1$ ($\psi_{ov}$) = 4.15° |
| $MAE_1$ ($\theta_{ov}$) excl. ($\theta_{ov_1}$ & $\theta_{ov_2}$) = 1.61° | $MAE_1$ ($\psi_{ov}$) excl. ($\psi_{ov_1}$ & $\psi_{ov_2}$) = 2.76° |
| $MAE_2$ ($\theta_{ov}$) = 0.55° | $MAE_2$ ($\psi_{ov}$) = 2.33° |
| $MAE_2$ ($\theta_{ov}$) excl. ($\theta_{ov_1}$ & $\theta_{ov_2}$) = 0.21° | $MAE_2$ ($\psi_{ov}$) excl. ($\psi_{ov_1}$ & $\psi_{ov_2}$) = 1.15° |
| $RMSE_1$ ($\theta_{ov}$) = 2.71° | $RMSE_1$ ($\psi_{ov}$) = 5.13° |
| $RMSE_1$ ($\theta_{ov}$) excl. ($\theta_{ov_1}$ & $\theta_{ov_2}$) = 1.62° | $RMSE_1$ ($\psi_{ov}$) excl. ($\psi_{ov_1}$ & $\psi_{ov_2}$) = 3.0° |
| $RMSE_2$ ($\theta_{ov}$) = 0.87° | $RMSE_2$ ($\psi_{ov}$) = 3.4° |
| $RMSE_2$ ($\theta_{ov}$) excl. ($\theta_{ov_1}$ & $\theta_{ov_2}$) = 0.27° | $RMSE_2$ ($\psi_{ov}$) excl. ($\psi_{ov_1}$ & $\psi_{ov_2}$) = 1.53° |

*Note*

Subscript 1: Error between Simulation (A) and Experimental Results—Without WBI Effects

Subscript 2: Error between Simulation (B) and Experimental Results—With WBI Effects

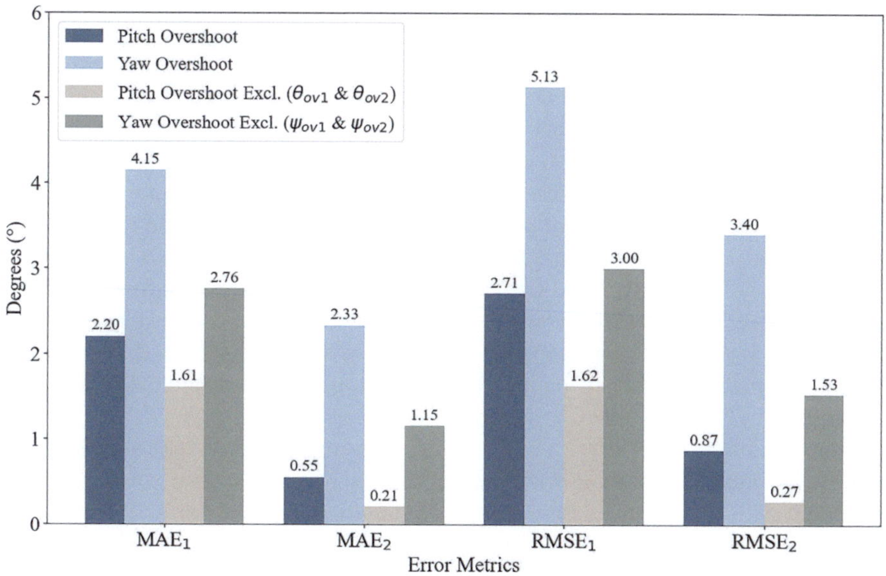


**Fig. 7.23** MAE and RMSE metrics for zigzag pitching and yawing overshoots

performance of the simulations, the MAE and RMSE metrics are also depicted in Fig. 7.23.

In Simulation (B), the initial turning time ($t_i$) was slightly shorter compared to Simulation (A), indicating a quicker response to control inputs when WBI effects were considered. However, the time of a complete cycle (T) was slightly longer in Simulation (B), showing stable and more sustained maneuvering. As anticipated, larger overshoot angles ($\psi_{ov}$) for different yawing maneuvers have been observed for Simulation (B) and are closer to the experimental results, thus indicating more pronounced yaw responses when considering WBI effects. Moreover, time overshoots ($t_{ov}$) observed for Simulation (B) also showed better agreement with the real-time response of the FSAUV during the underwater experiments, thus indicating capturing of better physical characteristics associated to the lift generation.

Overall, from MAE and RMSE analyses, Simulation (B) had lower errors compared to Simulation (A), particularly when excluding the first and second overshoot angles ($\psi_{ov_1}$ and $\psi_{ov_2}$). These findings suggest that considering WBI effects improves the accuracy of horizontal plane dynamics of FSAUV, particularly zigzag yawing maneuvers, resulting in better agreement with experimental data.

## 7.5 Summary

The chapter provides a thorough validation of the FSAUV's maneuvering simulations using the ITTC protocol in terms of various error metrics, including AE, RE, MAE, and RMSE. The simulations, covering zigzag maneuvers and other standard motions, were compared with free-running underwater experiments conducted in an inland lake in China. These experiments evaluated the FSAUV's underwater maneuvering capabilities, stability and control across six degrees of freedom.

The developed ASE approach for estimating added mass coefficients has been validated through simulations of circle and spiral maneuvers with the REMUS 100 AUV. The variations between the two ASE approaches showed minor variations of approximately 5% which is primarily due to differences in yaw and sway coefficients. Overall, both approaches provided consistent maneuvering results across all the measured parameters including velocities and heading rates. Subsequent to validations, the proposed ASE technique, have been applied to estimate the added mass coefficients to build the FSAUV dynamics model.

The ASE-based SNDM was validated through simulations of various maneuvers of FSAUV, including zigzag pitching, zigzag yawing, circle, and spiral motions, compared with experimental data. Based on the error metrics, the ASE techniques as well as nonlinear dynamics model of FSAUV demonstrated high accuracy and consistency, validating its effectiveness for model-based controller design and underwater operations. Moreover, the performance of the novel control plane configuration of FSAUV that is horizontal bow and stern fins of the FSAUV in generating lift during zigzag pitching maneuvers demonstrated that both fins, actuated individually or collectively, generated reliable pitch responses during maneuvering simulations. The results showed that the combined deflection of the bow and stern fins closely aligned with the average of individual fin deflections. Additional analysis of angular velocity, heave velocity, and vertical position curves validated the fins' effectiveness in controlling the AUV's pitch dynamics across all configurations.

The validation of the improved ASE technique for cross flow drag coefficients, 6-DOF FSAUV dynamics highlighted the importance of accurate cross-flow drag coefficient estimation. Accordingly, the lower values of $C_{d_c}$ that 3D flow across the AUV having $C_{d_c}^{3D}$ provided improved results between simulated and experimental results, particularly in complex maneuvers like spirals. Quantitative comparisons revealed that optimized $C_{d_c}^{3D}$ values better captured FSAUV dynamics, especially in tighter turns and complex 6-DOF motions.

Finally, simulations incorporating wing-body lift interference effects revealed larger overshoot angles in zigzag pitching and yawing maneuvers compared to simulations without these effects. However, the resulting maneuvering curves showed closer alignment with experimental results. The differences between Simulation (A) and Simulation (B) likely stem from treating the FSAUV's geometry separately, which altered flow dynamics, impacting lift forces, moment, vortex generation, and inertial coefficients. Additionally, coupling effects between different degrees of freedom, such as surge, sway, and heave, may influence overall dynamics. These observations were further validated through free-running underwater maneuvers, emphasizing the importance of accurate modeling to capture the complexities of AUV dynamics, particularly wing-body lift interference effects using the ASE approach. Moreover, from the perspective of control theory, the model-based controller provided better results to achieve desired heading and pitching in terms of better and faster convergence, when WBI effects are modeled in AUV dynamics.

## References


1. ITTC: Recommended procedures and guidelines-uv full scale manoeuvring trials, 7.5-04-02-02 (2021)
2. Ahmed, F., Xiang, X., Wang, H., Zhang, J., Xiang, G., Yang, S.: Investigating wing-body lift interference effects on the dynamics of a novel flight-style AUV with bow-wings: maneuvering simulations and experimental validations. Ocean Eng. **326**, 120778 (2025)
3. Prestero, T.T.J.: Verification of a six-degree of freedom simulation model for the remus autonomous underwater vehicle (2001)
4. Ahmed, F., Xiang, X., Zhou, G., Xiang, G., Yang, S.: Dynamic modeling and maneuvering of remus 100 AUV: The impact of added mass coefficients. In: 2023 42nd Chinese Control Conference (CCC), pp. 1424–1429. IEEE (2023)
5. Ahmed, F., Xiang, X., Wang, H., Zhang, J., Xiang, G., Yang, S.: Nonlinear dynamics of novel flight-style autonomous underwater vehicle with bow wings, part i: Ase and cfd based estimations of hydrodynamic coefficients, part ii: nonlinear dynamic modeling and experimental validations. Appl. Ocean Res. **141**, 103739 (2023)

FSC
www.fsc.org
MIX
Papier aus verantwortungsvollen Quellen
Paper from responsible sources
FSC® C105338

If you have any concerns about our products,
you can contact us on
**ProductSafety@springernature.com**

In case Publisher is established outside the EU,
the EU authorized representative is:
**Springer Nature Customer Service Center GmbH**
**Europaplatz 3, 69115 Heidelberg, Germany**

Printed by Libri Plureos GmbH
in Hamburg, Germany